# SIR FRANCIS DASHWOOD

*By the same author*

KING AND COMMONS, 1660–1832

# SIR FRANCIS DASHWOOD

*An Eighteenth-Century Independent*

———◆———

## BETTY KEMP

**MACMILLAN**
London · Melbourne · Toronto

**ST MARTIN'S PRESS**
New York
1967

© Betty Kemp 1967

MACMILLAN AND COMPANY LIMITED
*Little Essex Street London WC 2*
*also Bombay Calcutta Madras Melbourne*

THE MACMILLAN COMPANY OF CANADA LIMITED
*70 Bond Street Toronto 2*

ST MARTIN'S PRESS INC
*175 Fifth Avenue New York NY 10010*

PRINTED IN GREAT BRITAIN

TO BRUCE

# Contents

# List of Plates

# Preface

I AM grateful to the late Sir John Dashwood for the original permission to use the Dashwood manuscripts now deposited in the Bodleian Library, and to Sir Francis Dashwood for permission to reproduce some of these and for showing me his papers at West Wycombe. I have also to thank the Earl of Malmesbury for permission to use the parliamentary diary of James Harris, and the Earl of Bute for permission to use the transcripts of the Bute Papers, which are housed in the offices of the History of Parliament Trust.

# Independency: and Sir Francis Dashwood

INDEPENDENCY in eighteenth-century political life was not a freak, or a frill. It was not just a refusal to wear any of the available political labels, on the grounds that none of the parties was pleasing, but a belief that party labels, and the sacrifice of freedom which these entailed, were incompatible with the constitution. 'Independent' was, of course, a descriptive term. Just as the conduct of independents in parliament had, in a party sense, no consistency, so most independents did not owe their seats to any efforts or influence other than their own, and some of them prized their constituents' independence so highly that they refused to undermine it even by canvassing. In 1775 the antiquary Richard Gough drew up a model of an address from an independent candidate to his electors:

> I offer myself a Candidate to represent the County [or Borough] of ————, with a determined resolution neither to solicit, or influence, the votes of the free electors. Superior to such influence myself, I cannot condescend to bribe or intimidate my countrymen. I stand forth, therefore, on no other ground than public virtue. . . . I shall neither make nor authorize any other application than this. As I have no ends of my own to serve, I profess myself of no party; and resolved to follow the dictates of my own conscience, with respect to my duty to my Country, my Sovereign, and my Constituents.[1]

But independency was more than a group of independents. It was a constitutional creed, at a time when the constitution of a state was believed to be of paramount importance because it determined, in something like the Aristotelian sense, the way of life of its people. In England, accordingly, the nature of the constitution was thought to be not accidental, or separate from, her political, social, and cultural achievements: it was their basis and their begetter.

The fact that independency was a constitutional creed at a time of

---

[1] John Nichols, *Literary Anecdotes of the Eighteenth Century* (1812 ed.), vi. 304–5.

general concern with the constitution would, by itself, make independency important. But it has other claims. The basic idea of independency was simple, and perhaps not greatly disputed. It was, that the true function of the House of Commons as a whole, and its members as individuals, was to criticise the government, not to support it. A division of the House into parties prevented the exercise of this critical function and so distorted the Commons' proper relationship to the government. The independents claimed that this first principle, that the House of Commons should be independent of the government, was tacitly enshrined in the constitution as it was imagined in 1689 and in the Revolution settlement. Their opponents did not deny this, but answered that parties, placemen, and all the paraphernalia which the independents chose to call 'corruption', did not in fact pervert the constitution or render the House of Commons dependent or unfree.

Zeal for the independence of the House of Commons has been given less emphasis, as one of the reasons why parties were disliked, than the restriction of the king's right to choose his own ministers which, it is said, parties imply. This emphasis is a retrospective one, a reflection of events, particularly of the greater concern, in later times, for the smooth working of the executive government. In the eighteenth century, to all sides and to everyone except, in practice, a handful of harassed ministers, the prime concern was not the smooth working of the executive government but its proper subordination, limitation, and control. This control lay with the House of Commons, or nowhere. It was not defence of the king's prerogative but defence of the Commons against the king's influence that was the inspiration of independency. A friend of independency wrote in 1747:

> To be free then, is to have a House of Commons that is so: Free from all Influence and Corruption, independant of the arbitrary Will of the Prince, independant of his Ministers, independant of their Smiles and Favours, independant of all Power but what is legal; in short, independant of every Thing, but that Liberty of which it has the Honour to be the Support and Guardian. . . . Ministerial Power is therefore only to be dreaded and guarded against with the utmost Care, Prudence, and Vigilance. Their Schemes and Measures are to be entertained with great Caution and Jealousy, and all *unconstitutional*

Acts punished with the greatest Severity; but how can this be done, but by an *independant House of Commons*, chose by independant Electors? [1]

The House of Commons could not be independent unless it contained men who were not committed to party, so that governments should have some doubt about their ability to carry the House with them on every measure they proposed to it. In fact, in the years from 1741 to 1781 between 150 and 200, and more often nearer 200, members of the Commons were independent in this sense. Amongst them were men who were not only independent themselves but fighters for independency, indefatigably introducing and supporting measures to reduce the government's control over the Commons. The existence of this smaller group, not the size of its achievement, was a proof of independency. Its achievement was small. Great achievement was perhaps unlikely, for, though combination would have destroyed independency, lack of combination lessened independents' chance of success. Moreover, because their view of the true nature of the constitution could be represented as not being very different from that of men who wore a party label, independents were accused of being fearful of imagined dangers. They were time after time confused with the current anti-government party, which, in a constitutional age, inevitably claimed that the men it wished to replace in office were acting unconstitutionally. All ministers, and most zealous politicians, looked on independents as children in the art of politics, and despised them even while courting them. Nor was it always easy for independents to resist the insidious argument that office would, after all, give them more hope than opposition of realising their programme. As Dodington told Dashwood in 1751, in vain, that 'no good can be done to this country, but by good men getting into office',[2] so Fox told Shelburne in 1762, with more effect, that 'it is the place-man, not the independent Lord, that can do his country good'.[3] Yet, even

---

[1] *An Address to the Electors of Great Britain. In which the Constitution of England is considered and asserted; particularly, the original Design, Nature, Privileges and Power of the House of Commons, as opposed to Ministerial Influence and Corruption. And the Independancy of Parliaments earnestly recommended, as the only Means to make the Nation happy.* By an Independant Elector, pp. 12, 13.

[2] *Political Journal of George Bubb Dodington* (ed. J. Carswell and L. A. Drale (Oxford, 1965)), p. 114 [*Diary*].

[3] Lord Fitzmaurice, *Life of William Earl of Shelburne* (1912), i. 113.

though success for the independents may have been unlikely, one cannot hope to understand them if one assumes that 'the logic of events', as well as the politicians, was arrayed against them. If the logic of events always leads to what happens, it has no meaning either as an explanation of what happened or as a rod of judgement for what did not happen, for the failures. Discard it, and one can see more clearly what the independents wanted, and how they hoped to achieve it, though one is still perplexed in the attempt to see what effect their programme would have had.

Independency stood for a free, uncommitted House of Commons, scrutinising government proposals on their merits and not automatically either supporting or opposing them. Independents believed that this was the 'true constitution': that is, the intention of the constitution. They therefore defined their purpose as the creation, or restoration, in fact, of a constitution which was generally approved in theory. Its perversion they attributed to developments which had taken place since 1689, and especially since 1714, more particularly the use of places and pensions in order to build up and keep together a body of government supporters in the House. The first plank in the independents' programme was therefore a place bill, to exclude placemen from the House or at least to limit the number of members holding places. The second plank was the repeal of the Septennial Act, and the substitution of a rule preferably of annual parliaments, which would give the government no time to manipulate the Commons, or, if this was impracticable, at least triennial ones. To these two constant demands others were from time to time added, equally aimed at the threat of an encroaching executive: free elections, the restoration of the clause in the Act of Settlement which had required privy councillors to sign the advice they gave to the monarch; the restoration of ministerial equality and the end for ever of 'sole' ministers; the murder of that 'midnight assembly' the cabinet; reliance on a militia instead of on a standing army.

Two answers were given, at the time, to these demands. One was to deny the existence of the things complained of, or to deny that they had the effect imputed to them, as Walpole denied that he was sole minister and as many placemen denied, both honestly and accurately, that their places bound them to support the government. The other was to stigmatise the independents' remedies as impracticable, on the grounds that the things they complained of were the very things that made the constitution work. The argument from denial was clearly no argument at all: Walpole was in some sense a sole minister, though not in all the senses he was accused of; not all placemen felt able to ignore their places, and all governments hoped that not many of them would. The argument from impracticability was more disingenuous, and has found much favour with posterity. It claimed that placemen were necessary, not so much on the grounds that they strengthened the government as on the grounds that they provided a counterpoise to the power of the House of Commons, which, greatly increased since 1689, would otherwise be overwhelming. Placemen, far from being pernicious, were valuable, for they — almost single-handed — made the balance of the constitution a reality. This argument turned the tables on the independents, painting them not as friends and restorers of the constitution, but as its enemies. No doubt many workaday independents gradually became aware of and resented this new view of placemen. One who did so early was Strange, who, in the debate on a motion for a place bill in December 1742, said

> the doctrine of corruption has this day been pushed farther than ever I believe it was in this House. It has been represented not only as a harmless but as a necessary implement of government; and all the laws we have for excluding pensioners, and several sorts of officers, from having a seat in this House may, by the same sort of reasoning, be proved to be subversive of our constitution, and introductory of anarchy, confusion, and arbitrary power.[1]

The doctrine that Strange thought unfair proved attractive, and has had great influence. Nevertheless, it could again be contended that the twist later given to it distorts what contemporaries said. Historians have seen placemen as an intermediate stage in the development of party, necessary to give the government firm support in the House of Commons until the day when party should perform this function. Contemporary apologists, however, did not say this. They defended placemen because they preserved the balance of the constitution, not because they made for strong government. The argument from impracticability went further than this, of course. Independents

---

[1] *Parliamentary History*, xii. 882–3 (3 Dec. 1742) (hereafter *Parl. Hist.*). The motion was lost only by 196 to 221.

were laughed at as victims of idealistic nonsense, romantics who only needed the experience of office to teach them that placemen were necessary, or jeered at as place-seekers hoping to force themselves into office by preaching a popular doctrine out of office.[1]

None of these answers to the independents is a good one: the truth is that they failed, and their opponents succeeded. Clearly the facts the independents complained of were not imaginary. Placemen and parties were certainly intended to give the government as much influence as possible over the House of Commons. Of course it is true that, even at their most effective, the influence they gave the government was very much more precarious than the influence it was to have in the halcyon days of party after 1867, and perhaps more precarious than the opponents of influence imagined. But this is irrelevant. The only question that is really open is whether this influence saved the balance of the constitution, by giving the king just enough power to balance the Commons, or whether it upset the balance, by giving him enough power to outweigh the Commons. This question was asked very often after 1780, in the great period of administrative reform. The gradual whittling away of places and consequent decline of influence raised acutely the whole question of the parliamentary function of patronage. Those who believed it to be essential to the working of government, and therefore to the constitution, then found themselves defending the 'old constitution', which to the independents was 'the corrupted constitution', in alliance with opponents of parliamentary reform. In this period, however, parliamentary reform, which to the independents had meant independency, was taking on a new meaning. Reformers were concerned less with the independence of the House of Commons than

[1] Cf. Paul Whitehead, 'Epistle to Dr. Thomson', 1755 (*The Poetical Works of the English Poets* (ed. A. Chalmers, 1810), xvi. 223).

> Vain shall the Muse the various Symptoms find,
> When every doctor's of a different mind.
> In xx's palm, be foul corruption found,
> Each court-empiric hold, his grace is sound.
> In Sackville's breast let public spirit reign,
> Blisters! (they cry) the cause is in his brain,
> So, Talbot's want of place is want of sense,
> And Dashwood's stubborn virtue, downright insolence.

with the right of the people to vote for it, and shorter parliaments were thought desirable less because they reduced the government's control of the Commons than because they enabled the people to judge and control their members' conduct in parliament. The demand that members of parliament should be independent was lost in — and was in the end to be killed by — the demand that they should be dependent on the people. This was Radicalism, the child of independency, though soon so unlike its father that the relationship is easily forgotten.

In the earlier stage, before 1780, the defence of patronage was usually less sophisticated, for the general assumption was that the independence of the House of Commons, not the smooth working of the executive government, was the most vital element in the constitution. Thus Walpole, faced with charges of corruption, did not defend it, but merely denied that his sway over the Commons came from corruption. This difference can perhaps define, roughly, the period of independency. It was first notably advocated in the mid-1730s, with particular reference to Walpole, and, partly because of changed circumstances and partly because of the rise of radicalism, it hardly survived after 1781. For the first half of this period most independents usually opposed the government; after 1760 many of them supported it. None of them, of course, could at any time be relied on either to oppose or to support it.

An attempt to see this period through the eyes of the independents produces a picture which at first sight seems oddly old-fashioned: corruption reconsidered, and seen not as a device for making the constitution work, but as a constitutional development which not only fools thought undesirable; party regarded as a perversion of the constitution; agitation for place bills and annual parliaments seen as a serious attempt at constitutional or parliamentary reform; Bolingbroke, and some less spectacular pamphleteers and theorists, better understood; the accession of George III, and Bute's ministry, seen as very much more than a mere change of king and an unwise choice of minister. One does not need to accept the absolute truth of this picture in order to think it worth presenting, and to think it worth hunting for information about the kind of men who thought it true. Sir Francis Dashwood was one of these men, and his career almost coincides with the period of independency. He sat in the House of

Commons from 1741 to 1763. He was an independent, and was labelled variously Tory, independent Tory, Jacobite, and, by Dupplin in 1754, 'an opposition Whig unconnected with any of the leading parties'.[1] He accepted office as soon as George III came to the throne, and held office of some kind for the next twenty years, without becoming a party man.

Francis Dashwood was born in December 1708, and died at West Wycombe Park in Buckinghamshire on 11 December 1781. He was the grandson of Francis Dashwood, of Vellow-Wood in Somerset, Turkey merchant, member of the Saddlers' and Vintners' Companies, and alderman of London in 1653, who founded a prominent city and merchant family, and died in 1683. Two of his sons, Samuel and Francis, were also Turkey merchants. His eldest son, Samuel, knighted in 1684, was alderman, sheriff, Lord Mayor 1702-3, member of parliament for London 1685-7 and 1690-5, acquired land in Lincolnshire and founded a family there. His third son, Francis, also an alderman of London, was member of parliament for Winchelsea 1708-10. In 1698 he bought the manor and rectory of West Wycombe in Buckinghamshire jointly with his brother Samuel, and in 1705 bought Samuel's half-share. He was created a baronet in 1705. This Francis Dashwood, founder of the West Wycombe family, married four times, and set the stage for a very wide family connection for his eldest son, the second child of his second marriage. By his first marriage, with Mary Jennings, daughter of John Jennings of Westminster, alderman of London, he had two daughters, Mary, who in 1703 married Sir Fulwar Skipwith of Newbold, Warwickshire, and Susannah, who in 1702 married Sir Orlando Bridgeman of Ridley, Cheshire. Mary Jennings died in 1694. By his second marriage, with Lady Mary Fane, sister of the seventh Earl of West-

---

[1] Pitt's definition of his own position as an 'Independant' in 1779 is perhaps sufficient comment on the fact that the meaningful word here was 'independent'. 'I should not scruple to profess that my Sentiments and Principles are . . . not in favour of the present Administration. . . . But I do not wish to be thought inlisted in any Party or to call myself anything but an Independant Whig, which in words is hardly a distinction, as everyone alike pretends to it' (*Historical Manuscripts Commission, 10th Report, Appendix IV* (Westmorland MSS.) 26, Pitt to Lord Westmorland, 26 July 1779). But 'independent Whig' will not suffice for Dashwood.

morland, he had a daughter Rachel, born in 1706, and Francis. In 1738 Rachel married Sir Robert Austen of Hall-Place, Bexley, Kent, who died without children in 1743. She died in 1788. Dashwood's third wife was Mary King, niece of John King, who had been vicar of West Wycombe and afterwards Master of the Charterhouse, and died in 1739. They had two sons, John, born in 1716 and Charles, who died unmarried in 1740, and two daughters, Henrietta, and Mary, who in 1732 married John Walcot of Bitterley, Shropshire. Under John King's will, all but Mary took the name of King in addition to Dashwood. By his fourth marriage, with Lady Elizabeth Windsor, daughter of Thomas Windsor Hickman, first Earl of Plymouth, Dashwood had no children. They were married in 1720 and she died in 1737.

Nothing is known of Dashwood's education except that he was at Eton at the same time as Pitt, his exact contemporary, who all his life had a respect and liking for Dashwood, telling Horace Walpole in 1776 that, of all his old acquaintances, only Dashwood had asked him 'how he did'. Dashwood's mother died in 1710, his father in 1724. In 1726 he began the Tour of Europe with an eight months' visit to France and a return journey through Germany. In 1729–31 he was in Italy, staying in Florence and in Rome, where he became acquainted with the Abbé Niccolini and began a friendship which lasted until Niccolini died in 1769. On his return, in 1732, Dashwood took the initiative and chief part in founding the Society of Dilettanti. In 1733 he accompanied George Lord Forbes, later third Earl of Granard, on a visit to St. Petersburg. Forbes, Envoy Extraordinary to the Empress Anne, was charged with negotiating a commercial agreement with Russia. On the way they stopped at Copenhagen, and Dashwood, who returned alone, stopped there again on his way back. At some time, probably in the late 1730s, Dashwood visited Greece and Asia Minor. In 1739 he was again in Italy, taking a house in Florence, mixing in Niccolini's circle, meeting scholars and antiquaries and, amongst English travellers, Horace Walpole and Lady Mary Wortley Montagu. He returned to England in the summer of 1741, in time to offer himself as a candidate for parliament. His constituency was New Romney, which had been represented by his brother-in-law, Sir Robert Austen, in the parliaments of 1727 and 1734.

In parliament Dashwood came very quickly to be regarded as an able opposition speaker. He did not play a prominent part in the debates which led to Walpole's resignation and apparently did not support the subsequent inquiry into his conduct. He strongly opposed the employment by England of Hanoverian troops. He supported a motion to tax places and pensions at a rate double that of the land tax. On the eve of the Jacobite march from Scotland into England he proposed an inquiry into corruption, and outlined a plan of constitutional reform. He prepared a militia bill. He was clearly one of the most prominent of the independents in the House. At the time of the elections of 1747, when Frederick, Prince of Wales wished to effect an alliance with the Tories, it was Dashwood whom he approached for help, just as it was Dashwood whose support Dodington tried to enlist at the time of his resignation from office and junction with Frederick in 1749. Just before the elections Dashwood wrote and published a pamphlet, in the form of an *Address* to the electors. The pamphlet urges the need to free the House of Commons from the influence of the king and his ministers, and sets out the independents' programme: a place bill, the repeal of the Septennial Act, a militia bill. Other pamphlets written at the time of the elections counsel the choice of independent members, and warn electors against candidates who are ' *Place-Men* and *Pensioners* '; but Dashwood went further than this. He advised the use of a weapon which is associated, later, with radicalism, and, earlier, with Shaftesbury's Whig party: pledges, exacted by constituents from candidates for election to parliament. Dashwood's pamphlet is one of the things that separates him from the Tories and makes him look more like a 'true' 1689 Whig or, in Talbot's phrase, a 'real Whig'. But what Dashwood says about pledges goes beyond 'real Whiggism'.

In June 1745 Dashwood married Sarah, daughter and co-heir of George Gould of Iver, Buckinghamshire, and widow of Sir Richard Ellys of Nocton and Wyham, Lincolnshire, who had died in 1742. Ellys, grandson through his mother of the patriot John Hampden, was a theologian and a Greek and Hebrew scholar, an antiquarian, a great bibliophile, a puritan in religion. He was member of parliament for Boston from 1719 to 1734. He had no children and his Lincolnshire property was left to his widow for her lifetime. Dashwood's marriage gave him an interest in this property, on Lincoln Heath and near the river Witham, and strengthened the interest in Lincoln-shire which he had before this, both through the Dashwoods and through the Fanes. He bought property there, particularly in Dunston, the village next to Nocton. His marriage also gave him access to a large library and collection of antiques and pictures. Lady Dashwood died in 1769, again leaving no children. In June 1746 Dashwood was elected a Fellow of the Royal Society, and in April 1749, at the ceremony of the opening of the Radcliffe Library in Oxford, the degree of D.C.L. was conferred upon him.

In the parliament of 1747–54 Dashwood was again member for New Romney. He was the leading member of a small group of independents whose support in the House Dodington tried hard to win for his 'scheme of opposition'. This scheme would, Dodington hoped, include a group in the Commons and a parallel group in the Lords, led by the Earl of Westmorland. After Frederick's death in March 1751 Dodington renewed his efforts to form a 'party of constitutional principles . . . reduced into writing'. He failed to per-suade Dashwood that the proper object of opposition was office. Instead, Dashwood subscribed to another expression of true Whig-gism, Stanhope's Declaration. In May 1751 Dashwood was one of the handful of critics of the Regency bill in the Commons, as in January he had been one of the few who opposed the burning of the 'Jacobite' pamphlet 'Constitutional Queries'. In May 1752, when Dashwood refused to support a party willing, 'on certain terms', to join the Pelham government, Dodington gave up hope of winning him from his independency.

It was about this time that Dashwood's interest in building, improvements, and public works became conspicuous. The first Commons committee he sat on, in December 1741, was appointed 'to consider the Laws in being, with respect to the Repair and Pre-servation of the public Roads'[1] of England. This was the beginning of his membership of a notably long series of committees to discuss bills and petitions for the repair of roads and the establishment of turnpikes in all parts of the country, the building of bridges, and the improvement especially of London but also of other cities and boroughs. He was prominent in the movement to drain the fens and improve the navigation of the river Witham, which finally led to the

[1] *Commons Journals*, xxiv. 31 (8 Dec. 1741).

Witham Drainage Act of 1762, and he sat on a number of Commons committees for bills concerned with draining and navigation. In 1747 Dashwood introduced a poor-relief bill, providing for voluntary public works in order to relieve the unemployed. Three years later he undertook what the bill recommended, employing the poor of West Wycombe on building a new road just outside the village. In the early 1750s he began to make extensive alterations to the house at West Wycombe and to landscape the gardens. In 1751 he built Dunston Pillar, or 'Lincoln lighthouse', to guide travellers across the wild and unenclosed Lincoln Heath. At about the same time he began to repair and restore Medmenham Abbey. He sat on all important Dilettanti Society committees, and led the society in urging the establishment of a public academy for painting and architecture. He became a member of the Society for the Encouragement of Arts, Commerce, and Manufactures, founded in 1754.

In December 1755, in the uneasy years after Pelham's death, another approach was made to Dashwood: not this time from Dodington to join an opposition, but from Henry Fox to join a government. This also Dashwood refused. The approach was induced partly by the wish to attract a prominent independent to the government's side, partly by Dashwood's apparent alliance with Pitt. They had, of course, from time to time been on the same side in the 1740s, but less dangerously. They were brought together in the mid-1750s by their zeal for a militia bill. In December 1755 Pitt and George Townshend secured a committee to inquire into the existing militia laws, and Dashwood wrote a pamphlet urging the need to reform them. Both the bill Townshend introduced in March 1756 and the amended bill of January 1757 incorporated the main principles of the bill Dashwood had prepared in 1745. The second bill was passed in June 1757, when Pitt was in office, and Dashwood became the first colonel of the Buckinghamshire militia. In the same year Dashwood played the leading part in the defence of Byng in the House of Commons, showing not only courage but quick-wittedness and skill.

From the beginning of George III's reign it seemed likely that Dashwood would again be offered office and that this time he would probably accept it. It had indeed been thought that Pitt would offer him office in 1757, and it is possible that he did so and was, like Fox, refused.  In 1761 Dashwood changed his constituency from New Romney to Weymouth.  Bute named him in January 1761 as one of the three men without whom he would not join with Newcastle. In March 1761 Dashwood became a privy councillor and Treasurer of the Chamber, and in May 1762, in Bute's administration, Chancellor of the Exchequer.  In this office he was responsible for the first post-war budget.  This made provision for a large reduction in expenditure and a small increase in taxation, which took the form of additional customs duties on imported wines and cider, and an additional excise duty on cider made at home.  The excise duty, the 'cyder tax', raised a storm of opposition, reminiscent of the outcry which greeted Walpole's excise scheme in 1733 and as little related to the merits of the proposal.  No doubt an excise duty of any kind was a likely target for popular clamour: Niccolini believed that 'il nome V'accisa in Inghilterra è piu odioso di quello de Pretendente'.[1] The Whigs' attempt to make the cider tax a focus of united opposition to Bute failed, in so far as the bill passed both Houses.  Nevertheless, Bute's administration was doomed, for Bute was determined to stay in office only until the peace was made.  The treaty of Paris was signed on 10 February, and on 8 April, a week after the king gave his assent to the cider bill, Bute resigned.  Dashwood resigned too, for Grenville, Bute's successor, was a commoner and so combined the offices of First Lord of the Treasury and Chancellor of the Exchequer.  Dashwood was appointed Keeper of the Great Wardrobe.  The Earl of Westmorland had died in August 1762 and the barony of Le Despencer, held to be in abeyance on his death, was called out in Dashwood's favour.  Grenville tried to keep Dashwood's goodwill, and seems on the whole to have been successful. When Rockingham replaced Grenville in July 1765 Dashwood was dismissed from the Wardrobe.  In December 1766 Pitt, now Earl of Chatham, made him Joint Postmaster-General.  He held this post until his death in 1781.

After leaving the House of Commons Dashwood's interest in politics dwindled.  He attended the House of Lords regularly and played a prominent part in its committee work, but his intervention in political debates was rare.  In February 1766 he opposed the repeal

[1] Bodleian Library, MSS. Dashwood d.d. (Bucks) [Dashwood MSS.] B 11/4. Niccolini to Dashwood, 23 May 1763.

of the Stamp Act. On personal grounds, his wife's illness, he refused Grafton's request that he would second the Address in 1767, but he seemed willing enough to give general support to Grafton's government. His friendliness with Bute and Chatham continued, and he seems to have been on good terms with North. He befriended Franklin, who was dismissed from his office of Postmaster-General for America in 1774. It seems likely that Dashwood's opinions on the American question changed, probably after the government's decision in March 1770 not to repeal all the duties imposed in 1767 but to retain that on tea, and in July 1770 Franklin praised Dashwood's 'Plan of Reconciliation between the two Countries' and hoped that it might be adopted. More is known in these years of Dashwood's work at the Post Office than of his political views. He was a good Postmaster-General, having a care for efficient administration and supporting the Post Office in its attempts to free itself from the claims of political interest.

Dashwood's interest in building and improvements continued, as did his interest in antiquities and in modern experiments. In 1763 he repaired and rebuilt the church at West Wycombe in an attractive Italianate style and provided it with an organ; in 1763–4 he built a mausoleum near the church. He took the lead in the Dilettanti Society's encouragement and financial assistance to Stuart and Revett, and to their publication, in 1762, of the first volume of the *Antiquities of Athens*, an important stimulus to the neo-classical Greek influence in England. Two years later Dashwood encouraged the Society to send its own expedition to Asia Minor, and was chairman of the committee which organised it. It was a tribute to Dashwood's interest in Greek architecture that Revett, who built very little, designed several buildings at West Wycombe. He designed the Ionic portico on the west side of the house soon after he returned from the Dilettanti expedition to Asia Minor in 1766. He is said to have designed the east portico also, earlier, and, later, he built other temples in the garden. In 1769 Dashwood became a Fellow of the Society of Antiquaries, and was one of the first members of the Dilettanti Society to do so. His membership of the Society of Arts brought him into contact with David Hartley, son of the philosopher. In the 1760s Dashwood experimented with the use of copper for roofs, as a precaution against the spread of fire, and in 1774 he participated in one of Hartley's earliest experiments with fireproof rooms. In September 1771 Dashwood held a jubilee fête in the park at West Wycombe, to celebrate the completion of Revett's west portico; in 1774 he organised an impressive and moving ceremony there to commemorate the death of the poet Paul Whitehead. On both occasions the proceedings included a procession, accompanied by vocal and instrumental music, winding through the gardens and up the hill to the church, where an oratorio was performed. Interest in organ music was clearly the basis for Dashwood's acquaintance with the family of Samuel Wesley, for the religious reform that Dashwood favoured was not of Wesley's kind. In 1773 — at a time of controversy over the question of subscription to the Thirty-Nine Articles, and over the content of the Liturgy — Dashwood compiled a revised Book of Common Prayer, *An Abridgement of the Book of Common Prayer*, which was printed on his private printing press at West Wycombe. It had an important and unexpected influence in America.

Dashwood visited Oxford from time to time: he gave a book to the Bodleian Library, went with Franklin to the installation of North as Chancellor of the University in 1773, and was said to have had a hand in the planning of the new Magdalen bridge, begun in 1772. Dashwood's interest in the improvement of London went back to his membership of the Commons committee of 1744 to consider a bill for the better lighting of the City of London. For more than thirty years afterwards he was a member of most of the Commons and Lords committees which discussed the paving, lighting, and cleansing of London and Westminster streets, the clearing and widening of some of the passages and squares, the repairing and building of bridges and the embankment and navigation of the river. He was a vice-president of the Foundling Hospital and of the General Medical Asylum founded in 1777.

All this, and rather more, of Dashwood's life and career is documented, notwithstanding large gaps in chronological sequence. The picture that emerges is far more than an illustrative one. In politics, Dashwood was an independent in the sense that he thought Whig and Tory an outdated nomenclature, as Bolingbroke did. Dashwood's constitutional views were, however, 'old Whig' rather than 'old Tory', and his belief that Walpole and his successors were not 'real' or 'true' Whigs was linked not with a liking for Toryism but with adherence to the principles of 1689 Whiggism. For a definition of 'real Whig' and 'real Tory' he looked not to Bolingbroke but to Talbot, a man called republican and commonwealthman. Yet 'real Whig' will not quite do as a label for Dashwood, for his independency points to the future as well as to the past—to Wilkes as well as to Shaftesbury — and contains an element which must be called radicalism. In office, both in the first government after his election to the Commons that seemed to him to hold promise of being not incompatible with independency, and for the next twenty years, Dashwood showed a concern to free administration from the shackles of political interest. This concern stemmed naturally from his political independency, but it accords too with the canons of good administration enunciated by the economical reformers of the 1780s. In private life Dashwood was a man of intelligence, discrimination, and some originality. 'Honest', 'courageous', 'fearless', 'steady', are phrases used by contemporaries to describe his political conduct; phrases like 'careless of popularity', 'quick and generous', 'ready patron of new ideas', are contemporary comments on his character. He was, like many political independents, of an independent turn of mind, self-reliant, inquisitive, finding his own practical solutions to practical problems. But the range of his interests, and of his achievements, is unusual.

# 2

## An Independent in the House of Commons 1741–61

As a member of the House of Commons in the three parliaments between 1741 and 1761 Dashwood was often called 'Tory', and sometimes 'Jacobite'. These labels have never been challenged, and indeed, taking as a guide Bolingbroke's views in the 1730s, there seems at first sight good reason to describe Dashwood as a 'Tory independent'. He opposed all the Whig governments of these years, and his opposition was based on the creed of independency. He condemned the enslavement of the House of Commons which was Walpole's legacy to political life, and demanded as a remedy measures designed to loosen the government's hold over the Commons: place bills, the repeal of the Septennial Act, a stop to corruption. Nevertheless, there are unmistakable signs that the label 'Tory' is wrong, and that 'independent' needs qualification of another kind. Dashwood did not think himself a Tory, let alone a Jacobite. What makes it appropriate to modify his label is not so much his actions in parliament — for many Tories did support place bills and condemn septennial parliaments — as the sentiments on which his actions seem to have been based. Two of Dashwood's closest associates were Philip, second Earl Stanhope,[1] and William, second Baron Talbot.[2] Neither of these men was a Tory, though both were independents. Talbot, indeed, in 1734 offered a particularly

[1] 1714–86; son of James, first Earl Stanhope of Chevening; F.R.S. 1735; member of American Philosophical Society (on Franklin's recommendation) 1773. His letters in the Dashwood MSS. show that he and his wife were on terms of personal friendship with Dashwood.

[2] 1710–82; son of Charles, first Baron Talbot, of Barrington Park, Glos., and Hensol Castle, Glam.; M.P. Glamorgan 1734–7; Steward of Household 1761; cr. Earl Talbot 1763, Baron Dynevor 1780. He stood in 1734 as 'Whig' candidate against the dominant Mansel family and championed the independent interest in Glamorgan until his death. I have to thank Mr. P. D. G. Thomas for lending me a typescript copy of his chapter 'Glamorgan Politics 1688–1760', to be published in the Glamorgan County History.

attractive and convincing explanation of his independency. He made a plea, which is less suspect than Bolingbroke's, for dropping the terminology of Whig and Tory, and demonstrated that the principles of a 'real Whig' were no longer the principles of those who called themselves Whigs.

> An implicit faith is inconsistent with my principles, and contrary to my nature. I was taught very early in life to think for myself. The lesson suited my temper; I soon learnt it; I will for ever retain it; my opinion never yet hath been sacrificed, nor ever shall be; the compliment is too great for any man now living to expect, too mean for me to pay.
>
> I wish the nominal distinction of Whig and Tory was abolished, as the words only, not the sense remain; a Ministerial Whig and a State Tory, when in power, are so exactly alike in their conduct, that my discernment is not sufficient to distinguish one from the other. The principles of a real Whig, in my sense of the term, are these, That the Government is an original compact between the governors and governed, instituted for the good of the whole community; that in a limited monarchy, or more properly regal commonwealth, the majesty is in the people, and tho' the person on the throne is superior to any individual, he is the servant of the nation; that the only title to the crown is the election of the people; that the laws are equally obligatory to the Prince and people; that as the constitution of England is formed of three legislative branches, the balance between each must be preserved, to prevent the destruction of the whole; that elections ought to be free, the elected independent; that a Parliamentary influence by places and pensions is inconsistent with the interest of the public; and that a Minister who endeavours to govern by corruption, is guilty of the vilest attempt to subvert the Constitution; that a standing mercenary army, in time of peace, is contrary to the laws, dangerous to the liberties, and oppressive to the subjects of *Great Britain*.[1]

There seems no doubt that Dashwood subscribed to these views: it was probably statements of theory like this that led Frederick, Prince

[1] To these constitutional principles Talbot added freedom of the press, religious toleration, concern for trade and the colonies. Tory principles he defined as 'quite the reverse, for with them the Prince is above the law, Parliaments ought to be independent [? dependent], the freedom of the Press restrained, a standing army is necessary for the dignity of the Crown, and the security of domestic tranquillity . . . freedom of thought and debate occasions heresy in the Church and dissension in the State' (Talbot to Sir John Rundle, [May] 1734, *Letters of Thomas Rundle to Mrs Barbara Sandys, with introductory memoir by James Dallaway* (Gloucester, 1789), pp. 238–44).

of Wales to call Dashwood and Talbot 'republicans'. Stanhope, too, seems to have been something of a political theorist, and the views expressed in the Declaration he wrote in 1751 are not unlike Talbot's. Stanhope's son, the radical Lord Mahon,[1] stood as a Wilkite candidate for Westminster in 1774 and, like Wilkes, issued pledges to his constituents for his conduct in parliament. The content of Mahon's pledges was much the same as the content of the promises suggested in Stanhope's Declaration. The difference is in procedure. Promises made to each other, by a group of like-minded members of parliament, are replaced by pledges given by candidates to their constituents. This change marks the step from independency to radicalism. Yet in 1747, four years before Stanhope's praise of independency, Dashwood's *Address* had already suggested the new procedure. Moreover, his pamphlet not only recommended the exaction of pledges but justified them on grounds which both Mahon and Wilkes would have approved: the dependency of members of parliament on their constituents, and of the House of Commons on the people. 'Radical independency' is a contradiction in terms; but Dashwood wrote at a stage when it seemed not impossible to combine them.

The 1741–7 parliament lived its life in the shadow cast by Walpole's resignation. Its confusions were due primarily to the incoherence and disunity of the coalition that engineered his fall and the consequent instability of all governments except that of his supporter, Henry Pelham. In this parliament Dashwood seemed an independent Tory, and he was, moreover, one of those to whom the label 'Jacobite' was applied. This label had a thousand meanings. It was certainly not simply awarded, as Horace Walpole suggested, for particular vehemence against his father, and, although in December 1741 Dashwood seemed to Horace Walpole to be 'one of the most inveterate'[2] of the opposition, his inveteracy took a more impersonal

1 Charles Stanhope (1753–1816); unsuccessful candidate for Westminster 1774; active in county petitioning movement of 1780 and chairman of Kent Committee; M.P. Chipping Wycombe 1780–6; called 'Citizen Stanhope' because of sympathy with French Revolution; like his father, interested in science and in mechanical devices.

2 *Correspondence* (ed. W. S. Lewis), xvii. 249 (Walpole to Horace Mann, 24 Dec. 1741).

form than pursuit of Walpole. In January 1742, before Walpole's resignation, Dashwood supported a motion to bring in a bill to limit the number of placemen in the Commons. He also spoke in the debate on Pulteney's motion for a Select Committee of twenty-one 'to sit and examine whatever persons and papers they should please',[1] relevant to the conduct of the war. The defeat of this motion, like the defeat of Sandys's motion to remove Walpole the year before, showed that Walpole's superb oratory still had effect;[2] but the motion failed only by 250 to 253, while Sandys had only 106 votes to 290 for his direct personal attack on Walpole.

The months following Walpole's resignation on 11 February 1742 served to emphasise the difference between those of his opponents who succeeded him, like Sandys, Carteret, and Pulteney, or wished to do so, like Dodington, and those whose attitude to his successors remained much the same as their attitude to Walpole had been. Dashwood was one of these. On 10 December 1742 he voted against the government on the question of taking the Hanoverian troops into British pay.[3] A year later, on 6 December 1743, he spoke in support of Edmund Waller's motion for an Address to the king, asking that 'the Hanoverian troops should not be continued in the service of Great Britain' after 25 December.[4] This motion was lost by 181 to 231 votes. Stanhope proposed a similar motion in the Lords, speaking against the 'Hanoverian mercenaries', and Westmorland supported him. On 11 January 1744 Dashwood spoke and voted against continuing to maintain British troops in Flanders.[5] Dislike of Hanoverian troops and continental war was a Tory watchword, but it was not peculiarly Tory, for Pitt shared it and was indeed its

[1] *Correspondence* (ed. W. S. Lewis), xvii. 297–8 (Walpole to Mann, 24 Dec. 1741). Horace Walpole allowed that Dashwood made one of the 'several glorious speeches on both sides', even though he was misguided enough to contradict 'my friend Coke who . . . mentioned how great Sir Robert's character is abroad'.

[2] Lady Hartford thought Walpole's victory in 1741 'more to his honour than any occurrence which has happened in the course of his ministry' (*Pomfret-Hartford Correspondence*, ii. 219, Lady Hartford to Lady Pomfret, 19 Feb. 1741).

[3] *Parliamentary History*, xii. 1053–7. The voting was 260 for the government, 193 against.     [4] Ibid. xiii. 139.     [5] Ibid. 394.

most violent exponent until he joined Pelham's government in 1746. After this, in April 1746, Dashwood and Pitt were for the first time on opposite sides on the question of using Hanoverian troops and engaging in a continental war, and Pitt, defending his own change of front, was 'resolute and contemptuous of the present Tory opposition'.[1]

Other actions in this parliament showed more clearly what people meant by calling Dashwood a Tory and a Jacobite: he was one of a group of members who thought Walpole's fall no reason to abate their demands for an end to his 'system', and sought to achieve this by introducing place bills, pension bills, and motions for the repeal of the Septennial Act. Dashwood became conspicuous as a critic and would-be amender of Addresses to the king. At the beginning of the third session, on 1 December 1743, he supported, with what Philip Yorke described as 'absurd zeal', the very extreme motion proposing not to thank the king for his speech, and was successful in forcing it to a division.[2] Not all the opposition supported this move; according to Yorke the 'leaders' had decided not to divide on the Address 'which they allowed to be the most unexceptionable of any that had been proposed in their memory'. But Dashwood's zeal was perhaps not quite as absurd as Yorke pretended: he was supported, among others, by Pitt, Grenville, Lyttelton, and Dodington, and the voting was 149 to 278. On 15 February 1744 Dashwood supported an amendment to the Address of loyalty to the king, in reply to his message announcing that a French fleet was in the Channel and that the Young Pretender was in France and preparing an invasion. The amendment, proposed by the Tory Sir John Philipps, asked for an inquiry into 'the conduct of the Marine, and the times of the fitting out and sailing of the Brest squadron'.[3] This was a clear suggestion of mismanagement or worse. Dashwood went further. He

> dealt very much upon the causes and the political mismanagements, which occasioned the Revolution in 1688 — a weak, avaricious, narrow-minded prince on the throne, a great part of the nation proscribed and forced into disaffection, daily encroachments made upon the constitution. No wonder there was an unwillingness in the people

---

[1] Add. MS. 32707, f. 68.    [2] *Parl. Hist.* xiii. 138.
[3] Ibid. 645.

to support the government, which the Earl of Bedford intimated in his famous answer to King James . . . to the same purpose he [Dashwood] told a story out of Livy, that the Romans refused to march against foreign invaders until they had abolished the tyranny of the decemvirate.[1]

This speech, according to Yorke, 'gave deserved offence'; the fact that it was described by Sir William Yonge, Secretary at War, as having 'the most of a Jacobite tendency of any speech that was ever pronounced in parliament' is an illustration of the strange connotations of the word Jacobite. The voting was 123 for the amendment, 287 against, and it was therefore dropped. On 8 December 1744, after Granville's resignation and the formation of the Broad Bottom administration, Dashwood supported Henry Archer's amendment, in committee of Ways and Means, to a resolution for a land tax of 4 shillings in the pound, a maximum war-time figure. The amendment proposed to add to the land tax a tax of 8 shillings in the pound 'upon places and pensions'. Archer recommended this tax because it would 'operate as a place bill' and because, by lessening the value of places and so the undue influence supposed to arise from them, it would 'corroborate and strengthen' the Qualification Act, and 'fortify the laws of elections'.[2] Dashwood recommended it on the grounds that

> To reduce these towering giants of the common-wealth to the same size with the rest of the people, to cut off that exuberance which serves only to excite insolence on one part, and detestation on the other, cannot surely be thought improper or unjust, nor will those who appear to look upon place-men with so much tenderness, think them injured by screening them from the tenderness of the people.[3]

The amendment was defeated by 95 votes to 53. It was followed on 29 January 1745 by Thomas Carew's motion for annual parliaments, which was lost only by 145 votes to 113. Carew's speech in support of his bill illustrates well the attitude of independents to the 'new ministers and *quondam* patriots' who, if they had fulfilled the promises they made when Walpole was in office, would themselves have brought in both this bill and a place bill. More positively, Carew's arguments for annual parliaments show, as Dashwood's constitutional arguments do, how radicalism could grow out of an

---

[1] *Parl. Hist.* xiii. 647.    [2] Ibid. 993–8.    [3] Ibid. 1033.

appeal to the past. Annual parliaments, Carew held, were 'our ancient constitution'. They were prescribed in law by the two statutes of Edward III's reign which stated that 'a parliament shall be annually holden', and 'every one knows that long prorogations or adjournments were not then introduced or known: so that the meaning of both these laws must be, that a parliament should be every year chosen as well as held'.[1] But Carew was far from advocating annual parliaments simply because they were authorised by law and by the ancient constitution. This was their constitutional justification; what made them desirable was that they would enable 'the people' to keep a tight control over their representatives. Members of parliament, he believed, should be independent of the king and his ministers, but not independent of the electors, for 'we are, properly speaking, the Attornies of the people. Is it prudent, is it reasonable, that any man should give a power of attorney irrevocable for a long term of years?'[2]

In the autumn of 1745 Dashwood was again called Jacobite. On 17 October, just as the Young Pretender was preparing to march from Edinburgh into England, Dashwood proposed to add a clause to the Address in reply to the King's Speech. Philipps seconded his proposal, and on the same day Westmorland 'spoke about Grievances'[3] in the House of Lords. Dashwood thought the Address too short. He urged that

at a time when we are in such imminent domestic danger; at a time when we may have need for the hands as well as the purses of the people, surely, we ought to do something to convince them, that we have a regard for their rights and privileges, as well as for the posts, places, and lucrative employments that many, perhaps most of us enjoy.

He drew a distinction between the 'constitution' and the 'establishment': corruption made it possible that 'under the latter the former may be destroyed, and, consequently, the people divested of their rights and privileges'. 'The people', he believed, were aware of the

[1] Ibid. 1058.          [2] Ibid. 1060.
[3] Debrett, *History, Debates, and Proceedings of both Houses of Parliament, 1743–74* (1792), ii. 11–18. Westmorland made a long speech (the only one in the Lords on the Address) deploring corruption, but did not propose an amendment.

distinction, and had shown this in 'the instructions that have been given in all parts of the United Kingdom, to their representatives in this House'. He believed that 'we cannot do a better service to our sovereign, than by passing such laws as are necessary for putting a stop to the progress of corruption, . . . and, as the people have loudly called for some such laws against corruption being passed, we cannot take a more proper opportunity for introducing them, because it will confirm and strengthen that spirit, which now appears among the people without doors in favour of our present establishment, and will make them more ready to venture their lives in support of the government'.[1] Accordingly, he proposed that the Address should include the following paragraph:

> And in order to the firmer establishment of your Majesty's Throne on the solid and truly glorious Basis of your people's affections, it shall be our Zealous and Speedy Care to frame such bills as (if passed into laws) may prove more effectual than any hitherto obtained for securing to your faithful Subjects, the perpetual enjoyment of their undoubted right to be freely and fairly represented in Parliaments frequently chosen, and exempted from undue influence of every kind; for easing their minds in time to come of the apprehensions they might entertain of seeing abuses in offices rendered perpetual without the seasonable interpolation of Parliament to reform them, and for raising in every true Lover of his King and Country the pleasing hopes of beholding these Realms once more restored to that happy and flourishing Estate as may reflect the highest honour on your Majesty's Reign and cause posterity to look back with veneration and gratitude on the Source of their National felicity.[2]

The proposal had little support. No doubt most of its potential friends were swayed, as even Strange[3] was, rather by the argument

[1] *Parl. Hist.* xiii. 1337–42; Debrett, *History*, ii. 37–41.

[2] Dashwood MSS. B 7/2 (written in Dashwood's hand).

[3] James Smith Stanley (1717–71), eldest son of eleventh Earl of Derby; M.P. Lancashire 1741–71; a firm and respected independent, often on the same side as Dashwood; called himself 'a Whig in principle'; Feb. 1757 defended Byng; June 1757 refused Fox's offer of office; Nov. 1762 Chancellor of Duchy of Lancaster; Jan. 1763 proposed that House should sit on anniversary of Charles I's death, and that the statute prescribing 'such a saint's day' should be repealed; Feb. 1763 supported peace terms; opposed increased grants for members of royal family; Mar. 1763 supported cider

that the time was inopportune for reform, than by Dashwood's argument that reform would strengthen the government. Pitt, the self-styled 'friend to every thing that could reasonably be offered for securing the independency of parliaments', was anxious that he should not be thought a party to Dashwood's amendment, and flatly denied that constituencies had instructed their representatives 'to bring in any such bills'. It was, Pitt declared, essential to oppose an

> amendment offered at a time so extremely improper as the present. . . .
> Shall we employ ourselves in contriving bills to guard our liberties from corruption, when we are in danger of losing them, and everything else that is dear to us, by the force of arms? . . . Do gentlemen wish to . . . create a contention about the Constitution, that the Kingdom may fall an easy prey to the enemy? If, Sir, I did not know the Honourable Gentlemen, who made and seconded this motion, I should really suspect their having some such design.[1]

Pitt was, of course, incorrect in stating that constituents had not instructed their members. He must have been as aware as Dashwood was of the instructions issued at the time of Walpole's resignation,[2] and the discussions about them in the *Craftsman* and other journals, and he may well have read the anonymous pamphlet *A Hint upon Instructions*, which deplored the 'Political Doctrine strenuously enforced by the *Modern* Male-contents, *That the Electors have an absolute, and indubitable right to* Instruct, *and* Advise *their members how to* Act, *and give their Votes upon every occasion in Parliament*; *And that They are accountable for every Step they take, as* Representatives, *to those who Elect Them.*'[3]

On 25 October 1745, just a week after Dashwood's amendment to the Address, the House of Commons gave leave for the introduction of a bill 'for the better Regulation of the Militia in that part of

tax; Feb. 1766 voted and spoke against repeal of Stamp Act, but not dismissed by Rockingham.

1 J. Almon, *Anecdotes of the Life and Character of William Pitt, Earl of Chatham* (1792), i. 92–93.

2 *Parl. Hist.* xii. 416–27, lists 18 counties, 12 cities, and 15 boroughs which sent petitions, and prints several. It states that other boroughs also petitioned.

3 *A Hint upon Instructions from the Electors to their Representatives in Parliament, &c.* (London, 1742), pp. 5–6.

*Great Britain* called *England*'.[1] Dashwood was a member of the committee appointed to prepare the bill. After the Restoration the militia had been reorganised on the basis of the general levy,[2] but its effectiveness declined after 1689, with the authorisation of a standing army, and a period of neglect set in. Nevertheless, even if some sort of a standing army was generally accepted as inevitable, this did not mean that it was generally accepted as the sole form of national defence. Accordingly, an efficient militia became the symbol not only of patriotic self-defence but also of liberty, the counterpoise to a standing army and, in the last resort, the nation's defence against it. It was a 'constitutional force', the safeguard alike of ancient Rome and modern Switzerland. To Dashwood, therefore, just as the invasion in 1745 was an argument for constitutional reform, not against it, so it increased the desirability of reforming the militia and not relying for defence on the standing army or on mercenary soldiers. He drafted a bill,[3] providing for a militia of 100,007 private men and 18,083 officers, divided into 175 regiments and three independent companies. It was to be raised on a county basis and paid for out of public funds. The quota for each county, based on its land tax assessment, the cost, and the estimate that this could be met by an extra 5*d.* on the land tax, were based on calculations made for Dashwood by the mathematician Peter Davall.[4] The committee

[1] *Commons Journals*, xxv. 12. The bill was ordered to be printed three times: on 12 Feb. (ibid. 151), on 12 May (after the committee stage), and on 20 June (after the House had considered the committee's amendments). But it was printed separately, not in the *Journals*, and is not included in either of the collections of eighteenth-century parliamentary papers (*Papers printed by Order of the House of Commons from the Year 1731 to 1800*, 110 vols. (1807); *Reports from Committees of the House of Commons, 1715–1801, reprinted by Order of the House of Commons*, 16 vols. (1803)). See Appendix V.

[2] 13 Chas. II, st. I, c. 26; 13 and 14 Chas. II, c. 5. The abolition of tenures by knights-service did not remove the liability of every subject to serve in the general levy, which remained the basis of the reconstituted militia until 1757.

[3] Dashwood MSS. B 8/2. The bill is in Dashwood's hand: several pages are missing.

[4] d. 1763; lawyer and mathematician; Master in Chancery 1759; Fellow of Royal Society 1740, Secretary 1747–59; Fellow of Society of Antiquaries; member of Spalding Society 1753; translated *Memoirs of*

discussed Dashwood's plan and Davall's figures and it is reasonably certain that the bill that was introduced into the Commons on 12 February 1746 was Dashwood's. The bill was considered by a Committee of the Whole House in May and by the House in June. Apparently it was then dropped, for there is no record of its third reading. But the scheme 'w^ch is call'd yours, well becoming a Guardian of his Country'[1] did more than give another label — 'militia patriot' — to Dashwood, for its main principles were repeated in the bill introduced ten years later, in March 1756 and in the bill which became law in June 1757.

Dashwood's proposed amendment, in October 1745, and the reasons he gave for it, was much speculated upon.[2] Stripped of its context, the motion is just a statement of the creed of independency, together with the suggestion that the people have declared their support for it. Dashwood elaborated both the creed and the suggestion in 1747. The Pelham government, triumphant after the failure of Bath and Granville to form an administration in February 1746, and strengthened by the accession of the Cobhamites and Pitt, dissolved parliament in June 1747. Just before the dissolution, but not before it was generally expected, Dashwood wrote his *Address*.[3]  In

*Cardinal de Retz* 1723; assisted with drafting of bill to regulate commencement of year, 1751, and wrote *Vindication of New Calendar, Tables and Rules annexed to the Act for regulating the commencement of the year*, 1761; one of mathematicians asked to advise on merits of elliptical arches for Blackfriars Bridge 1760.

1 Dashwood MSS. B 8/1. H. D. to Dashwood, 19 Mar. [1746].

2 One of those who commented on it was Lady Bolingbroke, who wrote to Lady Denbigh about 'la queue . . . [au] chevalier Dashwood'. But the information she gave about its content was inaccurate (H.M.C. *Denbigh MSS*. v. 188. 17 and 24 Oct. 1745).

3 *An Address to the Gentlemen, Clergy, and Freeholders of all the Counties in Great Britain, and to the Mayors, Jurats, Bailiffs, Aldermen, Common-Councilmen, and Burgesses of all the Cities, Towns-Corporate, and Boroughs throughout the said Kingdom of Great Britain. The following necessary and friendly Advice is humbly offered, by a Cordial Admirer of Truth and Liberty, and a Zealous Friend of this Constitution.* London. Printed for E. Amey, at Charing-Cross. 1747. 7 pp. Three manuscript drafts of this, one dated 9 June, are in Dashwood (MSS.) B 7/2. It was published anonymously: a copy is in the British Museum (643 1. 28(12)). See Appendix I.

1745 he had asserted the relevance of the people's wish to end corruption, as expressed in the instructions issued to their representatives; in 1747 he went further, urging that the programme of independency could be assisted if constituents demanded pledges from candidates. He described the reforms necessary to restore the constitution to its intended condition of balance and harmony and, above all, to restore the House of Commons to independence. The first of these concerned the timing of elections, the link between Commons and people. Dashwood warned electors that the

> dissolving of a Parliament, is always acknowledged and understood to be a violent Measure, merely Ministerial, and cannot be National, and bespeaks some extraordinary political Jobb to be put in Execution, that will not bear the Light, and must mean to declare, that it is not safe to suffer the Elections to take Place after the Secret is out.

He reminded them that 'you once had a Right to judge of the Behaviour of your Representatives every three Years', and expressed his astonishment that all constituencies had not instructed their representatives to secure the repeal of the 'unjust, odious, destructive [Septennial] Act'. This condemnation of septennial parliaments was followed by a piece of radical doctrine which completely denies the theory of representation, and is only doubtfully compatible with independency at all: the claim that the right to elect carried with it 'a Right therefore to make Terms on behalf of yourselves and the Nation, with these you constitute and appoint to represent you'. These terms should be precise: a point insisted on by Cobbett when discussing the relations between members and constituents in 1832. Constituents should impose them on members of parliament by making them

> (previous to their Elections) sign and seal Duplicates, wherein they shall declare solemnly, that they will not adhere to, support, or put Confidence in, any Administration whatever, nor grant any Aids of Money to the Crown, until these just Rights and Demands of the People are procured, by the three abovementioned Acts of Parliament being obtained: namely, the Repeal of the Septennial Bill, which enables Men to represent the Commons of *Great Britain* for the unreasonable Term of Seven Years. An Act to constitute an effectual and numerous Militia throughout the Kingdom, and a further Place-bill, at least to exclude Officers, as abovementioned.

28

The *Address* ends with a suggested form of promise, a 'Declaration which all honest Men will not refuse to sign, if required, and what all prudent Men will require to be signed by those who offer themselves as Candidates to serve in Parliament'. It is drawn up in legal form, like a contract, and contains the phrase

> And I declare by these Presents under my Hand and Seal, that I accept of my Seat in Parliament upon these Terms; and that I understand this to be the Intention of my Constituents.

This is even more radical, for it replaces the idea of free election by the quite novel idea of something like a legally enforceable contract between members and constituents.

Just before the 1747 elections there seems to have been a proposal [1] that Dashwood should offer himself as a candidate for the city of Lincoln, an open borough, but he did not do so and was returned again for New Romney. He appeared as a matter of course in a list of 'Lords and Commons in Opposition', probably drawn up soon after the meeting of the new parliament.[2] His prominence in opposition, and his potential value as an ally, are reflected in the approaches made to him by Frederick, Prince of Wales at the time of the elections. On 4 June Dashwood and Talbot were invited to meet Frederick and two of his party, Baltimore and Dr. Lee, at Carlton House. Frederick read them a 'Paper' of proposals, and Dashwood and Talbot were authorised 'to give the most positive Assurances to the Gentlemen in the Opposition, of his upright Intentions', and to say that he 'invites all well-wishers to this Country & its Constitution to coalise & unite with him'.[3] As a basis of

---

[1] Dashwood MSS. B 10/1. Coningsby Sibthorp to Dashwood, 10 and 22 June 1747. Sibthorp asked for Dashwood's support, if he was not himself a candidate, and assured him that 'my sentim^ts & just indignation is equaly strong ag^st the late measures as what you have kindly express'd y^rself in'. He was elected.

[2] Dashwood MSS. D 1/4. The list (undated) is in the hand of Samuel Sandys, with the title in Dashwood's. It contains 24 members of the Lords, 125 of the Commons. It was probably compiled in the autumn of 1747: all the members named (28 of them new members) sat in the 1747 parliament, except William Curzon (M.P. Clitheroe 1741–7, d. 1749) and Robert Fenwick (M.P. Lancaster 1741–7, d. 1750), and several died early in 1748.

[3] British Museum, Add. MS. 35870, ff. 129–31. Parson Etough

union Frederick declared his intention 'to abolish for the future all Distinctions of Party and, so far as it lies in his power, . . . to take away all Proscriptions from any Set of men whatever, who are Friends to this Constitution'. He promised to support, and to promote 'when it is in his power', a bill for a property qualification of £300 a year for J.P.s, a militia bill, a bill limiting the number of army and navy officers in the Commons, an inquiry into 'Abuses in Offices', and to be content with a Civil List of £800,000 a year. The gentlemen who considered this paper, mostly Tories, may not have been very impressed with Frederick's promises: the place bill he suggested was a modest one and there was no mention of the repeal of the Septennial Act or the abolition, or even reduction, of the standing army. In any case it was not easy to bring the Tories to the idea of a firm alliance with the heir to the throne. In January 1748, long after the elections, Frederick was still awaiting a reply, and Dashwood pacifying Baltimore with the assurance that 'the great affair in question, is seriously in agitation'.[1] When the reply was at last sent, on 8 February 1748, it was cautious and non-committal, and this probably accorded with Dashwood's own feeling. It expressed gratitude, and appreciation of Frederick's intentions, but it mentioned no specific measures and made no comment on those mentioned by Frederick:

> The Lords and Gentlemen to whom a Paper has been communicated containing his Royall Highness the Prince[s] gracious intentions upon several weighty and important points of the greatest consequence to the honour and interest of his Majesty[s] Government and absolutely necessary for restoreing and perpetuating the true use and design of Parl[nts] the Purity of our excellent constitution, and the Happyness and Wellfare of the Whole Nation Do therein with the greatest satisfaction observe and most gratefully acknowledge the uprightness and generosity of those his Royal Highness[s] noble sentiments and resolutions; and therefore beg leave to return their most dutyfull and humble thanks for

describes Frederick's Proposal as 'the Method he [Frederick] took to induce the steady and determined adherents to the cause of Jacobitism to a Coalition with his particular Friends'. Etough names Dashwood as one of the 'most flagrant Jacobites', and adds, wrongly, that Frederick exerted his interest for Dashwood in the general election (*Free and Impartial Reflections on the Character, Life, and Death of Frederick Prince of Wales* (n.d.), pp. 54, 63).

[1] British Museum, Egerton MS. 2136, f. 7.

the same, and to assure his Royal Highness that they will constantly and steadily use their utmost endeavours to support those his wise and salutary purposes, that the *Throne* may be strengthened, Religion and Morality encouraged Faction and corruption destroyed the Purity and essence of Parliament restored and the Happyness and wellfare of our constitution preserved.[1]

Frederick's overtures were followed by a series of attempts to build an effective and united opposition. These were instigated by Dodington. In March 1749 he resigned his office of Treasurer of the Navy in Pelham's government and threw in his lot with the opposition, and in July Frederick made him his Treasurer of the Chambers. Dashwood was certainly inclined to prefer Dodington to the extremists who tried to undermine his influence with Frederick.[2] But Horace Walpole was wrong in saying that Dashwood 'was strongly for'[3] Dodington; it was, rather, that Dodington was strongly for Dashwood. He was important to Dodington's plans not because they were in political agreement but because Dodington believed that Dashwood's alliance might bring with it the support of independents and Tories in both Houses. Thus Dodington reported to Dashwood, on 18 July 1749, Frederick's promise that, on his accession, he would make Dashwood Treasurer of the Navy or Cofferer of the Household. Dodington himself was to be Secretary of State. He was gratified that Dashwood received the news 'with much pleasure, both what related to himself, and to me'.[4] It is however clear that Dashwood was less committed than Dodington would have wished, and Dodington was no doubt well aware of this, even if reluctant to admit it. He certainly hoped that Dashwood's 'Countenance, &

---

[1] Dashwood MSS. B 1/1. 'Answer to Prince of Wales.' There is a copy of the Answer in the Shaftesbury MSS. in the Public Record Office (28, no. 25), and in Add. MS. 38570, and a copy is printed in *Bedford Correspondence*, i. 330–2, where there are two small differences from the version in Dashwood MSS. B 1/1.

[2] See Dodington's complaint of 'the lyes that have been told him of me, by Lords Egmont, and Baltimore, &c': one of the lies was 'that my design when I came into the Family, was to turn them all out even to the women, &c' (*Diary*, pp. 82–83, 11 Sept. 1750).

[3] *Correspondence* (ed. Lewis), xx. 39 (Walpole to Mann, 23 Mar. 1749).

[4] *Diary*, p. 8.

Assistance, would be, always, at Hand',[1] but hardly expected his independency to be so easily stilled. In the spring and summer of 1750 Dodington pursued his schemes for building an effective opposition. At the end of July James Ralph was entrusted with a 'Paper', proposing a union of all the opposition, Whig and Tory, around Frederick, and commissioned to obtain the views of Dashwood, Talbot, Middlesex, Furnese and Oswald.[2] Dashwood's comment was that the 'Paper was not particular enough',[3] though he was 'ready to underwrite any State-Policy that insur'd the Interest of the State'. It seems likely that the particulars Dashwood wanted were constitutional ones. Another kind of criticism came from Edmund Waller. He objected that the proposal was narrowly based, coming only from a part of Frederick's court, together with two or three neutrals, and he believed that the principle of union ought to be 'a sensible opposition grounded on such facts as might serve to expose the administration to the bottom'. This was a simpler outlook: to find the focus of opposition in the policy of the particular men in office.

Although one suspects that Dodington's preference, other things being equal, would have been for 'a sensible opposition', he was convinced that opposition would only be effective if it was based on a 'union of parties'. For this he believed Dashwood's support to be vital. So in January 1751 Dodington tried again. This time he went to see Westmorland first, proposing to him, on 18 January, 'a cooperation, with a small group of peers, which he seem'd to approve of, and promis'd to endeavour to make it practicable', and on the next day approached Dashwood and Talbot, Furnese, Waller, and Oswald.[4] But by 21 March, when Frederick died, Dodington had made no progress. Frederick's death did not, in Dodington's opinion, make a united opposition any less desirable. Two days later, therefore, he called on Westmorland and begged him to take the lead, urging 'that their Lordships should form a set of propositions for the centre of union and then should call them [members of the Commons] together, to own them, and act upon them, either taking

---

[1] Dashwood MSS. B 11/1. Dodington to Dashwood, 28 Sept. 1749.
[2] Dodington, *Diary*, pp. 81–82. 1 Aug. 1750.
[3] H.M.C., *Var. Coll.* vi. 21. (Ralph to Dodington, 23 Aug. 1750.) The letter is now in the Houghton Library, Harvard University.
[4] *Diary*, p. 96.

places (if they were to be had on honourable terms) or acting without places'.[1]  Dodington's satisfaction with his interview, his belief 'that I had never before made such impression upon him [Westmorland]', was premature.  No set of propositions was produced, and on 10 April Dodington was back where he started: again he visited Westmorland and had a 'long conversation' with him and Stanhope, and again he believed he left them 'persuaded of the necessity of forming a Party, united by constitutional principles, reduc'd into writing, and sign'd by all the party'.  This time, however, he thought to encourage them by giving them a model: the 'paper' he had himself drawn up in July 1750.

> I told them that I had once drawn up such a Political Creed for the last opposition, but the gentlemen did not care to sign it . . . to make a beginning, if they pleas'd I would send them the paper mention'd, where possibly some hints might be of use. . . . I went home, and sent it directly, to the Earl of Westmorland.[2]

Dodington's 'political creed' was perhaps not of much use, but at least there was this time something to show for his efforts: a Declaration[3] composed by Stanhope.  The preamble, which consisted of a description of the purpose of government, the present state of the country, and the need for reform, Dodington thought 'extremely good'.  The body of the Declaration was less to his taste.  It was prefaced by an undertaking: 'We have, by way of Pledge, both to the Public and to each other, for the Sincerity of our Intentions, subscribed our Names to this Declaration'.  The Declaration consisted of agreed constitutional objectives: annual parliaments, or at least triennial ones; limitation of the number of placemen in the Commons to a maximum of fifty; a militia adequate for the purposes of defence; liberty of the press.  There followed, 'in order to demonstrate to the world, as far as Words and Actions can extend, that our

---

[1] Ibid., p. 108.        [2] Ibid., p. 111.
[3] Dashwood MSS. B 7/2.  See Appendix II.  There are rough drafts of the Declaration, and a final version headed 'Declaration drawn up in April 1751, and proposed to be subscribed by a number of members of both Houses of Parliament', in the Stanhope papers at Chevening.  The papers also contain a copy of Dashwood's amendment of 17 Oct. 1745.  No letters from Dashwood to Stanhope seem to have survived.  I am grateful to Mr. Aubrey Newman for lending me his microfilm of the second Earl's papers.

Intention is not to accomplish a change of Men, but of Measures', a promise to support any administration which would effect these reforms, and to do so without 'any tacit or express Bargain for the Gratification of any one or more Persons of our Number, with any Office, Trust, Honour, or Reward whatsoever'. This expression of a wish to see a reforming government, as distinct from a wish to be that government, accorded perfectly with independency. But Dodington could hardly be expected to approve it. It was, he lamented, the end of all hope of a united opposition, for 'the terms they propose to sign, are of a sort that imply an exclusion from coming into office'.[1] Disunity was in fact even greater than Dodington thought, for although Dashwood and Westmorland approved the Declaration the Tories did not. This, of course, was not because they agreed with Dodington's criticism of it, but perhaps partly because they were unwilling to commit themselves in writing, and partly because they did not like Stanhope's philosophy. If this is to be labelled, it must be called 'old Whig', not 'Tory'. The fact that Dashwood and Westmorland approved Stanhope's Declaration is an important indication of the nature of the difference between these three and the Tories. Dashwood's own difference from the Tories had already been shown by his 1747 *Address*, which was more radical than Stanhope's Declaration and may well have distinguished him not only from the Tories but from Stanhope and Westmorland too. These differences did not, however, destroy Dashwood's value to Dodington. Dashwood was certainly closer to the Tories than Dodington was, and more respected by them, quite apart from the fact that he was also, in Dodington's opinion, more constructive and therefore worth winning in himself. To Dodington, in fact, Dashwood was not a Tory but a bridge to the Tories.

Dodington's despair of union was confirmed in May 1751, by the easy passage of the Regency bill, which could, he thought, have served as a rallying point for opposition. Instead, as James Ralph said, 'to my infinite amazement, there seems to be neither concert nor Inclination to oppose'.[2] In the Lords Stanhope was alone in opposing the clause establishing a Council of Regency, and there was

[1] *Diary*, p. 115. 23 Apr. 1751.
[2] Dashwood MSS. I 1. Ralph to Edward Harley, third Earl of Oxford, 10 May 1751.

no seconder for Talbot's motion of opposition to the clause prolonging the existing parliament for three years, if the king was a minor, unless the Regent dissolved it sooner.[1] In the Commons only Dashwood and Thomas Pitt spoke against the bill on its first reading on 13 May 1751. 'The Tories', Dashwood told Dodington, who did not attend, were 'totally silent. The Court for it. Dr. Lee and Mr. Nugent speaking for it.' At the Committee stage the clause establishing the Regency council was strongly attacked, on constitutional grounds, by Speaker Onslow, who declared that 'the Royal Power must not be divided; that control is dividing it; that it never ought to be controlled, except when abused'.[2] But in spite of the weight of Onslow's name he had no support. 'I have, ever since I saw you', Dodington wrote to Dashwood on the day after the first reading in the Commons, 'been considering, & I think have well consider'd, the impracticability of uniting any four efficient Persons, upon any Principle, or Plan that may serve, or save their Country.' He counselled withdrawal from 'so ungracefull a Scene', though he defined his own withdrawal only as passing 'next week, Here [at Hammersmith]'. Once more he clearly hoped, without expecting, Dashwood would follow his advice.

> I wish that we might always think & act alike, or, at least, that what I do, may not meet with your Disapprobation, but not with the least View or Pretence to influence what your better Judgement shall direct, which [I] shall look upon, as your best Guide.[3]

The failure of the attempts to form a united opposition after Frederick's death meant less to Dashwood than it did to Dodington just because Dashwood did not accept the view that party, or union, should be primarily a means of achieving office. He had listened to Dodington's schemes of opposition, but Dodington never captured his firm support. After the failure of May 1751 Dodington had no choice but to turn to the idea of forming a party which would be willing 'on certain terms' to join the Pelham government. This, if he could have got his party, was not a forlorn hope, for Pelham's

[1] *Parl. Hist.* xiv. 1000 (10 May 1751).
[2] Walpole, *Memoirs of the last ten years of the reign of George II*, ed. Holland (1847), i. 124.
[3] Dashwood MSS. B 11/1. 14 May 1751.

policy was to stifle his potential opponents by including as many as possible of them in his government. Dodington's attempt to persuade Dashwood in May 1752 to join in an approach to Pelham[1] failed not because it was based on an unrealistic plan, but simply because Dashwood, not regarding office as of great importance, was not interested in stating the conditions on which he would accept it. Dodington therefore had no party to strengthen his approaches to Pelham. Nevertheless, Pelham affected to welcome him, 'told to me the bottom of his politicks', and promised that he would try to persuade the king to forget Dodington's desertion in 1749 and to remember that he had, after all, been a moderating influence on Frederick. Dodington therefore had some hope of office in the reconstruction that followed Pelham's death on 6 March 1754. This hope is reflected in Dodington's report of a dinner party he gave on 18 March.[2] It was very much a business meeting: Dashwood was there, and George Grenville, but not Westmorland or Stanhope. There was no talk of party, only of the rearrangement of offices which must follow Newcastle's transfer from Secretary of State to First Lord of the Treasury. Again, however, Dodington's hopes were disappointed. Newcastle proved that he could 'talk *Pelham*' as well as Pelham, but nothing came of his 'fine conversation', and by the time of the dissolution of parliament in April 'all the employments were given away' and there was nothing to show for Dodington's efforts except his own promise to use his electoral influence on the side of the government. He kept his promise, but was not any longer deceived by Newcastle's 'great professions of good wishes, good will, best endeavours, &c which weigh with me, as much as the breath they were made of'.[3]

Dashwood's independency and his carelessness of office were further defined during the next parliament, which met in May 1754. It was in this parliament that, according to Horace Walpole,

after so long a dose of genius, there at once appeared near thirty men [who] in their several degrees, comprehended all the various powers of eloquence, art, reasoning, satire, learning, persuasion, wit, business, spirit, and plain common sense.

---

[1] *Diary*, p. 158. 11 May 1752.     [2] Ibid., p. 256.
[3] Ibid., pp. 268–9.

His description of Dashwood, one of the thirty, as

> a man who loved to know, and who cultivated a roughness of speech [and] affected to know no more than what he had learned from a very unadorned understanding[1]

might perhaps be translated as a combination of 'learning' and 'plain common sense'.

The part Dashwood played in the debate on the disputed Oxfordshire election of April 1754 reveals something of the meaning he attached to independency. He had been present during that 'remarkably candid Election . . . [and] still more extraordinary Scrutiny'.[2] There were two Whig candidates, Sir Edward Turner and Lord Parker, son of the Earl of Macclesfield, and two Tories, Lord Wenman and Sir James Dashwood. Both Tories received more votes than either of the Whigs, but the Whigs demanded a scrutiny, and the sheriff returned all four, saying that he 'had not time to Compleat [the Scrutiny]' and leaving the decision to the House of Commons.[3] All four sat, and no action was taken until 18 November, when petitions were presented from both Whig and Tory candidates, and from the freeholders of Oxfordshire, complaining of the conduct of the election. Dashwood then proposed that the House should consider the question of the double return before it considered the petitions. This proposal, which even the radical Oldfield thought 'certainly reasonable', was defeated, and the House decided instead, by a very large majority, to consider both matters at the same time. The proposal that the sheriff should attend the House, to answer the charge that he had given 'a very unfair advantage to the court candidates, by allowing them to make their objections to all the voters through the whole poll, before the opposition gentlemen should object to one individual' was also defeated. The dice were in fact heavily loaded in favour of the Whig candidates, and after protracted debates they were declared, on 23 April 1755, to have been duly elected.

[1] Walpole, *George II*, ii. 143.

[2] Dashwood MSS. B 11/3. Sir Francis Skipwith to Dashwood, 9 June [1754]. Dashwood voted in the parish of Stokenchurch (*Poll of the Freeholders of Oxfordshire, taken at Oxford on the 17th, 18th, 19th, 20th, 22nd and 23rd of April 1754*. Printed at [Oxford: at] the Theatre (1754), p. 83).

[3] The votes were: Wenman 2033; Dashwood 2014; Parker 1919; Turner 1890.

Apart from the questions of bribery and the partiality of the returning officer, a question of principle was involved: the right of copyholders to vote at county elections.[1] Dashwood raised this question on 23 January. The legal position was clear enough. Copyholders were implicitly excluded from the franchise by the Act of Henry VI which gave it to 40s. freeholders, and a series of statutes had confirmed this. The last was an Act of 1746,[2] which required voters to take an oath that they possessed a freehold of at least 40s. annual value, and imposed a heavy penalty on unqualified voters. Against this there could be no argument except one of equity. Those who were moved by this contended that copyholders ought to be enfranchised because many of them were men of substance, qualified to sit as members of parliament and to serve on juries, and because many of them were more accurately described as 'customary freeholders' than as 'copyholders'. Many 'customary freeholders' had voted in the Oxfordshire election, and although it is true enough that most of them were Whigs, it seems clear that copyholders had demanded to vote in other county elections and that some sheriffs had allowed this. Their conduct may well have been no more impartial than that of the sheriff of Oxfordshire, but other factors determined that the Oxfordshire election should be spectacular. This was the first time the county had gone to the poll since 1710, and it did so largely because the Duke of Marlborough, against Newcastle's wishes, was ambitious to extend his Whig influence in a Tory county; the election was preceded by a long campaign, in which the city and the university took part. The fact of the double return, and the fact that this was the only disputed county election, meant that the question of copyholders' votes was bound to arise.

Dashwood himself wished to stand by the legal position: he maintained that there was, in law, a clear distinction between copyholders and freeholders, and that there was no such thing as a 'customary freeholder'. This view was later sharply criticised by a group of parliamentary reformers, with Oldfield as spokesman, who attacked the exclusion of copyholders from the franchise as a 'base and unjust relict of Norman oppression'.[3] But Dashwood was concerned with

[1] See Dashwood MSS. H 1.     [2] 18 Geo. II, c. 18.

[3] T. H. B. Oldfield, *An Entire and Complete History of the Boroughs of Great Britain, to which is prefixed An Original Sketch of Constitutional Rights*

another kind of parliamentary reform, which he defined as 'the independence of the House of Commons', not with the defence of freeholders for their own sake. Accordingly, he insisted that the vital question was not whether copyholders should be given the right to vote, but what authority was competent to give or deny them this right.[1] If the decision whether or not to allow copyholders' votes was left to the discretion of each individual sheriff, as in Oxfordshire, it would be the decision of 'the prime minister for the time being', and the effect on 'the independency of this House, and consequently upon our constitution' would be disastrous. The influence of the court, at present less strong in the counties than in the boroughs, would be greatly increased:

> The court has already an absolute command over too many of our boroughs, and if you add to this such a commanding influence as the court must have in every county by leaving this question undecided, you will render it ridiculous for any gentleman to put himself at the expense of standing a candidate at any election against the court interest, if he has no motive but that of serving his country in parliament. . . . We must take care to preserve the independency of this House, which can never be done, if we allow the ministers of the crown to have a commanding influence in our country elections, and this they will have, if we leave it in the power of the sheriff to reject or admit copyholders to vote at elections as he pleases.

Moreover, to let Oxfordshire become a precedent 'would very much increase the influence of our nobility at all future elections . . . put it into the power of the other House, by uniting together, to determine who shall be members of this'. It was therefore essential that the House should lay down a general rule, and should do so at once: to make a wrong decision would be a lesser evil than to leave the decision to be made by others. Dashwood therefore moved that

> all copyholders, holding their estates by copy of court roll, not having the words 'ad voluntatem domini,' or, 'at the will of the lord,' inserted

---

(1792), i. 79, 81; and see pp. 84–102 for his indignant refutation of 'the sentiments of Sir W. Blackstone . . . [and] some observations upon the misinterpretation of the law, and some inconsistencies that appear in the said learned author's opinions regarding this subject'. Oldfield said he espoused the cause of copyholders not out of particular tenderness towards them but because he believed that every tenant and every householder had a 'constitutional right' to vote.

[1] For his speech on 23 Jan. see *Parl. Hist.* xv. 432–7.

in the copies by which such estates are holden, have a right to vote at elections for knights of the shire to serve in parliament for that part of Great-Britain called England, within the meaning of the laws confining the said right of election to estates of freehold only.

This was an attempt to force the House to make a general ruling on the question of those copyholders who could least implausibly be regarded as coming near to being freeholders. A clear statement that they were entitled to vote would not entitle all other copyholders, though a clear statement that they were not so entitled would certainly cover all others. Dashwood hoped that his motion would be defeated, but in fact it was not voted on, for the government chose to counter it by moving for the order of the day, on the disingenuous ground that the general issue was too complicated to be solved quickly, and must wait until the Oxfordshire case was settled. No doubt the postponement of the general issue did hasten the Oxfordshire decision, and of course it left the copyholders' votes undisturbed. The precedent was, however, overturned when the general issue was solved three years later. Dashwood's view of the correct legal position had been supported by Blackstone in 1755, and was elaborated by him in a pamphlet[1] published in 1758. In the same year Dashwood's demand for a general ruling was satisfied. In March Sir John Philipps moved for a bill which should state that 'no person, who holds his estate by copy of Court-roll, shall be entitled thereby to vote for the election of Knights of the Shire',[2] and the bill was passed in June. In his *Commentaries*, published in 1765, Blackstone merely cited the 1758 Act and stated, without discussion, that 'no tenant by copy of court roll shall be permitted to vote as a freeholder'.[3] This was the statement which became the target for Oldfield's campaign for the enfranchisement of copyholders.

At the beginning of the third session of this parliament, on 13

---

[1] *Considerations on the Question whether Tenants by Copy of Court Roll, though not at the Will of the Lord, are Free-holders qualified to vote in Elections for Knights of the Shire* (London, 1758).

[2] Debrett, *History*, iii. 399–400; *Commons Journals*, xxviii. 112, 290. The Act was 31 Geo. II, c. 14, 'An Act for further explaining the Laws touching the Electors of Knights of the Shire for that part of Great Britain called England'.

[3] *Commentaries on the Laws of England* (1765), bk. I, ch. 2.

November 1755, Dashwood spoke in opposition to the Address or thanks to the king.[1]  In the same month, according to Horace Walpole, he spoke in a debate on the grant of pensions which 'called forth a display of abilities that revived the lustre of the House of Commons', and was one of those who contributed to this display.[2]  In this session Dashwood found himself again in alliance with Pitt, this time on the question of the establishment of a militia. Pitt had been dismissed in November.  On 8 December he seconded George Townshend's motion for a Committee of the Whole House to inquire into the laws relating to the militia.[3]  Dashwood supported him and, while the inquiry was taking place, wrote 'A sketch for a National Militia humbly submitted to the Consideration of the Public by a Member of Parliament'.[4]  On 21 January the Commons unanimously resolved that 'the laws now in being, for regulating the Militia, are ineffectual', and gave leave for the preparation of a bill 'for the better ordering of the Militia Forces in England'.[5]  Townshend introduced the bill on 12 March and Dashwood spoke in support of it.  It provided for a militia of 62,680 private men, to be

[1] *Parl. Hist.* xv. 536.

[2] Walpole, *George II*, i. 486.

[3] *Parl. Hist.* xv. 704.  A militia bill had been introduced by William Thornton (M.P. York 1747–54, 1758–61) in Nov. 1751 after the Commons had given a 'unanimous order to prepare it', as they did on 21 Jan. 1756. Thornton's bill had a first and second reading, and was ordered to be committed, but then, like the 1746 bill, 'it dropped' (Debrett, *History*, iii. 107–120).  In 1752 there appeared Thornton's *The Counterpoise* and also Charles Sackville's *Treatise concerning the Militia, in four Sections*, interesting for its blending of theory with constructive proposals and remarks on militias in other countries, especially Switzerland.  Sackville praised the 1745 scheme: 'this new species of Militia, by *County Regiments*' (p. 42).

[4] Dashwood MSS. B 8/2.  The manuscript is dated 29 Dec. 1755.  It is incomplete — only one and a half foolscap pages — and I have not been able to discover whether it was printed.  In the title, Dashwood substituted 'the Public' for his original 'the Legislature', as the audience to which he submitted his 'Sketch'.

[5] *Commons Journals*, xxvii. 395.  The bill was to come into force on 29 Sept. 1756.  It was ordered to be printed on 9 Apr. 1756, after it had been considered and amended in Committee of the Whole House (ibid. 577).  It is included in *House of Commons Papers*, 1731–1800. *Bills*, vol. ii, no. 84.

raised on the basis of county quotas, and chosen in each county by lot. In one important way it departed from the 1746 precedent: the quota prescribed for each county was not related to the amount it paid in land tax.[1] The bill passed the Commons in May, but after 'long debate' was rejected in the Lords, partly it seems on Hardwicke's argument that the population could not supply so large a militia, partly on the constitutional ground that the bill infringed the king's prerogative by requiring him to inform parliament before calling out the militia,[2] and partly because of objection raised to the powers which the bill gave to the Land Tax Commissioners. A year later, in January 1757, a similar bill was introduced, again by Townshend. It went through the same stages in the Commons. The clause requiring the king to notify parliament was taken out, but on 25 March Dashwood was successful in adding a clause empowering the king to summon parliament in time of emergency.[3] On the same day the bill was passed and sent to the Lords. This time they amended instead of rejecting it. Dashwood was a member of the Select Com-

---

[1] This was severely criticised in a letter to the *Gentleman's Magazine* in Oct. 1756 (pp. 458–60). The writer could not understand 'from what calculation, or rule of proportion, the numbers to be raised in each county &c was made'. He admitted that the land tax was not an equal charge but was 'at a loss to see how a more equal one could be ascertained'. He thought that what each country paid in land tax should be 'a guide to shew the number of men that ought to be raised in each county &c', and appended a table to show how this would work: if one man was raised for each £20 paid in land tax, the total raised would be 99,159. His figures are very little different from Davall's in 1746, and he confessed that he favoured a militia of 100,000. But if this were thought too large, then one man raised for each £30 of land tax paid would give a total of 63,053.

[2] Jenkinson discussed this objection to the bill in his pamphlet *A Discourse on the Establishment of a National and Constitutional Force in England* (written in 1756 but not printed until 1757; reprinted 1794), pp. 13 ff. He deprecated the attempt to revive the seventeenth-century quarrel between 'Lawyers and Antiquarians'; he thought it a pity that Charles II's Militia Act had not been amended in 1689. Now, he thought, the statement of parliamentary authority in the bill was both necessary and unalarming, merely a formal recognition of the fact that the 'Feodal Militia was properly the army of the King, the National Militia was the Army of the Kingdom' (p. 31).

[3] *Commons Journals*, xxvii. 816.

mittee appointed in May to consider the Lords' amendments. After two conferences between this Committee and Managers appointed by the Lords, agreement was reached.[1] The Commons accepted the reduction of the size of the militia by about one half, to 32,340, and the replacement of the Land Tax Commissioners by J.P.s. The Commons also accepted the reinstatement of the requirement that the king should inform parliament before calling out the militia, or, if parliament was not sitting, inform the council. Dashwood's clause empowering the king to summon parliament remained. For the rest, the Lords did not insist on their amendments. They passed the bill on 8 June, and the king gave his assent on 28 June.[2] Pitt's entry into the government on 18 June turned the bill into a government bill, and it has always been known as 'Pitt's Militia Act'. The size of the militia it provided was only about a third of that envisaged by Dashwood in 1745 and the county quotas were not related to their land tax assessments, but there can be no doubt of Dashwood's contribution to the shape of the bill.

Although Dodington's disillusionment with Newcastle in the spring of 1754 was great, his plans for a party and a united opposition had finally given way to schemes for joining the administration, and he did not look back. There is no evidence that Dashwood was at all interested in his schemes, but nevertheless Dodington tried to strengthen his own hand by including Dashwood's name in his negotiations. In May 1755 Dodington had a long conversation with Halifax about the 'insufficiency, falseness, and meanness of the Duke of Newcastle's Administration'. He reported, perhaps with his tongue in his cheek rather than naïvely, Halifax's response to his approach.

> Lord Halifax [he wrote] saw nothing to help him [the Duke], but my friends, Talbot, Dashwood, and me. I said I did not know how he could come by us, unless he would show us a real intention to extricate this country from the distress he had so much contributed to bring upon it.[3]

---

[1] Commons Journals, xxvii. 898, 915, 919, 920; Lords Journals, xxix. 170, 176, 177, 180.
[2] Commons Journals, xxvii. 920, 924. The Act is 20 Geo. II, c. 25.
[3] Diary, pp. 296–7. 29 May 1755.

And in October, when Dodington at last achieved not only conversation with Newcastle but also an agreement with him, Dashwood was not forgotten. Part of the agreement was

> Sir Francis Dashwood to be offered the Comptroller's staff, or something that is proper for, and would be agreeable to him; if he can be prevailed on to accept anything, which I very much doubt.[1]

Dodington's doubt was, of course, well founded. It is, however, probable that to Newcastle and to Henry Fox, who became Secretary of State and minister in the House of Commons in September, Dashwood was the most worth gaining of those whom Dodington called his friends. His value to them, however, did not lie in his friendship with Dodington. It lay partly in the fact that, in a political sense, he was not Dodington's friend, and partly in his apparent concert with Pitt. Pitt had sought Dashwood's help in September, in opposing 'the subsidies' to Russia, Hesse-Cassel, and Bavaria — the 'Topick of opposition'[2] in the autumn of 1755 — and in the supply debate on 15 December both of them spoke and voted against the subsidy treaties.[3] They were agreed on the necessity for a militia bill. It is not surprising therefore that a week before Dodington happily resumed office as Treasurer of the Navy,[4] and Henry Furnese became a Lord of the Treasury, Fox and Newcastle should have approached Dashwood. Apparently he was first offered and refused the Admiralty. On 16 December Henry Fox wrote to him saying 'he understood the Admiralty would not be agreeable to you' and offered instead the office of Comptroller of the Household or 'an Employment that shall, in your own Eye & that of the whole World be at least as good'.[5] This too Dashwood refused. He acknow-

---

[1] *Diary*, p. 334. 29 May 1755.

[2] Berkshire Record Office, Hartley-Russell MSS. D/EHy. James West to Newcastle, 25 Oct. 1755.

[3] *Parl. Hist.* xv. 662–4; Walpole, *George II*, ii. 61.

[4] Dodington was appointed on 22 Dec. to what he called 'my old place'. He had held it from 1744 to 1749 and in his negotiations with Newcastle in March 1754 said he would like it 'better than anything' (*Diary*, p. 260).

[5] Dashwood MSS. B 7/1. North described the Comptroller's office in 1781 as 'honourable, attended with a seat in the Privy Council, and . . . held by persons of the first rank and importance in the Kingdom' (Egerton MS. 2136, f. 166).

ledged the 'personal civilitys' in Fox's letter, 'more especially as this mark of regard was unsought, and certainly, until lately, unexpected by me'. He said that he would not take office without Westmorland's approval, and he named also as men in agreement with him, Talbot and Stanhope. But, in any case, the offer was irrelevant, for he had opposed Newcastle's administration not because he wanted office, but on constitutional grounds which had not in any way changed:

> It has allwayes been my express opinion, that those would be unworthy of, and useless to, an administration who should occasionally alter their opinions of any before adopted constitutional and great national points. With these my constant declarations, I am particularly assured the Duke of Newcastle has been acquainted; this is the language I have held to my two worthy friends Mr Dodington and Mr Furnese. Therefore I must entreat you (Sir) to be fully assured, and convinced, that neither the Admiralty, nor the Comptroller's Staff, nor anything better, were ever of primary consideration with me.[1]

It was again clear from Dashwood's defence of Admiral Byng in the House of Commons two months later that, though he was worth winning, Newcastle at least was unlikely to win him. Dashwood's defence showed not only independence, but also resourcefulness and understanding. Byng was condemned under the 12th Article of War, which, since 1749, had made 'cowardice, disaffection, or negligence punishable with death'. The court martial exonerated him from cowardice and disaffection, but felt, though not unanimously, that 'negligence' covered the misjudgement of which he could fairly be accused. Nevertheless, the court ended the letter conveying their decision with a unanimous recommendation to mercy and a statement of the 'distresses of our minds . . . in finding ourselves under a necessity of condemning a man to death from the great severity of the 12th Article of War, part of which he falls under, and which allows of no mitigation even if the crime should be committed by an error of judgment only'. Dashwood made all possible use of this letter. On 17 February, when the sentence was reported to the Commons, he spoke against Byng's expulsion from the House and moved for 'the letter of the court martial',[2] in order, 'by considering the warmth of their recommendation, to lead to some

[1] Dashwood MSS. B 7/1. 17 Dec. 1755.
[2] Walpole, *George II*, ii. 312.

45

application for mercy'. When this had no immediate success, Dashwood reinforced it by using the suggestion made by Keppel and other members of the court that, if released from their oaths of secrecy, they would have relevant information to disclose. On 26 February, two days before the date fixed for the execution, Pitt delivered to the Commons a message from the king that 'he has thought fit to respite the Execution of the same, in order that there may be an Opportunity of Knowing, by the separate Examination of the Members of the said Court, what ground there is for the above Suggestion'.[1] Dashwood then moved that the 12th Article be read. 'His opinion [of Byng's culpability] was', he said, 'totally changed by the trial. That at most he could only impute misjudgment to Mr Byng. To the court martial he must impute it more strongly, who, he thought, had condemned the admiral unjustly.'[2] He then obtained from the House leave to introduce a bill releasing members of the court martial from their oaths of secrecy, in order that they should be free 'to declare what had been their intention in declaring Mr Byng guilty'.[3] Dashwood and Thomas Potter prepared the bill, and it went through its first and second readings, committal, and report on the same day. On 28 February it was read a third time and passed by 153 votes to 23.[4] It went to the House of Lords on 1 March. They examined the members of the court separately, found insufficient support for the suggestion that they wished to be released from their oaths, and on the next day rejected the bill 'without debate'.[5]

[1] *Commons Journals*, xxvii. 738.

[2] Walpole, *George II*, ii. 318.

[3] *Parl. Hist.* xv. 805. This was perhaps the speech after which Horace Walpole told Mann 'the House was wondrously softened', but the king's message did not come 'on the next day', as Walpole says (*Correspondence* (ed. Lewis), xxi. 63–64, 3 Mar. 1757). Walpole's chronology does not tally with the *Commons Journals*; and his statements that Dashwood 'moved the repeal of the bloody 12th article', and that the king 'respited Mr Byng . . . till the bill could be passed', are inaccurate though they show where his sympathy lay. Walpole and Dodington have both been praised for the 'humanity' they showed towards Byng. It is time that Dashwood, who did more than either of them, was praised too.

[4] *Commons Journals*, xxvii. 739–40.

[5] Debrett, *History*, iii. 273. But the supporters of the bill in the Lords

The government's decision to ignore the court martial's recommendation to mercy, and its willingness to save what it could of its own reputation by subserviency to public clamour for vengeance on the man who had lost Minorca, is of course a miserable story. But behind it was Article 12, the real stumbling-block, not only because it allowed the court no choice of punishment, but also because 'negligence' is not capable of being precisely defined and 'admits of several degrees'.[1] Given this very difficult situation, there was everything to be said for Dashwood's solution — a bill freeing members of the court from their oaths of secrecy — as a possible way of moving the government. The pity is not that the Lords rejected Dashwood's bill, but that, when given the chance, few of Byng's judges were willing to speak strongly for it.

The harmony which, according to contemporary recorders, marked the parliamentary proceedings of the last years of George II's reign seems to have been ruled by only one expression of independency, apart from the bill clarifying the county franchise, which was introduced in March 1758. On 20 February 1758 Strange introduced a motion for leave to bring in a bill to shorten the duration of parliaments.[2] It was opposed on the grounds that 'while the nation was engaged on such a dangerous and expensive war, it would be improper to think of introducing such an alteration in the form of government', and defeated by 190 votes to 74. The argument that the time was inappropriate for reform may well have been Pitt's: it is the one he used against Dashwood's amendment of 17 October 1745. It was in these years of harmony that Dashwood's practice of independency, which made him unwilling to undermine his constituents' independence, forced him to change his constituency. He was elected for the third time at New Romney in April 1754, but after 1756 his position there became precarious. The right of election lay with the mayor, jurats, and commonalty. In 1756 there

were so impressive that Debrett, without naming them, gives their arguments three pages (ibid., pp. 383–6). The Lords ordered the proceedings of their examination of the Court to be printed, and Debrett prints them on pp. 272–82.     [1] Ibid. 283.

[2] *Commons Journals*, xxviii. 97; Debrett, *History*, iii. 398. It seems likely that Dashwood supported Strange, but there is no evidence one way or the other.

were seventeen electors and Dashwood thought the corporation 'not venal'. In August the other member, Henry Furnese, died. Three candidates appeared in the field: Rose Fuller; Edward Dering, son of Sir Edward Dering, member for Kent from 1733 to 1754; and Thomas Scrope. Scrope soon saw that he had no chance and withdrew. Fuller and Dering both tried to enlist Dashwood's support, but he refused to take sides. On 22 September 1756 he wrote to John Mascall, an elector:

> I wrote to Mr Steven Fuller some time ago to assure him that I wished not to interfere, but, that I should be guided by the majority of my friends in adhering to the person they should pitch upon.

Most of Dashwood's friends at first supported Dering, as did the mayor, Benjamin Cobb, and the election seemed likely to be 'a tight struggle'. The death of Cobb, however, in October 1756, and the contest over the election of a new mayor, lost Dering enough votes to tip the balance. He withdrew his candidature and in December Fuller was returned unopposed. In the following years both Fuller and Dering worked hard to extend their influence in New Romney. Each tried to get Dashwood's support against the other, but as he steadily refused to commit himself to either of them or to meddle in the affairs of the corporation, their influence was in fact extended at his expense. Dashwood's view of the proper conduct of candidates was shared by Westmorland. He wrote to Dashwood on 12 November 1758:

> I was never more astonish'd than at the account you sent me of the new Politicks at New Romney. One does not know what to do with such People. It seems to me not to belong properly to any Candidate to be joyning with this or that other Candidate, but to leave the Electors to dispose of things as they like best among themselves.[1]

and on 29 November he replied to electors who tried to persuade him to approach Dashwood, 'that the part of a Representative, was not to take the lead in the intestine divisions of a Corporation, but to do the business of the whole Body in Parliament fairly and honestly'.[2] This view did not prevail, and Dashwood's position was so clearly undermined by 1760 that at the general election of 1761 he did not stand for New Romney but transferred to Weymouth and Melcombe Regis.

[1] Dashwood MSS. B 9/1.          [2] Ibid.

48

## 3

## *An Independent in Office 1761–81*

EXCEPT during Rockingham's administration of 1765–6, Dashwood held office continuously from 1761 until his death in 1781. He was Treasurer of the Chamber 1761–2, Chancellor of the Exchequer 1762–3, Keeper of the Great Wardrobe 1763–5, Joint Postmaster-General 1766–81. He took office in 1761, not because his opinions had changed, but because he believed that the conditions of politics had changed. He remained, for the next twenty years as for the twenty years previously, an independent in politics, not a party man. This is true even of his tenure of office as Chancellor of the Exchequer in Bute's government. This was the most purely political of the offices Dashwood held, but it was not one of the great political offices of state. The Chancellor was Under-Treasurer, the most important member of the Treasury Board after the First Lord, and the First Lord's deputy. Until the middle of the nineteenth century the First Lord of the Treasury was, in a real sense, the finance minister, and if he was a commoner, he held the office of Chancellor of the Exchequer himself, as Walpole and Pelham, North and Pitt did. If the First Lord was a peer, responsibility for financial policy in the Commons fell to the Chancellor, but even then he did not normally sit in the cabinet.[1] Dashwood's tenure of the office was conspicuous, politically, because of his association with Bute in the Treasury and because he was responsible in the Commons for the cider tax which provoked an outburst of hostility commonly supposed to have contributed to Bute's resignation.

Given the drama of Bute's rise and fall, and the legend of his continuing influence over the rise and fall of the ministries which succeeded his, it is not surprising that the label 'Bute's friend' was affixed to Dashwood so firmly that it obscured earlier labels. But it

---

[1] Dashwood's successor, Grenville, held both offices; Grenville's successor, Charles Townshend, who was admitted to the cabinet two months after his appointment, was the first Chancellor to sit in the cabinet side by side with the First Lord.

is unfortunate that the obscuring has lasted, for the result has been a distortion not only of the reasons for his appointment, and of his conduct in office, but also of his career before 1762. In fact, the label does not explain Dashwood's appointment, and his career before 1760, which supplies a better explanation, was very far from being a slow progression towards office-holding under Bute. In disentangling Dashwood's appointment from Bute's, one is struck at once by the dissimilarity of their careers and allegiances before 1760. Bute had never sat in the Commons, and his parliamentary experience was confined to his having been elected once, in 1737, as a representative peer for Scotland. Dashwood had been a member of the Commons continuously for twenty years. His views had been well known for the whole of that time, his support had been sought by various opposition groups, he had been invited to take office. He had not held office in the household either of Frederick, Prince of Wales, or of George, as Bute had, and the approaches made to him, from 1747 onwards, show that he was certainly not committed to either court. Dashwood's associates were men of tried independency in George II's reign: Westmorland, Stanhope, and Talbot above all, and in the Commons, men like Lord Strange, Sir John Philipps, Henry Archer, Thomas Carew. It is true that Dashwood figured in the shadow cabinets which Dodington drew up for Bute in the late 1750s, as he had done in Dodington's plans for union earlier, but this, like Dodington's dinners to Dashwood and Bute, was a sign not of their political alliance, but that Bute, like others before him, was courting Dashwood.

There was, in any case, a more cogent reason for offering office to Dashwood than friendship or political agreement. This was Bute's wish to associate the independents with his government, and his recognition that Dashwood was one of the most prominent of them. From the beginning of the reign Bute intended to offer office to Dashwood as soon as he himself should enter the government. In January 1761 he told Dodington that he was not willing to discuss the possibility of an alliance with Newcastle until Dashwood, Talbot, and Charles Townshend were offered 'such places as he wish'd'.[1] In March, when Bute took office as Secretary of State, Dashwood was appointed Treasurer of the Chamber in succession to Townshend, and

[1] Dodington, *Diary*, p. 414. 16 Jan. 1761.

became a privy councillor. Townshend was appointed Secretary at War, and Talbot became Steward of the Household. All three took office without surrendering their independency. In May 1762, when Newcastle resigned and Bute became First Lord of the Treasury, Dashwood succeeded Barrington as Chancellor of the Exchequer.

Dashwood made his decision to accept office not because of personal friendship or political alliance with Bute, but because he believed that the new king was different from the old and that the new reign would reflect this difference. For many independents, one of the first signs of difference, discounting the King's Speech, which they knew was 'fabricated in the old shop', seems to have been the new king's attitude to the militia. In November 1760 George Townshend, spokesman of 'the friends of the Militia', raised the question of the renewal of the 1757 Act, and was satisfied with Bute's reply, as Bute was satisfied with the 'uncommon disinterested part, the Country Gentlemen' took, in agreeing to postpone the question to the following session.¹ Talbot told Bute of the 'pleasing effect' of George III's 'sense of the Utility of the Militia', and smiled at the unprecedented spectacle of 'many Cocoa-tree Gentlemen [who] violated their Sobriety last night by Drinking felicity to his Majesty in pint bumpers'.² Dashwood was not alone in believing that, because the conditions of politics had changed, independency had become compatible with support of government, even with office-holding. Westmorland expressed this view at the time of Dashwood's appointment as Treasurer of the Chamber:

> What heartfelt joy it must be [he wrote] to be mark'd out, and taken into the service of a Prince of such qualities; acting upon such solid Principles of reason, of honour, and of Vertue! and how do I rejoyce at your happy Lot, in not having dishonour'd your self, by any service of so different a stamp, as heretofore!³

---

1 Bute MSS. Bute to Townshend, 29 Nov. 1760. Dashwood thought the postponement unwise, and was convinced that the militia would not be renewed while 'the present Minister' [Newcastle] remained in power. (Dashwood MSS. B 8/1. 30 Nov. 1760.) It was renewed for seven years in Mar. 1762, just before Newcastle resigned.
2 Bute MSS. [Nov. 1760.]
3 Dashwood MSS. B 11/1. 13 Feb. 1761.

The same contrast was made when Dashwood became Chancellor of the Exchequer. Deskfoord, remembering that 'time was, that you and I doubted, if a Chancellor of the Exchequer could be an honest Man',[1] thought that time was past. Other independents, Stanhope, Sambrooke Freeman, George Prescott, for example, echoed something of Westmorland's view. Nor was Dashwood's appointment welcomed only by independents and country gentlemen. George Grenville, very much a man of business, wrote to Bute in May 1762:

> I rejoice extremely [at Dashwood's acceptance] as I am convinced that his behaviour will be full of honour and spirit towards the publick, and of friendship towards you. I shall allways see him with a great deal of pleasure and more particularly on this occasion.[2]

Bute's government faced great difficulties. Its essential task — to negotiate terms of peace and to make financial provision for the aftermath of war — was heavy and required the support of both Houses of Parliament. It faced the hostility of the two most powerful men in politics: Pitt, who resigned in March 1761 because he disapproved of ending the war, and Newcastle, who resigned in May 1762. Pitt prided himself on being 'single', but Newcastle's idea of being out of office was not unlike Dodington's idea of opposition: he was much concerned with thoughts of a quick return, and to this end he expected the men he had appointed to office in the long period of the Pelham ascendancy to join him now in opposition. Though Pitt and Newcastle were estranged, they might well coalesce again to defeat any terms the government proposed for the peace. Bute had no party and no following in politics. Faced with certain opposition, and possible union among the Whigs, his only hope of support seemed to be from the independent members of parliament, and it was by no means certain that their disposition to favour his government would last.

Against this bleak outlook, Bute's government had by December 1762 made undoubted and unexpected progress. The Preliminaries of Peace had been approved by both Houses of Parliament; Bute had gained an ascendancy in the cabinet; the government's strength in

[1] Egerton MS. 2136, f. 42. 6 June 1762.
[2] Bute MSS. 21 May 1762.

the Commons was growing. Pitt and Newcastle were still estranged, and Pitt had rebuffed Newcastle's attempt to heal the breach. Indeed, Pitt was said to have declared in July that 'there was no comparison between the Administrations (Bute's and Newcastle's)', and that if the Earl of Bute 'continued to act as he had done he would support his measures in Parliament as a friend to his Country tho' an enemy to himself'.[1] At the beginning of October Bute, in a minority in the cabinet in wishing to press for peace at all costs, and in particular opposed by Grenville and Egremont on the question of surrendering Havana, decided to enlarge what he called 'the narrow Bottom of the Cabinet'.[2] This meant making Fox, instead of Grenville, minister in the House of Commons. Grenville moved to the Admiralty, and Halifax succeeded him as Secretary of State. The preferment of Fox had disadvantages, for he was distrusted by the country gentlemen and his position in the Commons might well lose Bute as much support as it gained. Fox himself feared that his unpopularity would 'more than overbalance them [my abilitys]',[3] North agreed, and Denbigh, an independent in the House of Lords, thought that 'almost the whole body of the country gentlemen' might 'take umbrage at the lead in the House of Commons being given to Mr. Fox'.[4] Bute, however, was convinced that in order to outwit the Whigs he must have Fox, even if he alienated some of the country gentlemen, and perhaps Bute was right in thinking that he was running the lesser of two risks. Fox was well aware of the need to placate the Tories. He invited Sir John Philipps not only to the Cockpit meeting of government supporters held on the eve of session to hear the King's Speech read, but also to the smaller pre-Cockpit meeting the day before. The Tory Robert Harley, who described himself as 'unengaged', was invited to move or second the Address. 'I told him', Fox wrote to Bute,

it was imputed to HM and his Ministers, by the great authors of this Opposition, that the Court was accessible to Torys as well as Whigs, for which reason, I wish'd a Tory might be the mover or seconder of this Address, in order to shew that what they thought an imputation

---

1 Bute MSS. Dr. John Campbell to Bute, 21 July 1762.
2 Add. MS. 36797, f. 26. 10 Oct. 1762.
3 Bowood MSS. Fox to Bute, 10 Oct. 1762.
4 Bute MSS. Denbigh to Bute, 1 Nov. 1762.

was by HM and his Servants thought a virtue, and that Torys and Whigs should in every thing according to their merits be employ'd indiscriminately.[1]

Fox's assessment of the results of his efforts was not unfair:

> The appearance at the Cockpit [he told Bute on 24 November] was to the utmost of our wishes. The Torys see the situation of the King in its true light . . . we shall not only have numbers, but, which I more doubted of, and value more; a most eager co-operation of those we have.[2]

This co-operation was evident a week later, when Dashwood presented to the Commons a copy of the Preliminary Articles of Peace.[3] In the division on 1 December on the question of the date for debating the peace terms the government had 213 votes to the opposition's 74, and in later divisions the opposition vote dropped to 65 and 63. Nearly all the Tories and independents voted for the government. Moreover, after making a long speech of mixed praise and blame for the Preliminaries on 9 December, Pitt explicitly disassociated himself from the opposition and left the House before the vote was taken.

This was a real achievement, though perhaps it was not a real test of power, for opposition to peace terms — not easily kept distinct from opposition to peace — was, in the last resort, neither a popular platform nor congenial to Newcastle's pacific nature. In normal circumstances the task of making an acceptable budget might well have looked less difficult than the task of making an acceptable peace, but Bute was right in thinking that 'the happy Conclusion of the Peace' had made his enemies 'desperate', and, in the event, the government's financial proposals provoked a more dangerous opposition than its peace proposals had done. Less predictably, perhaps, they forged some sort of alliance between Pitt and Newcastle.

The part of the budget which made this alliance was the 'cyder tax', an additional excise duty on cider made in England. There were two existing taxes on cider: 6s. 8d. a hogshead on cider and perry 'made for sale, to be paid by the first buyer or retailer', and 4s. a hogshead, also paid by the retailer, as part of the annual 'malt duty',

[1] Bute MSS. 23 Nov. 1762.
[2] Bute MSS. 24 Nov. 1762.
[3] *Commons Journals*, xxix. 360 (29 Nov. 1762).

or duty on malt, mum, cider, and perry.[1] Dashwood's first proposal, when he opened his budget on 7 March, was an additional tax of 10s. a hogshead on cider sold, to be paid, as the existing duties were, by the retailer. The proposal at once brought Pitt from his neutral position, which had in fact inclined rather more to Bute's government than against it.

Pitt's first attack was not on Dashwood but on Grenville, who had argued that those who opposed the tax must suggest an equally productive one to replace it. In reply to this Pitt was 'ironical and sarcastic, answered nothing the other had said, nor appeared to be a master of the subject, yet by the mere power of words convinced many I believe who heard him, that he *had* answered, and knew more of the matter than his antagonist'.[2] In the middle of Grenville's reply Pitt left the House 'in the most insolent and contemptuous manner, that ever was seen'. The debate ended without a division, 'only that the cider tax was postponed by consent for further consideration at the request of the members of the cider counties'. As a result, the tax was reduced to 4s. a hogshead, but placed on the maker instead of on the retailer. Provision was made for compounding, at 5s. a head, by those who made cider simply to drink it in their own families, and for exemptions for the poor.

> This seemed to me [said Harris] a change much for the better, as enforcing the same purpose in point of profit, and making withall the tax more diffused, and the duty safe from fraud by being less.[3]

Some members no doubt agreed with Harris's sensible view, but, though the reduction in the amount of the duty may have reduced the numbers of the opposition, it did not decrease their violence.

[1] Board of Customs and Excise, Excise Revenue Accounts 1662-1827, ff. 26-27. The 6s. 8d. a hogshead was known as the 'old duty'.

[2] Harris, Parliamentary Diary, 7 Mar. 1763. James Harris (1709-80); M.P. Christchurch 1761-81; lord of Admiralty Dec. 1762-Apr. 1763, of Treasury Apr. 1763-July 1765; secretary and comptroller to the Queen 1774-80; classical scholar; of the journal he kept while a member of parliament only the part for 1760-6 and a few later fragments have survived.

[3] There can be no doubt that the modification was made after conference either with the 'members for the cider counties', as Harris says, or with the 'country gentlemen', as the *Parliamentary History* states (xv. 1307). This throws some light on the nature of the later opposition.

Indeed, it provided them with a new point of attack. Whereas Glover, for example, 'descanted tragically against a general excise, which he said he hoped had been crushed in 1733',[1] Pitt, whose views on 'a general excise' varied with the occasion, refined his argument and concentrated his invective against 'the dangerous precedent of admitting the officers of excise into private houses. . . . If this tax is endured, it will necessarily lead to introducing the laws of excise into the domestic concerns of every private family, and to every species of the produce of the land.'[2]

> The division was such [wrote Harris on 13 March] as no object but cider could produce — against the measure, all[3] the members and inhabitants of the cider counties of Devon, Somerset, Worcestershire, Gloucester and Hereford; part of the Tories; part of the Newcastle men.

These categories, of course, are not distinct. Cider members might well find that their loyalties as Tories or country gentlemen were stronger than their feelings about the cider tax; some clearly did so. The opposition was noisy, but there was little real doubt about the issue. The division on 13 March ended in 138 votes to 81. The opposition's last hope, at the committee stage, was a motion by Dowdeswell[4] to leave out the words 'Makers of Cyder . . . and lay it on the Buyers'. It was defeated by 181 votes to 112.

But the great point, as Temple said to Newcastle, was Pitt's attitude, not the fate of the opposition to the cider tax.

[1] Harris, Diary, 7 Mar. 1763.

[2] Almon, *Anecdotes of Pitt*, i. 250.

[3] This is exaggerated. One example of a 'cider member' who supported the tax was Norborne Berkeley, who spoke for the bill 'through a representative for Gloucester County — told us of his own independency — that he had been for the Jew-Bill, and avowed it to his constituents, though the year before a general election' (Harris, Diary, 23 Mar. 1763).

[4] William Dowdeswell (1721–75) of Pull Court, Worcs.; M.P. Tewkesbury 1747–54, Worcs. 1761–75; Chancellor of the Exchequer 1765–6; first became conspicuous in the Commons for his opposition to the cider tax, which turned him from a so-called Tory into a staunch Rockinghamite. The principle behind his motion in 1763 triumphed in his 'repeal' Act of 1766.

What He [Temple] had been about, unsuccessfully, for Six Months, viz. The bringing Mr. Pitt and us together, is now come about as It were of itself; That Nothing could be better.[1]

Pitt's views on excise were not easy to understand: he was accused of inconsistency, of being 'both for and against', and probably was. He had declared himself 'not afraid to mention the word excise' in 1751.[2] He explained on 23 March 1763 that he did not object to 'Excise under proper Limitations, without any entry into the House of the private person.'[3] Yet he had opposed Dashwood's cider tax from the beginning, and he and Dowdeswell were the spearhead of opposition in the Commons. Moreover, Pitt went so far as to call on Newcastle, begging him not to let the Bill go unopposed in the Lords, and urged Rockingham to arrange for a 'well drawn Protest'. Newcastle himself was doubtful of the 'prudence' of opposing a money bill in the Lords, but it seems that of all the other Whigs only Cumberland was 'strongly of opinion, that opposition at this time is improper, and hopes the Tax will pass in the house of Lords without one'.[4] Cumberland warned Newcastle of the folly of joining with 'a few Tory Lords'[5] who would certainly never join with him in any other cause. But Newcastle, pressed by all his 'Principal Friends', and anxious to conciliate Pitt, gave in and even spoke against the tax himself. The pattern of the voting was rather more favourable to the government than in the Commons: 83 to 21 on the second reading, 73 to 39 (including proxies) on the third reading on 30 March. There were two protests, but they were neither 'well

---

[1] Add. MS. 32947, f. 216. Newcastle to Hardwicke, 11 Mar. 1763.

[2] *Parl. Hist.* xiv. 970. He explained that he was not in the House in 1733 'when the famous Excise Scheme was brought upon the carpet. . . . But I have seen so much of the deceit of popular clamours . . . and I am so fully convinced of the benefits we should reap by preventing all sorts of unfair trade, that if ever any such scheme be again offered . . . I believe I should be as heartily for it as I am for the motion now under consideration [the subsidies].' In 1756, too, Dashwood's proposal for an excise on meat had, according to Sir George Lyttelton, not 'much shocked the House'. (Walpole, *George II*, ii. 181.)

[3] Harris, Diary, 23 Mar. 1763.

[4] Add. MS. 32947, f. 327. Albermale to Newcastle, 27 Mar. 1763.

[5] The 'cider Lords': Foley, Ward, Suffolk, Fortescue, Oxford, Lyttelton.

drawn' nor well supported: each of them had only three signatures, and Temple was the only prominent Whig amongst them.

Outside parliament the City of London, which had, as Harris remarked, no interest in cider[1] but had other reasons for opposing Bute's government, undertook 'to prescribe to the legislature and to take the Lead in setting an Example to other Boroughs, for Clamour'.[2] The City petitioned the Commons against the bill on 22 March, petitioned the Lords on 28 March, and on 30 March took the extreme step of petitioning the king to refuse his assent.

> The Petitioners have observed [they stated to the Commons] that a Bill is now depending . . . which subjects the Makers of Cyder and Perry to the Laws of Excise . . . [They] cannot help considering this unexpected Proceeding as preparatory to a general Extension of those grievous Laws; . . . [and] hope that the Meritorious Subjects of this Country may not feel the Extension of the Excise Laws among the First Fruits of Peace.[3]

As soon as the bill passed the City began to arrange a petition for its repeal. The cider counties followed suit, holding county meetings, setting up committees, and sending in petitions. A mixed crop of pamphlets appeared, Dowdeswell made a bid for the support of public opinion outside the cider counties, and 'Wilkes's pen was never idle', in the *North Briton* and elsewhere. Dowdeswell's pamphlet, *An Address to such of the Electors of Great Britain as are Not Makers of Cyder and Perry, by the Representative of a Cyder-County*, elaborated some of the arguments he had used in the Commons, and added others. He warned against the plausible but 'fallacious' parallel between the cider tax and the malt tax, accused Dashwood of intend-

---

[1] Owen Ruffhead also noted that the City of London was 'not immediately or scarce remotely affected' by the Act (*Considerations on the Present Dangerous Crisis* (1763), pp. 22, 33). Horace Walpole, asking 'What principle of union could there be between the City of London and two or three distant counties whose apples were to be taxed?' (*Memoirs of George III* (ed. G. F. R. Barker, 1894), i. 201), drew the conclusion that Bute resigned out of needless panic.

[2] Strange, who made this very fair charge, was in favour of rejecting the petition. Dashwood, however, moved its acceptance and his motion was carried. (Add MS. 32947, f. 267.) West to Newcastle, 23 Mar. 1763.

[3] *Commons Journals*, xxix. 601.

ing a 'Great Reformation in Revenues', and of taxing 'the independent part of this Kingdom', and condemned as Machiavellian the attempt 'to draw in Country-Gentlemen to a Co-operation in so severe and so extraordinary an Extension of Excise'. This was 'a Plan for *Power* not for Revenue'. There were, Dowdeswell said, 'great *Constitutional* Objections to *Excise of all Sorts*'; if it should ever be necessary to impose such a tax, it 'must be laid on the *Trader*, . . . the Occupier of Land and the Private Person in his Family are *not the proper Objects of it*'. He begged electors in counties not affected by the Act to understand that their turn would come next, for 'the Principles on which this Tax is supported will necessarily lead to introducing the laws of Excise into the *domestic* Concerns of every *private* Family', and urged them therefore to 'instruct your Representatives to *nip the Precedent in its Bud*'. On the technical side, Dowdeswell attacked the inequity of taxing different qualities of cider (some of which were too poor to be anything but 'Family-Drink') at the same rate. This argument is elaborated, with statistics and examples, in the *Case of the County of Devon with Respect to the Consequences of the New Excise Duty on Cyder and Perry*, which was published in 1763 by the Committee appointed at the County General Meeting 'to superintend the Application for the Repeal of that Duty'.

Yet, though the opposition was fierce, there is an air of farce about the battle, for some at least of those who engaged in it were well aware that the emotive power of the word 'excise' was so great that, with ordinary luck, the fiscal merits of the cider tax need not be discussed at all. Pitt's facetious reply, 'Gentle Shepherd, tell me where', to Grenville's defence of the duty as unavoidable, because the government did not know where they could lay 'another tax of equal efficiency', is perhaps a sign of this. So, on a higher level, is Dowdeswell's prim and laboured attack on procedure, his condemnation of 'the tacking of an exceptionable tax to one that is not so'[1] and of the iniquity of including, in the same bill, two different types of duty — an excise duty on cider and a customs duty on wine — as well as the loan for which the duties were to be security.

It was [he said] improper as Gentlemen might be for one though not for the other Tax, & might be for one Mode of Collecting it & not

---

[1] Add. MS. 32947, f. 236. Legge to Newcastle, 17 Mar. 1763.

for the other, & very hard to send it in that Shape to another House where It could not be altered.[1]

It was of course logical, and right accounting, to combine the tax and the loan in one bill, and as Dashwood pointed out there was a precedent in 1759 for including a customs duty and an excise duty in the same bill.[2]    Moreover, as Owen Ruffhead reminded his readers, this was not even the first time that there had been a tax on makers of cider.[3]    It is not unfair to conclude, from an examination of the arguments put forward, that the opposition from the cider counties was an interested one, and that the more general opposition was an illustration partly of the extreme distrust with which that 'engine of tyranny', the excise, was regarded, and partly of the ease with which that distrust could be exploited for party purposes.

The only valid criticism of the cider tax is, in fact, the purely political one: that a government which had such determined enemies was unwise to risk the sort of storm that Walpole had bowed to thirty years earlier.  Fox and George III both thought this.  Fox advised Bute to give in to the clamour and withdraw the bill after it had passed the Commons, 'in consideration of alienating the minds of country gentlemen';[4]  George III advised him to follow Walpole's example, not to 'wait to be drove into declaring that the tax on cyder may be alter'd next session:  that would have the appearance of being defeated' but to withdraw it on the grounds of 'the opposition made by the public to it, and as his [Bute's] wish for public tranquility not as his having himself objections to the tax'.[5]  Yet Bute's refusal was, from one point of view, clearly justified, for the bill passed both

[1] Add. MS. 32947, f. 236.   West's memorandum to Newcastle, 17 Mar. 1763.

[2] Hardwicke told Newcastle on 18 Mar. that this was a feeble argument, and that there were many precedents 'in your time, your Brother's, and I believe Sir Robert Walpole's'.  (Add. MS. 32947, f. 247.)   He rejected the idea that the House of Lords should oppose the cider tax 'as a Tack'.

[3] *Considerations*, pp. 16–17.   See also Appendix IV (*a*), 'On Cyder'.

[4] Fox to Bute, 29 Mar. 1763.  (Bute MSS.)   But after the City of London petitions Fox felt some doubt about giving up 'the tax and Parliament itself to the Common Council'.

[5] *Letters of George III to Lord Bute, 1756–66* (ed. R. Sedgwick, 1939), p. 206 (28 Mar. 1763).

Houses by fairly safe majorities. The political criticism remains. The passing of the bill showed the government's strength, but it did not improve its popularity. Moreover, the first step had been taken towards closing the ranks of the Whigs and the bill remained a tiresome issue in politics throughout Grenville's ministry and until its repeal by Rockingham in 1766. Against this there can be set the non-political arguments which had prompted the introduction of the bill, and, in addition, the government's awareness that the tax was being misrepresented and that many of the arguments used against it — for example, that excisemen were empowered to enter private houses at night — were wild and inaccurate. Precisely how one strikes a balance between political and non-political arguments depends, perhaps, on one's temperament, and the attempt to do so impartially is sadly apt to suggest confused thinking. William Belsham, for example, wrote in 1795:

> No sooner was this most unpopular, and therefore most imprudent, proposition brought forward than the Opposition, eager and joyful to embrace so inviting an opportunity of attack, opened all their batteries against it. . . . The arguments by which the nation had been so much inflamed thirty years before, at the period when Sir Robert Walpole attempted to carry into effect his famous project, were now revived, and anew enforced. . . . Still, however it cannot be justly doubted, that the duties of excise, levied on the proper objects, and guarded from abuse by just and equitable regulations, constitute incomparably the fairest, the easiest, the most productive of all the various modes of indirect taxation. But a wise Government will and ought to consult the general temper and disposition of the people on all the measures of Government, and more especially in the manner of raising the national supplies. . . . In the present instance . . . the Minister, who entertained doubtless very different ideas of political wisdom from his predecessor Sir Robert Walpole, resolved . . . to persevere, and the bill finally passed into a law.[1]

The *Annual Register* had shown similar uncertainties in 1763. It described the government's financial proposals as 'perfectly unexceptionable' apart from the cider tax

> concerning which very sober men might have had their doubts, and which gave to all the discontented the fairest opportunity, which could

---

[1] *Memoirs of the Reign of George III to the Session of Parliament ending* A.D. *1793* (1795), i. pp. 81–83.

be furnished, of raising a popular clamour, and inflaming the whole nation. . . . Nobody can forget the clamour, which a scheme of a more extended excise raised in the year 1733. One of the ablest ministers, that England ever had, was on the point of sinking under it. Though time has made many particular converts, and those too of no mean rank, to this plan, or at least to the principles of it, the general odium has not yet worked off, and it remained one of the most inflammatory topics, which could be held out to the public. . . . In short, no political project since the year 1733, not excepting even the Jew bill, ever threw the nation into so high a ferment. . . .

If it were once admitted, that cyder for private consumption was a fit object for a tax, there could be no doubt, that the excise was the only sure way of collecting it.

The excise has clearly the advantage over every other mode of collection, in point of cheapness, expedition, accuracy, and a power of preventing frauds, either in the Officer or in the dealer. . . .

Whilst these matters were agitated in parliament, every method was taken to continue the ferment without doors. The fury of the populace was let loose. . . . Virulent libels, audacious beyond the example of former licentiousness, were circulated throughout the nation, in which nothing was sacred and no character spared. . . . But still the ministry braved the storm, and except on the single question of excise, their strength in parliament seemed to be rather augmented than impaired.[1]

As far as opposition in parliament is concerned, the passing of the cider bill was a greater triumph for Bute than his success over the peace terms, and his victory is made more spectacular by the fact that Pitt's conduct was unprincipled and Newcastle's only less so to the extent that he tried to restrain Pitt and his supporters without losing their support. Bute's resignation at the beginning of April, after two great successes, was therefore a surprise to his opponents and to most of his supporters, though some of his friends, George Townshend and Dr. John Campbell for example, had known at least since January that he greatly wished to resign,[2] and that, as he told Bedford, he had the king's 'solemn Promise to be permitted to go out when Peace was once attained'.[3] His resignation was of course partly the explosion of the smouldering distaste for party politics which had been

[1] *Annual Register* (1763), pp. 33–38.
[2] See, for example, Bute to Campbell, 30 Jan. 1763. (Bute MSS.)
[3] Add. MS. 36797, f. 36. 2 Apr. 1763.

his reason for accepting office. He expressed this to Worsley as early as November 1762:

> You are no dabler in Party-Politicks: would to God I had nothing to do with them ... I need not tell you that could I separate my Station from my loved Master's Security, Freedom, and Independancy, England should soon be eased of complaints made against a Scotch Minister, however I may despise such Objection. . . . You know Worsley I never aimed at forming Party to support my own Consideration. I am ignorant of the means others use to acquire it; or to speak plainly, my Mind revolts at the methods practised on These occasions.[1]

Distaste and disenchantment apart, there is no doubt that Bute's resignation was based on a realistic appraisal of the 'War at Home' which followed the peace. The arguments Bute put to Bedford the week before he resigned were both shrewd and disinterested:

> I am firmly of the opinion that my Retirement will remove the only unpopular Part of Government. And I once gone, it will be very hard for me to believe, that the Duke of Newcastle will, with Lord Hardwicke &c &c, continue a violent or peevish opposition, in order to make Mr Pitt, Lord Temple, & Mr Legge, Ministers of this Country . . . I fondly hope therefore, I shall by my retiring, do my Royal Master much more Service, than I could have performed, by remaining in office.[2]

Neither the king nor Bute intended that the ministry should change in anything but its head. Bute's resignation was, as Gilbert Elliot said, the execution of a 'long intended purpose'; he retired 'in full favour, and supported by a great majority, . . . leaving the Government in the hands he most approves of'.[3] The king, though forced to let Bute go, was determined that his going should not be interpreted as a victory for his enemies. George therefore restated his own attitude: he would never employ 'those Ministers of the late Reign who have attempted to fetter, and enslave him', and he would continue to show 'all proper Countenance to the Country Gentlemen acting on Whigg Principles; and on these Principles only supporting His Government'.[4] Grenville, 'the only Person in whom He [the king] can confide so great a Trust', moved to the Treasury,

1 Add MS. 36797, f. 24.    28 Nov. 1762.
2 Add. MS. 36797, f. 38.    2 Apr. 1763.
3 Caldwell Papers, 2, i, p. 175.        4 Add. MS. 36797, f. 37.

and Sandwich replaced him at the Admiralty. As a commoner, Grenville took the office of Chancellor of the Exchequer as well as that of First Lord of the Treasury. Dashwood was appointed Keeper of the Great Wardrobe and summoned to the House of Lords as Baron Le Despencer. 'We, who are friends of Lord Bute,' said Elliot, 'are desired by him to concur heartily in support of the new administration.'

Bute told Dashwood of his decision to resign on 2 April, the same day as he told Bedford. Dashwood's reply, though cautiously worded, suggests that the decision disappointed him. He praised the peace, but expressed concern about 'the King's peace of mind'.[1] He had more experience of party politics than Bute, and so is unlikely to have been as distressed by the manœuvres of Pitt and Newcastle, and perhaps only Bute's plea of ill health restrained him, as it did Bedford and George Townshend, from pressing Bute to remain. Dashwood himself moved from the Treasury, not as an act of sympathy with Bute, but simply because Grenville did not need a separate Chancellor of the Exchequer, and no doubt Bute thought it unwise, given his close association with Dashwood in the Treasury, to suggest his transfer to another ministerial post. Dashwood respected Grenville without having much personal sympathy with him. Once at least he acted as intermediary between Bute and Grenville, and he thought it right that Bute should accede to Grenville's demand that there should be no communication between Bute and the king without Grenville's knowledge. Grenville consulted Dashwood about the attitude of the country gentlemen, and took Dashwood's advice to approach Talbot and Sir John Philipps. Dashwood also lent his name, in September 1763, in support of candidates friendly to Grenville in the by-elections for Bishop's Castle and for Kent, though giving the impression that he was not much interested in electioneering.[2]

The cider tax remained as troublesome an issue in politics as the Whigs could make it, but Grenville's awareness of this did not outweigh his conviction that the tax was necessary. Out of doors, the opposition did their best to use the cider issue to deprive Grenville of the support of the country gentlemen and to harry candidates at by-elections.

[1] Bute MSS. Dashwood to Bute, 3 Apr. 1763.
[2] *Additional Grenville Papers, 1763–5* (ed. J. R. G. Tomlinson, 1962), pp. 41, 44–45, 53–54.

In Gloucestershire, in April 1763, Lord Coleraine was forced 'to decline going on with the canvass' merely because one of his supporters was Norborne Berkeley, who had voted for the cider bill.

> The adverse party [Coleraine observed] promise the people their best endeavours towards the repeal of the Act next sessions, altho' in their hearts are pleased, and wish its continuance, in order to get ground for the old faction again.[1]

Egmont, begging Bute to persuade Talbot to attend the Glamorgan county meeting, 'to blast the intended opposition' and support Sir Edmund Thomas, painted a picture of an inflamed west country which matched Ruffhead's picture of an inflamed City of London.

> Gloucester is already in flames — Bristol, ever disposed to riot, is a very near neighbour — the Welsh Counties adjacent, Monmouth and Hereford, are made of stuff to kindle with a very little fire, and Somerset, Devon and Cornwall are divided from Glamorgan by the Severn only — these are the Counties most affected by the late Tax, and therefore more easily practised upon.[2]

In May a 'riotous Mob . . . did . . . grossly affront and insult' Sir John Philipps at Monmouth 'on account of [his support of] the Act . . . for laying an additional Duty on Cyder and Perry'.[3] In November the City of London petitioned for the repeal of the Cider Act, and in December Devon, Somerset, Herefordshire, Gloucestershire followed suit, complaining of the tax and especially of 'the Mode of collecting it under the Power of the Excise Laws'.[4] While the petitions were coming in Grenville met 'the cyder members' and told them that though he would not consider repeal he would not refuse to consider amendments to the bill. In January 1764 he was successful in modifying Dowdeswell's motion for a Committee 'to take the Cyder Act into consideration' in such a way that the Committee was precluded from considering repeal.[5] In Committee,

1 Bute MSS. Coleraine to Bute, 18 Apr. 1763. See *Additional Grenville Papers*, pp. 50–51, for further trouble in Gloucestershire in October 1763.

2 Bute MSS. Egmont to Bute, 25 Apr. 1763. Talbot did attend and Thomas was elected.                    3 *Commons Journals*, xxix. 706.

4 Ibid. 74, 694 et passim. Exeter, Hereford, Plymouth, Bristol also petitioned, as did a number of small boroughs.

5 Harris, Diary, 24 Jan. 1764; cf. *The Jenkinson Papers*, 1760–66 (ed. N. S. Jucker, 1949), p. 257 (Jenkinson to C. W. Cornwall, 22 Jan. 1764).

Dowdeswell lost by twenty votes his proposal that the tax be laid 'on the first buyer and retailer' instead of on the maker.[1] He was opposed by North, Strange, Jenkinson, Philipps, and Charles Townshend as well as by Grenville. On 7 February Grenville produced his own amendments: the reduction of the composition fee from 5s. to 2s., and the increase of the time allowed for payment from six weeks to six months. They were carried without a division. Grenville's compromise perhaps proved acceptable enough to win over those who had, in Harris's words, opposed 'on principle'. For when, on 10 February, Richard Bamfylde moved for repeal, with Dowdeswell's support, his motion was rejected by 204 to 115.[2] This left a hard core of irreconcilables, many of whom of course had little interest in cider.

In April 1765 Grenville was led by his own financial difficulties to devise a tax which, like the cider duty, provided the Whigs with a point of union. This was the American Stamp Act, which he first suggested to the Commons in March 1764.[3] Ultimately, the Stamp Act was to create greater difficulties than the cider duty, and to raise issues far more real. Immediately, however, the two financial expedients were linked together in Whig opinion and propaganda as twin Bute–Grenville iniquities. When Rockingham took office in July 1765 he was committed to the repeal of both.

Nevertheless, the Rockingham administration was formed not because Grenville fell a victim to united Whig opposition, but because George III was determined to rid himself of Grenville. To this extent Bute was right in thinking that his own resignation would loosen the Whig alliance. He was right also in his assessment of Grenville:

the only Person that in this situation could manage the Treasury. . . . I have known him since he was 12 years old, and will answer with my

---

[1] Harris, Diary, 31 Jan. 1764. The voting was 152 to 172.

[2] Ibid., 10 Feb. 1764. Sir Richard Warwick Bamfylde (1722–76; M.P. Exeter 1743–7, Devonshire 1747–76) was one of the independent supporters whom Grenville inherited from Bute. His views on the cider tax were, he said, 'not his own sentiments . . . but those which the instructions and petitions of his constituents *forced* him to maintain'. He voted against the repeal of the Stamp Act. [3] Ibid., 9 Mar. 1764.

life for his being an honest, conscientious, bold determined man. He was bred in the Treasury and has more and better Ideas of Oeconomy than any Man in the Kingdom.[1]

Grenville managed the Treasury and the House of Commons[2] better than he managed the king. George III, forced to do without Bute, began almost at once a series of overtures to Pitt, believing that a man who, like himself, was opposed to 'all distinctions of party', could not refuse his appeal. These overtures were commonly supposed to be inspired by Bute. Pitt did refuse them, or at least his demands were so extravagant that George could not accept them. Grenville was therefore alienated to no purpose, and George was driven to accept conditions from men he disliked far more: Newcastle, Conway, and Rockingham. The first of their conditions was

the removal of some of my Lord Bute's friends, and particularly my Lord Despenser. . . . Lord Bute's most intimate friend.[3]

Egmont's letter telling Dashwood of his dismissal shows how much Egmont disliked it and how unwillingly the king agreed to it.

I never till this day [he wrote] felt repugnance in the Execution of the King's Commands. . . . It is improper of me to make any Comment of my own upon this unpleasing Occasion farther than to express my personal Concern to your Lordship in y$^e$ strongest Manner; Nor can I presume to say more in His Majesty's Name, than to assure your Lordship that notwithstanding this Event you may depend on the Continuance of his Regard, as for one whose Services he knows to have been faithfull and Sincere.[4]

---

1 Add. MS. 36797, f. 43. Bute to G. Townshend [7 Apr. 1763].

2 There are many testimonies to his management of the Commons. See, for example, Barrington's statement: 'George Grenville has done admirably, indeed triumphantly, in the House of Commons' (H.M.C., *Lothian MSS.*, p. 250. Barrington to Earl of Buckinghamshire, 9 May 1764); and John Tucker's comment on 'the reputation Mr Grenville has gained this session and how redily it has been acknowledged from all quarters of the House' (Dashwood MSS. B 11/8. Tucker to Dashwood, 23 Mar. 1765).

3 *A Narrative of the Changes in the Ministry 1765–67*, ed. M. Bateson (Camden Society, 1898), p. 28. Newcastle to White, 29 June 1765; cf. George III to Bute, 10 Jan. 1766 (*Letters from George III to Bute*, p. 241). 'After many cruel scenes' only Dashwood and Sir Fletcher Norton were removed; others followed after the repeal of the Stamp Act.

4 Dashwood MSS. B 3/2. Egmont to Dashwood, 10 July 1765, endorsed

Dashwood's stature in Whig eyes was seen again a few months later when in February 1766 he spoke and voted in the House of Lords against the repeal of the Stamp Act. 'This', wrote Newcastle, 'was the first appearance in the House of Lord Bute or his friends taking any open part in opposition to the administration.'[1] It seems to have so shaken Newcastle that he asked the king whether he wished to make any changes in his ministry. The king said he did not, and was interpreted as implying that he was not himself now opposed to repeal. The 'repeal of the cyder tax' went hand in hand with the repeal of the Stamp Act. On 7 February 1766 Dowdeswell, now Chancellor of the Exchequer, proposed once again that the tax should be removed from the makers and paid only by 'dealers and factors', and Pitt seconded the motion. Pitt's estimate of the loss of revenue by repeal bears no relation to the actual revenue from the 1763 duty, but in any case he was not interested in revenue:

> The loss might be £20,000 a year — what was that to a blemish upon liberty — we should not by the present cyder act continue such a blemish on the constitution, as to disfranchise six large countys by letting excise men into their houses.[2]

Grenville, North and Shelburne were among those who opposed repeal. On 18 March, a week after the Lords passed the repeal of the Stamp Act, the Commons passed Dowdeswell's 'new cyder bill' by 148 to 48. It replaced the tax of 4s. on the maker with one of 6s. on the retailer. The Lords did not divide on the bill, and the king gave his assent on 11 April. 'Nothing could be more grateful or pleasing', wrote the *Annual Register*, 'than the repeal of that [the cider] law; and the inhabitants of the cider counties had, upon this occasion, a taste of the same pleasure, which their brethren in America about the same time enjoyed.'[3]

The idea of 'Bute's friends' continued to haunt the minds of politicians. It was not only that they were a convenient whipping-

'Lord Egmont's letter about my Dismission'. Dashwood's reply, a dignified acquiescence, contains a phrase which is echoed in comments made about him by others: 'It is a great comfort to me to have acted through Life a Steady uniform part.'

[1] *Changes in Ministry, 1765-7*, p. 47 (Newcastle to White, 27 Feb. 1766). Bute also opposed repeal.

[2] Harris, Diary, 7 Feb. 1766.     [3] *Annual Register* (1766), p. 47.

boy; they were also the object of general courtship. This is perhaps less a tribute to their strength [1] than an admission of weakness on the part of those who wooed them. But everyone, it seems, wooed them, especially after the repeal of the Stamp and Cider Acts, as 'everyone' is said to have wooed North's friends after his resignation in 1782 and the end of the war with America. At a meeting of ministers in May 1766 Conway described Bute's friends as 'the most able men in parliament', and Egmont gave his opinion that 'without a thorough Coalition with you [Bute] and your friends he could not think this Administration could stand'.[2] Richmond, too, believed that only a 'union with Bute' could save Rockingham's administration, and in June urged Rockingham to give office to Dashwood and six others.[3] Rockingham either did not try, or failed, or was too dilatory in his wooing, for in July the king 'told his Ministers that he finds he cannot go on with them & has sent to Mr Pitt to come up & settle a Ministry entirely to his own Satisfaction'.[4] The king's wish was 'through Mr Pitt to build an Administration on as general a basis as the Times will permit, [and] to see as many of those gentlemen who were contrary to my inclinations removed, reinstated'.[5] As far as Bute himself was concerned Pitt's attitude was simple: he discounted Bute as a factor in the situation, declaring himself content with the king's 'declaration of last Year $y^t$ Ld Bute should not interfere in Political Matters'. Pitt's interpretation of this was that 'Bute's friends' might be employed, but not by that name, and not in consultation with Bute. The king named Dashwood and three others he 'wish'd brought again into Office', and Pitt 'said He did also'.[6] Neither the king nor Pitt referred to Dashwood as 'Bute's

[1] Harris put their numbers in Dec. 1765 as 50 or 60 'in both Houses' (Diary, 18 Dec.).

[2] Letters from George III to Bute, p. 246. George III to Bute [3 May 1766].

[3] Fletcher Norton, George Hay, Welbore Ellis, Robert Nugent, Hans Stanley, Northumberland (A. G. Olson, The Radical Duke, the Career and Correspondence of Charles Lennox third Duke of Richmond (1961), p. 19.)

[4] Dashwood MSS. B 19/2. G. Hobart to Dashwood, 10 July 1766.

[5] Letters of George III to Bute, p. 250 (George III to Bute [12 July 1766]).

[6] Correspondence of George III (ed. Sir J. Fortescue), i. 176. George III's memorandum, Aug. 1766. The other three were Northumberland, Norton, and Ellis.

friend'. It seems indeed to have been generally expected that Pitt would give office to Dashwood. He was, for example, the only one named by Burke when he wrote of those likely 'to be brought in' by Pitt[1]. Pitt himself, in his speech of 14 January on the repeal of the Stamp Act, had gone out of his way to praise Dashwood's consistency and courage, and added: 'I see his employment is taken from him; had I been employed, he is one of the first persons I should have endeavoured to keep in'.[2] In the event, Bute's ghost was too strong for Pitt. To assert his independence of it, he appointed Dashwood to office, not at the beginning of his administration, but in December 1766. Dashwood then became one of the Joint Postmasters-General, with Hillsborough as the other. At the same time, Jenkinson, who had been Bute's private secretary, and Secretary to the Treasury under Grenville, was made a lord of the Admiralty, Nugent became a lord of Trade, and Harcourt a groom of the bedchamber. Newcastle affected to find it difficult to believe that Pitt had really appointed Dashwood and Harcourt.[3] This, Newcastle wrote, was

> if true, the most material thing of all . . . if true it shows my Lord Chatham has thrown off the mask, and publicly owns and courts my Lord Bute's friendship and support. . . . What will become of all this, God only knows.[4]

Others drew the same conclusion. Horace Walpole noted the 'junction of Lord Chatham and Lord Bute, and the full support of the crown being given to the former'.[5] Macclesfield saw 'Lord Chatham endeavouring a connection with the Earl of B[ute] as the only means of supporting himself'.[6] The tones were less tragic

[1] *Correspondence of Edmund Burke*, i (ed. T. W. Copeland), 264.

[2] Walpole, *George III*, ii. 188; cf. Almon, *Anecdotes of Pitt*, i. 298. Franklin also reported Pitt's praise of Dashwood (A. H. Smyth, *Writings of Benjamin Franklin* (1905–7), iv. 407).

[3] William Harcourt (1743–1830), son of Simon, first Earl Harcourt (governor of George III as Prince of Wales 1751–2; d. 1777) and brother of second Earl, whom he succeeded in 1809; M.P. Oxford 1768–74; lieutenant-general 1793; field-marshal 1820.

[4] Albemarle, *Memoires of the Marquis of Rockingham* (1852), ii. 28. [3] Dec. 1766.

[5] *Correspondence* (ed. Lewis), xxii. 473 (Walpole to Mann, 8 Dec. 1766).

[6] *Jenkinson Papers*, p. 438.

1. Sir Francis Dashwood in 1739. An engraving by J. Faber
after the painting by Adrian Charpentier

2. West Wycombe Park in 1773, by Thomas Daniell

than Newcastle's, but there was general agreement with his opinion that the significance of the appointments, and especially Dashwood's, was that Pitt had decided to 'defy the world and openly take my Lord Bute by the hand at once'.

The general mistake was in thinking that Bute himself had any part in these negotiations. The men who were called 'Bute's friends' in December 1766 had little to do with Bute. As far as Pitt was concerned they had nothing to do with Bute. If they could be counted as a group, as the Whigs insisted that they could, this was so mainly because of their dismissal from office by Rockingham.[1] Dashwood seemed the chief of them because he had left the Treasury with Bute and had been dismissed from the Wardrobe by Rockingham when he formed his ministry in July 1765. But this was not Pitt's reason for appointing Dashwood. Pitt was determined that the label 'Bute's friend' should hold no political meaning; he did not believe that, with Dashwood, it did. The political significance of Dashwood to Pitt in December 1766 was, in fact, an echo of his political significance to Bute in April 1762: Pitt, like Bute, sought the support of independents rather than of party men. Pitt had had plenty of experience, over the last twenty-five years, of Dashwood's independency and his consistency, and may not have been averse to making amends for his own conduct over the cider tax. Dashwood's social and territorial standing was of course greater in 1766 than it was in 1762. Pitt probably thought this an advantage, and hoped that it would strengthen his ministry where he himself thought its weakness most serious — in the House of Lords, and in the face of the great Whig peers. Nevertheless, there can be no doubt that the

[1] J. Brooke, *The Chatham Administration* (1956), pp. 18–19, gives a 'modern' interpretation of the significance of the 'return to office of men who had served under Grenville but opposed the Rockinghams'. 'The Court was their party, office their goal, and opposition foreign and uncongenial. The Rockingham ministry had been an unnatural interlude in the smooth normality of their lives. Pitt's return to power was the signal for the birds to come back to their nests.' This I find — as far as Dashwood is concerned — simply not in accordance with facts, and the same seems to me true of A. S. Foord, *His Majesty's Opposition, 1714–1830* (1964), which, with a similar desire to make Dashwood a place-seeker, describes him in 1747 as one of 'a small group of [Tory] place-hunters' (p. 265), and in 1761 as one of the '[Tory] place-hunters [who] became placemen' (p. 333).

winning of Dashwood was a greater prize for Bute than it was for Pitt. In 1762 Dashwood was a prominent independent member of the Commons, well worth any government's wooing; after 1766 his interest in politics clearly waned. He attended the House of Lords regularly and sat on a large number of committees, but they were concerned with non-political questions — roads, canals, drainage, enclosures, the improvement of London and other cities and towns. He showed no desire to use his territorial standing to exert influence in the Commons.

Even so, it is not surprising that Grafton set store by Dashwood's support for the ministry. Nor is it surprising that North, who counted on and received the support of many independents, and had been on the Treasury board with Dashwood during Bute's ministry and left it when Rockingham succeeded, should have continued Dashwood in office. He was contented with his post and no more disposed than he had ever been to seek high political office. He remained, in the 1770s, independent in outlook, disposed on the whole to support North's government but not supporting it always, aloof from parties and connections.

Dashwood was an independent in office in another sense. It was not only that the holding of office did not take him from political independence; it was also that his attitude in office was influenced by his views of political independency. He was something of an administrative reformer, believing that political considerations should not be allowed to override administrative ones, and doing so as a natural corollary of his belief that patronage and party should not dominate the political world.

Dashwood's tenure of the office of Chancellor of the Exchequer was short, and circumscribed by problems of the return to peace. Nevertheless, it provides unmistakable evidence of an interest in administrative reform. In June 1762 he wrote to Bute about 'the necessity (as it appears to me) of regulating, and fixing by a Sign Manual from his Majesty, the Fees'[1] payable to the Deputy Clerk and Office Keeper in the office of the Treasurer of the Chamber. Although these fees, he said, depended on 'long uninterrupted custom', they were not authorised in law, and this was equally true of other fees and gratuities, for example the fees paid by those ap-

[1] Egerton MS. 2136, f. 50.

pointed to offices for the preparation of patents of appointment. He suggested that fees in the office of Treasurer of the Chamber should be abolished. 'I have', he wrote,

> ever disapproved the practice of perquisites and Gratuitys, a practice so shamefully extorted from the Livery servant[1] up to the Chancellor. If his Majesty should please to make a general reform in this branch of Corruption, (as far as the nature of thing would admit) I should receive his Majesty's commands with the greatest Satisfaction, and should think a deduction of £500 a year [from salary] . . . of little consideration, in comparison with the general Utility so salutary a measure would produce.

A step in this direction was taken at about this time in the Treasury itself. In 1758 a separate 'Office for making up the Accounts of the Revenue in the Treasury' was formed. Its business was 'to make up books containing accounts of income and issues of Customs, and the other duties and revenues payable at the Receipt of the Exchequer'. It was staffed by a Principal Clerk and other clerks; in 1766 and perhaps from the beginning there were six of them. Reformers at the end of the century regarded the Revenue Department as a model establishment, on the grounds that for many years 'no fees, gratuities, or perquisites whatever' had been paid to any of its officers, who were all paid entirely by fixed salary.[2] The Principal Clerk received the whole of his salary from the customs revenues — that is, 'being chiefly engaged in the concerns of the Public', he received his 'proper recompense at their hands' — and the other clerks received £100 each from the Civil List and the rest from the Customs revenues.[3] It is not entirely clear when this novel method

[1] This was no empty parallel. Vails were forbidden at West Wycombe and at Nocton. Stanhope, an associate in independency, forbade them at Chevening (B. Connell, *Portrait of a Whig Peer* compiled from the papers of the *Second Viscount Palmerston* (1957), p. 25).

[2] Reports of Commissioners appointed by Act 25 Geo. III, c. 19 to inquire into the FEES, GRATUITIES, PERQUISITES, and EMOLUMENTS, which are or have lately been received in the PUBLIC OFFICES therein mentioned. *Parl. Papers* (1806), vii. (H.C. 309), 2nd Report, pp. 71–72.

[3] The recommendation of the Commissioners on Fees that the Clerks too should be paid entirely from the customs revenues was adopted in 1793 (15th Report of Select Committee on Finance, 1797. *Parl. Papers* (1st series), xii. 288).

of payment 'by the Public' was introduced but there is evidence to suggest that it may have been in May 1762.

There can be no doubt of the significance of an interest in the method of paying public servants at this time, more than a generation before the great period of administrative reform inaugurated by the Public Accounts Commission appointed by North in 1780 and the Commission to inquire into Fees appointed by Pitt in 1785. One of the cardinal doctrines of reform was that all public servants should be paid entirely and only by fixed salary. The Public Accounts Commissioners stated this doctrine unequivocally in their sixth Report:

> We are of opinion that, in place of all these Salaries, Fees, and Gratuities, there should be substituted and annexed to each of these Offices, of whatever Rank or Denomination, One certain Salary, paid to the Officer by the Public Quarterly . . . The Advantages it [this Rule] holds out to the Public, its Simplicity, and Aptitude to be accommodated to all Offices, however distinguished, afford great Reason to believe that it may be applied to every Department of Government.[1]

To implement this, it was necessary that gratuities should be abolished and that fees paid by the public for services rendered should be fixed and regulated and paid not to the officer concerned but to the department, where they should form a Fee Fund appropriated to the payment of salaries. In 1782, four years before the Commissioners on Fees reported, the Treasury did this. It 'abolished the receipt of Fees, Gifts, Gratuities, and Perquisites by individuals; appointed a Clerk for the special purpose of receiving the fees usually taken at the Treasury, and established a List or Table thereof. . . . Out of the fund thereby constituted they directed fixed salaries to be paid to the Secretaries and Clerks.'[2] This may not unfairly be considered the end, or nearly the end, of a process begun in 1762 with the new method of paying the Clerks of the Revenue Room.

---

[1] 6th Report of Commissioners to examine, take, and state the Public Accounts of the Kingdom, and to report what Balances are in the hands of accountants, which may be applied to the Public Service; and what Defects there are in the present mode of receiving, collecting, issuing, and accounting for public money, 9 Feb. 1782. *Commons Journals*, xxxviii. 714.

[2] 2nd Report of Commissioners on Fees, *Parl. Papers* (1806), vii. 55–56.

Another 'branch of Corruption' which was attacked during Dashwood's tenure of office and later condemned by the Public Accounts Commissioners was the custom by which Receivers of Taxes did not pay the money they collected immediately into the Exchequer. In July 1762 the Treasury called for a statement of arrears of land tax and of the tax on houses, showing what part of the arrears had been collected but not paid into the Exchequer. As a result of the information returned, the Treasury directed the Commissioners of Taxes to write to the Receivers-General of sixteen counties 'stating to each of them the particular sum which appears from his own account to have been now for so long a time actually in his hands, and urging the immediate payment thereof, as well as strictly injoining him to keep up for the future a more speedy course of payment of all such money as shall from time to time come into his hands', and to twelve other Receivers (including the Receiver for the King's Household) asking why they had collected so little by the end of the year.[1] In November the Commissioners of Taxes were instructed to inform four still-delinquent Receivers that 'if they do not make immediate payment into the Exchequer of the publick money now actually in their hands, they will be superseded without further notice'. On the same day the Commissioners were ordered to send to the Treasury monthly accounts of 'all the publick money which appears to be in the hands of each Receiver respectively arisen by any Taxes or Duties, either of former years or of the current year'.[2] The sentiments on which this reform was based accord exactly with the views of the Public Accounts Commissioners, who stated, in their first report:

> The Revenue should come from the Pocket of the Subject directly into the Exchequer; but to permit Receivers to retain it in their Hands, expressly for their own Advantage, is to furnish them with the strongest Motive for withholding it. A private Interest is thus created, in direct Opposition to that of the Public.[3]

---

[1] Public Record Office, T 29/34, ff. 328–9.  21 July 1762.

[2] T 29/35, ff. 3, 4.  5 Nov. 1762.

[3] *Commons Journals*, xxxviii. 76.  The Report is dated 27 Nov. 1780. The reforms of 1762 hardly outlasted Bute's ministry. By 1764 balances were again being retained, and when Pitt tried to implement the Public Accounts Commissioners' recommendations the Receivers claimed compensation.

This was not all. Inquiries were made in June 1762 into the names, numbers, and salaries of the staff of the Commissioners of Taxes and other revenue departments, and in July and August into the gross and net produce of the taxes they had collected over the last fifteen years.[1] In August even the Commissioners of Excise — always held up as a model for other revenue departments — were required to explain why the revenue from the malt duties was paid over more slowly than it should be,[2] and this was followed in March 1763 by a bill for preventing fraud in the collection of malt duties.[3] In September the Auditors of Imprest were reprimanded for laxity in examining the accounts of John Sharpe, a former Solicitor to the Treasury, and in October the Treasury drew up rules for the Auditors to observe in their future handling of the Solicitor's accounts.[4]  In January 1763, after a review of the collection of Window Duties, the office of Comptroller-General of Window Duties was suppressed and his duties transferred to the Commissioners of Taxes.[5]

The ideas of administrative reform expressed by the Commissioners in the 1780s no doubt germinated during North's administration, and were made politically potent by the controversy over the American War.  It seems, however, that the seeds were sown earlier than this, in the soil of Bute's administration, and that administrative reform may claim a real connection with independency.  The fact that the reforms during Dashwood's period of office were crowded into a few months of precarious power strengthens their claim to be regarded as attempts to do what Pitt succeeded in doing later.  Beyond this, there is a personal link, both at the political and at the administrative level, that cannot be ignored.  Shelburne, who proposed the inquiry

[1] T 27/28, ff. 300, 316.
[2] T 27/28, f. 326. Dyson to Bindley, 19 Aug. 1762. [3] T 29/35, f. 51.
[4] T 29/34, f. 352 (29 Sept. 1762) and T 27/28, f. 337 (5 Oct. 1762). The Auditors (whose remuneration came almost entirely from fees) were severely castigated by the Public Accounts Commissioners (see especially Reports 8–14. *Commons Journals*, xxxix. 45, 325, 522, 771; xl. 111, 653; xli. 9) and suppressed by Pitt in 1785. They were replaced by five Commissioners for Auditing the Public Accounts, who were paid by fixed salary (25 Geo. III, c. 52). Pitt's reform owed a good deal to the suggestions of Lord Mountstuart (Bute's son), who was one of the Auditors in 1785. (Chatham Papers, P.R.O. 30/8/302.)
[5] T 29/35, f. 30. 26 Jan. 1763.

into public expenditure in December 1779 and planned to submit to parliament in 1783 a bill for regulating fees in financial departments, was Bute's protégé and was roused to interest in administrative reform in 1766 by his concern about fees in the Secretary of State's office. North, who enlarged the scope of the 1780 inquiry and chose the men who conducted it, and so in a sense was the father of its recommendations, was a member of Bute's Treasury Board in 1762–1763. Jeremiah Dyson, appointed Secretary to the Treasury in May 1762, had in 1751, when Clerk of the House of Commons, regulated the fees payable for private bills. He sat on the Treasury Board from 1768 to 1774 but died in 1776. Charles Jenkinson, who prepared the bill establishing the 1780 inquiry, and was North's mainstay and Pitt's lieutenant, began his political career as Bute's private secretary. Stamp Brooksbank, Commissioner of Excise from 1775 to 1785, who in 1782 produced detailed plans for funding fees and abolishing useless offices, began his official career in February 1763, when he was appointed secretary to the Excise. Sir William Musgrave, who in 1782–3 drew up plans for a comprehensive reform of the collection of the Customs duties, was appointed Commissioner of the Customs in March 1763. The fact that the zeal for reform and the mixed moral and utilitarian indignation expressed by the Commissioners is reminiscent of the independents' praise of 'economy' and condemnation of 'corruption' is perhaps a similarity rather than a link. But the similarity is certainly there, and the reforms of 1762–3 may serve as a reminder that the independents' strictures on corruption were not humbug.

This is perhaps also suggested by Dashwood's acceptance, in March 1763, of Sir John Philipps's proposal for an inquiry into the public accounts presented to parliament in that session and at any time since the beginning of the war, only persuading Philipps to agree that the inquiry should be made by a Select Committee of the House instead of by Commissioners. The proposal was, traditionally, an opposition demand, which might be forced on a government but which no government was expected willingly to concede. Legge could not understand Dashwood's conduct, which was not the result of weakness, for 'they might very easily have got rid of all Committees if they had chosen it';[1] Newcastle could explain it only in political

[1] Add. MS. 32947, f. 86. Legge to Newcastle, 24 Feb. 1763.

terms: 'that My Lord Bute has yielded to the Tories, to carry on this Enquiry, in Earnest; & perhaps, with a View, to come at me, to please Them'.[1] George III, commenting on Talbot's support for a similar proposal in the Lords, perhaps came nearer the truth. Talbot's

> conduct the whole winter [he wrote to Bute] has been unaccountable, either silent in the house or attacking friends and commending foes; ... the unhappy system that has been follow'd but too often since I have mounted the throne of preferring men who have opinions of their own, has aided to weaken Government ... a Talbot, a Dashwood, a Strange, are forever running counter.[2]

It was understandable enough at this particular time that George should be exasperated by refusal to regard office as a bar to independency. His pettishness contrasts with the pleasure Bute expressed in the appointment of Strange as Chancellor of the Duchy of Lancaster in November 1762. 'I do indeed believe', Bute wrote, 'that Office will not add to your Lordship's zeal for the Service of your King and Country, nor alter your conduct an jota; but . . . were it always in my Power, Gentlemen with this noble Turn of Mind, should be the only subjects I would recommend to my Prince.'[3] It seems that Talbot, who was very much of 'this Turn of Mind', was also expected to make 'reforms in his office': another hint that independency had administrative as well as political implications.

It is understandable, even if unfair to Philipps, that his proposal for an inquiry by Commissioners should have reminded Newcastle and his friends of the punitive Commissions of William III's reign and Anne's. Philipps, however, wanted primarily 'an Effectual Enquiry', and his belief that Dashwood also wanted this was so strong that he withdrew his own motion and supported Dashwood's motion for a Select Committee of twenty-one members, chosen by ballot, 'to examine & state the Estimates & publick accounts which have been delivered to parliament either in the present or any former

---

[1] Add. MS. 32947, f. 183. Newcastle to Devonshire 5 Mar. 1763. Newcastle had no doubt that there was an alliance between Bute and the Tories, but could not decide who was master: in the same letter he complains of the 'Submission' of the Tories to Bute.

[2] *Letters of George III to Bute*, p. 198. 7 Mar. 1763.

[3] Add. MS. 36797, f. 22. 17 Nov. 1762.

sessions of parliament since the commencement of the late War'.[1]
Grenville supported Dashwood's motion, but Fox behaved in a way
Newcastle thought befitting a minister, and showed his opposition.
Of course political events, which were to favour Shelburne when he
demanded an inquiry sixteen years later, did not favour Philipps, and
the ground on which his Committee's Report fell soon turned stony.
Nevertheless, the content of the Report suggests that Philipps's
proposal for an inquiry into corruption was not merely part of a
vendetta against Newcastle, nor a 'show of patriotism',[2] as Horace
Walpole called it, and that Dashwood's support cannot be fairly discounted, as it has in fact been, as a 'sop to the country gentlemen'.
The Committee had at its disposal a very large number of accounts
and, convinced of the 'Impracticability of a General Examination
during the present Session', it decided to investigate the different
branches of expenditure one by one, and began with the Board of
Ordnance. It paid particular attention to the methods by which
contracts were obtained. Here, its pronouncement in favour of
contracting by advertisement, and its statement that by 'more open
Bargains for Contracts . . . the board would have been better served
and considerable Sums saved to the Public'[3] is, in spirit, not different
at all from similar pronouncements by the Commissioners of Public
Accounts twenty years later.

Dashwood's main task during his ten months in office was the
framing of the first post-war budget, and here ideas of independency
had relevance only in the negative sense that his financial proposals
showed no wish to placate either the country gentlemen or any other
taxpayers. He opened his budget on 7 March. Supplies granted by
parliament for the service of the year were reduced from £18,625,046
in 1762 to £10,246,609 in 1763.[4] To meet this the land tax and the

[1] Add. MS. 32947, f. 61. West's memorandum to Newcastle, 22 Feb.
1763.                    [2] Walpole, *George III*, i. 191.

[3] *Report from Committee appointed 4 March 1763 to take into consideration
the various Estimates and Accounts presented to the House in this present or in
any former Session of Parliament which relate to the application or expenditure
of the Public Money since the commencement of the late War* (1763) (printed
separately).

[4] The main reason for the discrepancy between this figure and that given
by Debrett in the tables of Supply and Ways and Means 1743–73 which he

malt tax were both retained at their war-time rates, with an estimated yield of £2,750,000, £2,000,000 was to be taken from the Sinking Fund, £1,800,000 raised by Exchequer Bills and £3,500,000 borrowed by way of annuities and two lotteries.

As security for the loan of £3,500,000 additional duties were imposed on imported wines and cider and on cider and perry made at home, with the Sinking Fund as collateral security.[1] The large floating debt was reduced by funding a sum of £3,670,739 (representing £3,075,316 of navy debt and £595,423 of ordnance debt) into annuities bearing interest at 4 per cent.[2] This was a successful con-

published in 1774 (*History*, vii. 414) is simply that Debrett ignored the fact that land- and malt-tax deficiencies were, by parliamentary authority, met out of supply. The amount of these deficiencies was normally, as Dashwood noted, in the neighbourhood of £300,000: the actual figure for 1763 was £329,208. 'An Account, shewing how the Money given for the Service of the Year 1763 has been disposed of, until the 8th Day of *March* 1764' (*Commons Journals*, xxix. 922–4) gives the full details of Supply and Ways and Means that are in Dashwood MSS. B 1/5, and of course shows land- and malt-tax deficiencies.

[1] The Sinking Fund had gradually ceased to be used for the purpose for which it had been formed — the redemption of debt — and was regularly used instead both to provide security for the interest on new loans (or to back up some other security) and to supplement Ways and Means. The Sinking Fund was one of David Hartley's great anxieties: he charged Grenville, for example, with exaggerating the size of his Ways and Means by 'using' a larger sum from the Sinking Fund than it would in fact produce, but he calculated that in 1763 the 'disposeable revenue' was £2,202,000 (*State of the Nation* (1765), p. 31).

[2] Dashwood's figure of £10,117,120. 9s. 6d. for Ways and Means includes also:

Surplus of Annuity Fund 1761 ... ... £47,120. 9. 6
and Militia Money 1762 ... ... ... £20,000

It does not include funded navy and ordnance bills, and Debrett's figure does not, but the *Annual Register*'s does. The *Annual Register*'s figure of £14,199,375 requires comment. It estimates the land-tax yield at £37,855 more than the traditional (and unrealistic) £2,000,000. And, as well as including a sum for the funded navy and ordnance bills (£3,670,739), it duplicates (perhaps through sheer inadvertence) the sum of £393,661 which is included in Supply for the navy 'ordinary'. Thus, the *Annual*

version scheme, in that nearly all the stock was taken up. It was also a desirable operation. The size of the navy debt was a constant problem in the eighteenth century, in peace as well as in war, and the funding ensured that the large war debt was not carried over into peace-time. The scheme was copied by Pitt at the end of the war with America. According to Claudius Amyand, Secretary to the Board of Customs, Dashwood's 'Expedient for the Navy Debt . . . won general approbation'.[1] It was approved by Legge,[2] who was considered to have 'a clerk-like knowledge of finances', Grenville praised it as a true measure of economy, and the banker James Coutts told Bute

> I cannot help applauding the motion, though as a holder of a large sum of Navy Bills I do not like it, because the certainty of my payment being postponed at least balances the advantage of my principal and interest being secured.[3]

Moreover, forty years later Sir John Sinclair compared the younger Pitt's post-war debt operations unfavourably with Dashwood's, for Pitt funded navy debt at 5 per cent, against Dashwood's 4 per cent, when the discount rate was 20 per cent instead of 10 per cent as it had been in 1763. Sinclair quoted with approval a letter, printed in the *Morning Herald* of 15 January 1789, which maintained that 'by contrasting the management of the navy debt in 1763 with the management in 1784 and 1785, the difference between right and wrong will be seen', and gave figures to show that 'thus Pitt did unnecessarily load the people with two hundred and ninety thousand pounds taxes *per annum*, in perpetuity, by following his own measures

*Register* arrives at a twice-inflated 'surplus' of £677,366 (though it prints this as £577,366). Rectifying these mistakes brings the 'surplus' down to Debretts' £245,820, which still takes no account of land- and malt-tax deficiencies.

   1 Amyand to Dashwood, 5 Feb. 1763. Dashwood MSS. B 1/1. Amyand (1718-74) was M.P. Tregony 1747-54, Sandwich 1754-6; Keeper of King's Library 1745; Under Secretary of State 1750-6; Commissioner of Customs 1756-65; Receiver of Land Tax for Middlesex 1765-74.
   2 According to Harris 'Mr. Legge and everyone' approved the measure (Diary, 5 Mar. 1763).
   3 Bute MSS. 5 Feb. 1763.

in 1784 and 1785, instead of pursuing the plain path and precedent laid down in 1763'.[1]

The funded national debt had almost doubled during the war. In January 1763 it stood at £122,603,836, bearing an interest charge of £4,402,473. A memorandum headed 'The National Debt', written by Dashwood, is an attempt to bring into the picture, in a way that eighteenth-century budget statements did not, revenue as well as new parliamentary grants. He estimated the 'nett produce of the revenue for 12 months' at £10,000,000:

| | | |
|---|---|---|
| Excise about | 5,000,000 | including Malt |
| Customs not quite | 2,000,000 | |
| other Inland Duties | 1,000,000 | |
| Land tax | 2,000,000 | |
| | 10,000,000 | |
| *Less* Land and Malt | 2,750,000 | used for the Supply |
| | 7,250,000 | of the year |

Against this is charged:

| | | |
|---|---|---|
| Interest on National debt at the peace: | 4,600,000 | |
| King's Civil List: | 800,000 | 5,400,000 |
| | | 1,850,000 which is about the sum that will accrue to the Sinking Fund.[2] |

Additional duties were placed on the most profitable existing source of revenue: imported and home-manufactured alcoholic beverages. On wines imported from France the additional duty was £8 a tun; on other imported wines, £4 a tun; on cider imported, £2 a tun. To the existing duties on cider made in Great Britain there was added a tax of 4s. a hogshead, payable by the maker. The new duties on imported wines were expected to raise something like the amount raised by additional duties at the same rates imposed in 1745. Over the years 1756–60 these had brought in an average of £61,043 a year. This seems to have been a reasonable estimate: the total yield for the three years from July 1763 to July 1766 was probably

---

[1] *History of the Public Revenue* (3rd ed., 1804), iii. 298–9.
[2] Dashwood MSS. B 7/3.

something like £187,000.[1]  The new £2 a tun import duty on cider was, like the existing £12 10s., protective only: together, they produced only £3 in the three years 1764–6.[2]  No estimate survives of the probable yield of the 'cyder tax' — the new excise duty on cider made at home — and it would clearly have been very difficult to make one.  It was probably hoped that a tax of 4s. on the maker of cider would bring in not less than a tax of 10s. on the retailer, and it was estimated that this would produce £38,050 a year.  In fact the yield over the three years that the 4s. duty lasted was £141,293: £32,461 in 1763–4, £62,044 in 1764–5, £46,788 in 1765–6.[3] Nearly a third of this came from composition fees: £5,219 in 1763–1764, £28,006 in 1764–5, £19,561 in 1765–6.  These figures leave no doubt that the 'new mode' — that is, taxing the maker instead of the retailer — was financially profitable.  Reversion in 1766 to the 'old mode' of taxing the retailer drastically reduced the revenue,

[1] There are no records of receipts from customs duties (comparable to the Excise Revenue Accounts) before 1785.  The 1852 Select Committee on Import Duties on Wines procured from the Inspector-General of Imports and Exports an 'Account of Importations of Wine into *England*, from 1697 to 1785 inclusive' (*Parl. Papers* (1852) (495), xvii. app. i. 863–4), and printed his explanation that the information available was incomplete 'inasmuch as by far the larger portion of the earlier records of this office was destroyed by fire in 1814' (p. 865).  The yield from the 1763 wine duties (for England only) can be calculated from the import figures in the Account: a total of £184,931 for the three years 1764–6.  One way of estimating the total yield is to subtract, for each year, from the annual 'secured' interest of £140,000 the deficiency at the end of the year plus the yield from the cider duty.  The deficiency year ends on 10 Oct., and the excise year on 5 July, so the result can only be an approximation, though probably a reasonably good one: it is, for the three years, £186,995.

[2] The duty was increased by another £3 a tun in 1766, by the Act 'repealing' the cider tax.

[3] Most of the following estimates are taken from Dashwood MSS. B 1 and B 3, and most of the figures for yield from papers in the archives of the Board of Customs and Excise, especially Excise Revenue Accounts 1662–1827; Excise and Treasury, vol. 16 (1758–64) and vol. 17 (1763–8); a State of the Revenue of Excise since Michaelmas 1662; and Quantities, Rates, & Amounts of Excise Duties 1684–1798.  The figures in the book of Quantities are corrected ones, and I have adopted them, where relevant, in preference to those found elsewhere.

even though the rate of duty was raised from 4*s*. to 6*s*.: the yield fell to £9,649 in 1766–7 and £5,889 in 1767–8.

Although Dashwood's original proposal in the House of Commons was to place the new duty on cider on the retailer, it seems that he had previously considered the possibility of placing it on the maker. One may guess that he preferred this but thought it inexpedient. It is interesting that a conference with 'the country gentlemen' should have resulted in transferring the tax to the maker, for this certainly increased the inquisitorial visits to private houses that Pitt so deplored. Presumably the country gentlemen accepted a lower tax, even though it affected more of them, with provision for compounding, as the lesser of two evils. From the point of view of the revenue a tax on the maker was preferable to a tax on the retailer, and this is why expert opinion favoured it. It was simpler, easier to assess and to collect, more difficult to evade. It was easy to see who made cider, much more difficult to discover what happened to it after it was made. Malt and candles were already dutied in this way; there seemed good reason to draw a parallel between makers of beer and makers of cider. A system of compounding and exemptions, as with the malt duty, would relieve small private consumers.

The chief professional advocate of taxing the maker rather than the retailer of cider was John Bindley, Secretary to the Excise Board from December 1761 and a Commissioner from February 1763 to December 1764, when he resigned in order to enter politics.[1] Bindley had experience of excise collection from both sides: he was (like

[1] Bindley (1735–86) was a friend of Charles Jenkinson and of Charles Townshend, and gave advice about the revenue to both. His political career was short and undistinguished. His hope of standing for West Looe in Dec. 1764 was frustrated by his connection with the cider tax (*Additional Grenville Papers*, p. 225). He then offered his services to Grenville in the Customs department (Add. MS. 38204, f. 7), but was refused. He was a successful candidate at a by-election for Dover in Dec. 1766, but unsuccessful at Reading at the general election of 1768. He then returned to distilling, failed, and in 1769 was made a bankrupt. In 1770 North apparently refused his offer of 'my whole services' and in 1771 he went into business as a wine merchant. His jumping from one side to the other of the excise fence perhaps did not inspire trust. In the 1770s he frequently grumbled to Jenkinson, whom he rightly considered a 'Man of Business', that North did not appreciate his suggestions (e.g. Add. MSS. 38206, f. 230; 38216, f. 129).

Wilkes, who reviled the cider tax in the *North Briton*), the son of a London distiller, and he had been a distiller himself. Throughout the 1760s and 1770s he bombarded every government except Rockingham's (which had its own bombarder in David Hartley) with schemes for increasing the public revenue. Although Bindley's influence over general revenue policy fell far short of what he thought due to him, there can be no doubt that he deserved his reputation as 'the first proposer of the cyder tax', in the restricted sense that he had strongly urged that the tax be placed on the maker. Indeed, it was his opinion that all excised commodities should be taxed at the source, and that the tax should be paid by the maker irrespective of whether he afterwards sold the commodity or consumed it himself.[1] This opinion was shared by Henry Saxby, Secretary to the Customs, and probably by others in both departments.

Dashwood had estimated that the cider tax he first proposed — 10s. on the retailer — would, with the new wine tax, bring in about £100,000. This was £40,000 less than the interest for which the two taxes were security. To fill the gap Dashwood had considered, but did not put to the Commons, two new taxes: an increase in the stamp duty on insurance policies and bills of lading, estimated to produce nearly £25,000, and a stamp duty on tickets of admission to public entertainments. The first of these was implemented by Grenville in 1765. The second was proposed by North in the 1770s, and approved by parliament, but abandoned in face of opposition. This was one of the taxes recommended by Sinclair, who thought it capable of 'raising a considerable sum . . . without doing any material injury to the persons by whom such public places are conducted'.[2] It is not known why Dashwood abandoned the idea of introducing these two taxes, but presumably he was restrained by the argument that, in the first year of peace, it was impracticable to impose more than one new tax. Unless the wine and cider duties brought in more than £100,000, therefore, the Sinking Fund would have to supplement them by something like £40,000 a year. In fact, the average annual deficiency over the three years from October 1763 to October 1766 was less than £40,000: the figures were £49,742, £29,212, £12,758.[3]

[1] Appendix IV (*b*).　　　[2] *History of the Public Revenue*, iii. 256.
[3] Deficiencies were a normal feature of eighteenth-century estimates of

An eighteenth-century budget statement was a statement of the revenue and expenditure which parliament had to vote in the particular year to which it applied, not a comprehensive statement of all revenue and expenditure for that year. The balance that was struck, therefore, was a parliamentary balance, incomplete and in some ways irrelevant as a guide to the country's financial position. This method of balancing, together with the known inadequacies of estimating, means that the data which would justify describing any particular budget as 'good' or 'bad' do not exist. It is, however, clear that Dashwood was successful in meeting the challenge of the end of the war. He made sensible provision for the transition to peace, by drastically reducing expenditure and at the same time slightly increasing instead of reducing taxation. He produced a realistic temporary solution of a problem which was not solved permanently until much later: a large navy debt due to persistent underestimating by the Navy Office. This entitles him to be regarded as a competent Chancellor of the Exchequer, and his claim to be rather more than this must rest, as indeed must North's and Pitt's, on his disposition not merely to work the system, but to reform it. The tax on cider was part of his policy of slightly increasing taxation and the placing of the tax on the maker instead of on the retailer was well justified on financial and economic grounds. The prominence of the 'cyder tax' was as accidental as the prominence of Walpole's excise was in 1733; it was opposed for political reasons and in 1766 it was modified for political reasons. Sinclair, who, without naming Dashwood, praised his handling of the navy debt and recommended his proposed tax on tickets for public entertainment, also recommended the revival of the cider tax. 'Cyder and perry', Sinclair thought,

> have been too gently dealt with. .... The mode formerly thought of for taxing these commodities, however, having been once abandoned by

---

tax revenue, and a deficiency in one year was not followed by a revised estimate in the next. For example, the duties imposed on offices, houses, and windows in 1758 had, on average, a deficiency of about £50,000 a year. The annual land and malt taxes continued to be estimated each year at £2,750,000 though it was known that they would have a deficiency of about £300,000 (cf. Dashwood MSS. B 7/3). This deficiency was supplied each year, rather than reduce the estimate. The deficiencies of the 1763 wine and cider duties were, in comparison with others, small.

3. Cider cartoon, 1763

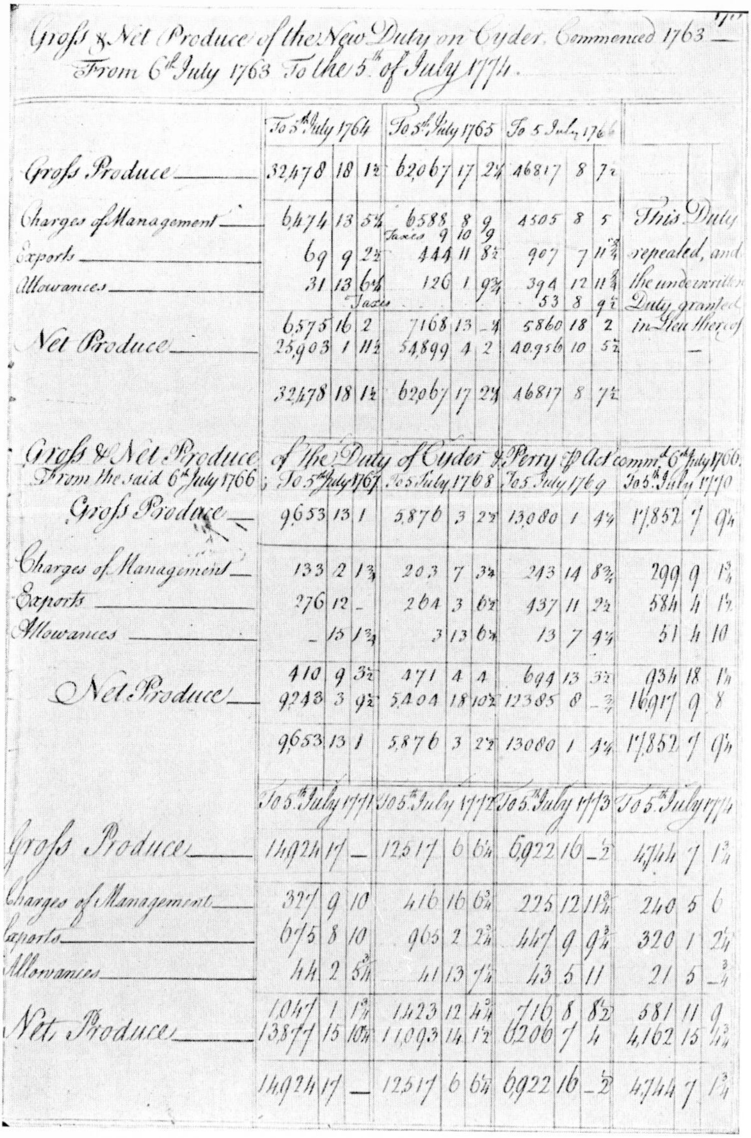

Gross & Net Produce of the New Duty on Cyder, Commenced 1763 — From 6th July 1763 To the 5th of July 1774.

| | To 5th July 1764 | | | To 5th July 1765 | | | To 5 July 1766 | | | |
|---|---|---|---|---|---|---|---|---|---|---|
| Gross Produce | 32,478 | 18 | 1½ | 62,067 | 17 | 2¼ | 46817 | 8 | 7½ | |
| Charges of Management | 6,474 | 13 | 5¼ | 6588 | 8 | 9 | 4505 | 8 | 5 | This Duty |
| | | | | Taxes 9 | 10 | 9 | | | | |
| Exports | 69 | 9 | 2½ | 444 | 11 | 8½ | 907 | 7 | 11¾ | repealed, and |
| Allowances | 31 | 13 | 6¼ | 126 | 1 | 9¾ | 394 | 12 | 11¾ | the underwritten |
| | | Taxes | | | | | 53 | 8 | 9½ | Duty granted |
| | 6,575 | 16 | 2 | 7168 | 13 | –¼ | 5860 | 18 | 2 | in Lieu thereof |
| Net Produce | 25,903 | 1 | 11½ | 54,899 | 4 | 2 | 40,956 | 10 | 5½ | — |
| | 32,478 | 18 | 1½ | 62,067 | 17 | 2¼ | 46817 | 8 | 7½ | |

Gross & Net Produce of the Duty of Cyder & Perry ℔ Act commd. 6th July 1766. From the said 6th July 1766;

| | To 5th July 1767 | | | To 5 July 1768 | | | To 5 July 1769 | | | To 5th July 1770 | | |
|---|---|---|---|---|---|---|---|---|---|---|---|---|
| Gross Produce | 9,653 | 13 | 1 | 5,876 | 3 | 2½ | 13,080 | 1 | 4¼ | 17,852 | 7 | 9¼ |
| Charges of Management | 133 | 2 | 1¾ | 20,3 | 7 | 3¼ | 243 | 14 | 8¾ | 299 | 9 | 1¾ |
| Exports | 276 | 12 | – | 264 | 3 | 6½ | 437 | 11 | 2½ | 584 | 4 | 1½ |
| Allowances | – | 15 | 1¾ | 3 | 13 | 6¼ | 13 | 7 | 4¼ | 51 | 4 | 10 |
| | 410 | 9 | 3½ | 471 | 4 | 4 | 694 | 13 | 3½ | 934 | 18 | 1¼ |
| Net Produce | 9,243 | 3 | 9½ | 5,404 | 18 | 10½ | 12385 | 8 | –¾ | 16,917 | 9 | 8 |
| | 9,653 | 13 | 1 | 5,876 | 3 | 2½ | 13080 | 1 | 4¼ | 17,852 | 7 | 9¼ |

| | To 5th July 1771 | | | To 5th July 1772 | | | To 5th July 1773 | | | To 5th July 1774 | | |
|---|---|---|---|---|---|---|---|---|---|---|---|---|
| Gross Produce | 14,924 | 17 | – | 12,517 | 6 | 6¼ | 6,922 | 16 | –½ | 4,744 | 7 | 1¾ |
| Charges of Management | 327 | 9 | 10 | 416 | 16 | 6¾ | 225 | 12 | 11¾ | 240 | 5 | 6 |
| Exports | 675 | 8 | 10 | 965 | 2 | 2¾ | 447 | 9 | 9¾ | 320 | 1 | 2¼ |
| Allowances | 44 | 2 | 5¾ | 41 | 13 | 7¼ | 43 | 5 | 11 | 21 | 5 | –¾ |
| | 1,047 | 1 | 1¾ | 1,423 | 12 | 4¾ | 716 | 8 | 8½ | 581 | 11 | 9 |
| Net Produce | 13,877 | 15 | 10¼ | 11,093 | 14 | 1½ | 6,206 | 7 | 4 | 4,162 | 15 | 4¾ |
| | 14,924 | 17 | – | 12,517 | 6 | 6¼ | 6,922 | 16 | –½ | 4,744 | 7 | 1¾ |

4. ' Gross and Net Produce of the New Duty on Cyder '

the legislature, cannot well be revived in precisely the same form; though it is certain that the repeal was merely the effect of party spirit, and not of principle or conviction. But a cyder tax might be raised by imposing a duty upon apple trees, or orchards, without the possibility of any well-founded objection: or a tax might be levied upon pears and apples, when they are gathered in order to be manufactured into cyder and perry, in the same manner as the duty on hops is at present collected.[1]

For a man of Dashwood's views, with an interest in administration and a dislike of party politics, the Post Office offered positive attraction. It was an administrative rather than a political office. In this it differed less than is commonly supposed from the office of Chancellor of the Exchequer, whose political importance in the Commons, arising from his responsibility for the government's financial policy, was in a sense accidental. The Post Office was a revenue department, though it was more independent than the other revenue departments because the Joint Postmasters were ministers, able to sit in the House of Lords though debarred by statute from sitting in the Commons. Like other revenue departments, the Post Office was valuable to the government for two not easily compatible reasons: on the one hand it collected revenue, and on the other hand it was a potential source of political patronage. Unlike other revenue departments, the Post Office also performed a great public service, the carriage of mail. All revenue departments could claim that the efficient collection of the revenue was more important than political considerations, and one, the Excise, made good its claim. Only the Post Office could add to this claim the contention that the good of the public service ought to override the government's need for patronage. This contention fitted exactly with Dashwood's general views of government and patronage. It is for this reason that his period as Joint Postmaster, in giving evidence of his concern for good and efficient administration, also shows the way in which an independent in office reacted to the encroachment of political interest upon administration.

The Post Office was a young department, established by statute in 1711. It had more actual or potential links with politics than any other revenue department. Every parliamentary constituency had a

[1] Op. cit. iii. 239–40.

number of local Post Office officials, and their appointment could be claimed not only as a part of government patronage, but by members of parliament as part of their local patronage. Moreover, the Post Office extended certain privileges to members of parliament, in particular the valuable and expensive privilege of sending letters, packets, and newspapers free of charge.

Dashwood's period as Joint Postmaster came at an interesting time in the development of the Post Office, and at a time of rapidly increasing business. The Post Office revenues had been merged in the general revenue of the country in 1760. The end of the farming of the Bye and Cross Roads Letter Post in 1764 meant that for the first time the Post Office administered directly the four services it provided: the Inland Post, the Foreign Letter Post, the Penny Post, and the Bye and Cross Roads Letter Post. A Post Office Act had been passed in 1765. His tenure of office ended just before the younger Pitt, under the influence of his friend Palmer, forced the Post Office to adopt mail coaches instead of the mail carts which most Post Office officials believed to be more conducive to the 'safety of the mail'.

Anthony Todd's favourable first impression of Dashwood in December 1766, as having 'an earnest desire to gain knowledge of the business',[1] was matched by many later tributes to his interest in the efficient working of the postal services. Todd's secretaryship was a period of reform, and there is no doubt that he owed much to Dashwood's support. Among the improvements introduced were the establishment of a Six Day's post between England and Ireland in 1767, the introduction of optional prepayment on letters sent abroad and the reform of the system of collecting letters from London Receiving Houses in 1769, and the establishment of a Penny Post Office in Dublin in 1773. Experiments were made with mail carts in order to increase both the speed and the safety of the carriage of mail, and these Dashwood encouraged and took part in. A Memorial[2] sent by the Post Office to the Treasury in November 1772 suggested other reforms, and, as these could not be effected without legislation, asked the Treasury to promote an act of parliament. The two most important, both signs of increasing business, were the introduction of a system of delivering letters to the person to whom they were

[1] Bute MSS. Todd to Bute, 24 Dec. 1766.
[2] General Post Office, Treasury Letter Book (1771–8), pp. 28–34.

addressed, instead of to the nearest Post Office, and further regulation of the privilege of franking enjoyed by members of parliament and by certain officials. It is clear that there was no reliable way of preventing the abuse of franking, and that the only real remedy for the large and increasing loss to the revenue was to abolish the privilege. Here the Post Office ran up against political interest. Dashwood's attempts to persuade North to take action failed, and the question even of putting further restrictions on franking was postponed. In another sphere, that of appointments, Dashwood was able to challenge the claims of political interest more directly, though not always successfully. He refused demands from members of parliament to appoint their local postmasters. He stood out against North's attempt to use Post Office patronage as a way of cementing political friendship. In 1771, for example, he refused a request for a favour which North pressed on him as 'a most real & essential assistance to the Interest of the Crown in the Cinqueports',[1] and in 1774 he refused to renew one of the contracts for the provision of packet-boats that the Post Office had decided to abolish although North pleaded that the contractor, Edward Lewis, was 'an excellent Member of Parliament . . . [and] I think the King's affairs in Parliament may suffer, unless such good & steady friends as Mr. Lewis have from Government all the Countenance & Favour that Justice & the Public Service will permit'.[2] When Franklin was dismissed from his post of Deputy Postmaster-General of America in January 1774, Dashwood protested strongly and successfully against the proposal to make the office 'a sinecure by our Appointment', that is, to appoint a successor who was not resident in America. He wrote to Todd:

I do and must confess, according to my (what some may call simple) Ideas, that the appointing a Deputy Post Master General for America who is never supposed or intended to set his foot in America seems to me unwarrantable and unjustifiable and would be liable to just obloquy and abuse.[3]

1 Dashwood MSS. B 2/1. North to Dashwood, 1 Apr. 1771.
2 Dashwood MSS. B 2/1. North to Dashwood, 29 Jan. 1774 (I have printed this in *Bulletin of John Rylands Library*, vol. xxxvii, p. 237).
3 Dashwood MSS. B 2/1. Memorandum to Todd, 4 Feb. 1774 (printed in ibid., p. 240).

Throughout the eighteenth century, concern for good administration stopped half-way if it was not prepared to challenge the supremacy of political over administrative interest. Dashwood had shown his resentment of the claims of political interest in other fields, for example that of parliamentary management, and as a minister he carried over this resentment into the field of administration. To see this attitude to administration as a natural corollary of political independency is not at all the same as to suggest that independents were administrators rather than politicians, or not quite of the calibre of first-rank statesmen. It is merely to emphasise that independents were, by the logic of their political principles, likely to be sympathetic to the emancipation of administration from politics and therefore, in office, more likely than party men to persevere with administrative reform. The younger Pitt, who described himself as 'independent' and was with equal truth described by others as 'King's man', is clear proof of this. Moreover, his career illustrates very well the problems that might be created by a politician who wished to effect administrative reforms. The politicians who were alarmed by Pitt's reforms saw, in a sense, more clearly than he did. They were alarmed because they were convinced that the working of the political and parliamentary system depended on the subordination of the administrative system to it, and believed, therefore, that patronage should be used not as a way of choosing efficient instruments, but as a way of obtaining political support. Pitt himself refused to admit the possibility of conflict between efficient politics and efficient administration, but there can be no doubt that his reforms, designed to strengthen the executive in one way — by freeing administration from politics — did also weaken it in another, precisely because the reforms succeeded.

# 4

## Without Doors

## (1)

DASHWOOD was accounted by his contemporaries a great traveller. Horace Walpole allowed him this title because he went farther afield than the usual Tour of Europe; others did so because they thought him a man of taste. Several of Dashwood's correspondents mention his travels, and they usually do so, naturally enough, without saying where he went. One of them was Robert Lowth,[1] who reveals something of Dashwood's interests in two long letters[2] written, he says, to tell Dashwood what he would wish to know. Lowth was a man of 'abilities, equally applicable either to elegant literature, or professional studies',[3] a theologian, a Hebrew scholar, a literary critic, and a minor poet. He travelled in Europe twice, in 1748 with Legge, on his diplomatic mission to Berlin, and in 1749–1750 with two of the Duke of Devonshire's sons, mainly in Italy. Lowth's first letter to Dashwood was written from Berlin on 11 May 1748, after a leisurely journey from The Hague through Holland, Hanover, and the Palatinate

> w$^{ch}$ gave us an opportunity of seeing the Elector Palatine's fine Collection of Pictures, w$^{ch}$ I believe would be reckon'd a fine one in any part of the World. [He thought Berlin] a very large and very fine Town: the Palace is truly magnificent, the public buildings in general are handsome & in good taste; the streets spacious & well-built, especially

---

[1] 1710–87. Professor of Poetry at Oxford 1741–50; Archdeacon of Winchester 1750; Prebendary of Durham 1755; Bishop of Oxford 1766; Bishop of London 1777. His works include: *De sacra poesi Hebraeorum* (1753); *Life of William of Wykeham* (1758); *Short Introduction to English Grammar* (1762); *Translation of Isaiah*; and 'various poetical pieces' such as 'The Choice of Hercules' and 'Imitation of the 6th Ode of Horace' 'applied to the alarming situation of this Country at the time of the Rebellion, 1745'. (See Chapter 5 for his attitude towards the reform of the Liturgy and Articles.)

[2] Dashwood MSS. B 11/7.      [3] *Annual Register* (1788), p. 2.

the new town; w$^{ch}$ in extent makes at least one third part of the whole; it was added in the late Kings time: there is one thing wanting very necessary to make it compleat, & that is Inhabitants. The highest acc$^t$ I have heard of y$^e$ whole number of them, makes y$^m$ 100,000; (one 5th part of w$^{ch}$ are y$^e$ Garrison) & y$^e$ Town is suppos'd to be capable of holding 4 times y$^t$ number. But you would wonder how even these are supply'd with provisions, if you were to see y$^e$ Country round about, w$^{ch}$ is a deep Sand that seems incapable of producing any of the fruits of the earth.

Then, since Dashwood's 'first enquirys will be after Voltaire', Lowth explained that he was 'out of favour', having

had the vanity and absurdity to publish all y$^e$ King's letters to him without his leave; you'll find them in the last Edition of his Works [Dresden, 1748]. You may not have been fully inform'd of what has befall'n him lately; he was forced to leave Paris on account of some impertinent verses address'd to y$^e$ Dauphiness; he went to K. Stanislaus's Court at Bar where he made a sort of claim of being admitted to his Majesty's table at dinner, w$^{ch}$ being refus'd, he had no other way of dissembling this disgrace, but by taking to his Bed: I have not heard whether he is yet come abroad.

There followed some account of the troubles of Algarotti, another of Frederick's protégés, and the speculation aroused on all sides by Frederick's great show of favour to Legge.

Lowth's second letter to Dashwood was written from Rome on 25 April 1750. He reported the sale of the two great collections of pictures in Parma and Modena, and regretted that the second should have been bought not by the king of England but by the king of Poland. He thought the state of opera — 'of which you will expect some acc$^t$' — 'very low at present in Italy', opera music 'light & thin' with 'nobody that is worthy to blow the bellows to Mr. Handel', and music in general 'much fall'n . . . they have many excellent Performers, but I believe very few good Composers', and unfortunately 'no Fidler of eminence will play any thing but his own Music'. The rest of the letter is a long description of the latest discoveries at Herculaneum, where excavation had begun in 1738, under the patronage of Charles VII of Naples. Excavation continued intermittently, but there was no official record of the discoveries until the first volume of *Antichità di Ercolano* was published in 1757. Until then, the description of the finds by Venuti, which was translated into

English in 1750, and letters and descriptions by private visitors like Lowth provided the only available information about the 'subterraneous city' and the discoveries made there.  As the king did not allow notes to be taken inside the cabinet of Portici, the suite of rooms where the discoveries were housed, they had to be made from memory. Lowth found the paintings disappointing:[1]

> I think there is not any of the large pieces yᵗ are better than many other specimens of Ancient Painting that have been produc'd before. The best of the Collection are certainly some small Figures, wᶜʰ are very elegantly design'd.  Of Statues they have found many pretty small ones, some large ones that are good; but the finest thing of all by many degrees is the Equestrian Statue of Balbus, of marble, as big as the Life, wᶜʰ I will venture to say excells Marcus Aurelius at the Capitol; and if so, I suppose will be allow'd to be the best of its kind remaining of the Ancients.

He then describes the Theatre, household furniture, and perishable articles including

> one entire Loaf: it is about the size of a common twopenny brown loaf, has the same form & appearance, & does not look so very stale neither: it is kept in a Glass case to secure it.  I did not examine it very nicely, but a Gentleman that saw it since observ'd some Letters on it, wᶜʰ he was told nobody could make out;[2] he view'd it very narrowly, and with supplying a few letters at the beginning, which I shall mark, is confident that he has hitt it off compleatly & truly as follows: ˙˙SILIGO CRANII E CICERE.  I send you this as the freshest &
> ˙˙˙

---

[1] Valuable support for Lowth's opinion both of the paintings and of the statue of Balbus is found in *Travels in Italy, by the late Abbe Barthélemy, in a series of letters written to the celebrated Count Caylus.  Translated from the French.* (London, 1802.)  See especially Appendix IV ('Remarks by Count Caylus upon the City of Heraclea or Herculaneum', written about 1746) and a letter to Caylus dated 20 Jan. 1751 (pp. 257–72), which criticises adversely 'the superficial account of Mr. Venuti', who claimed the paintings as the work of 'the first painters of Greece'.

[2] Barthélemy notes that the glass case in which the loaf was kept increased the difficulty of reading the inscription.  'It consists of two lines.  In the second, I thought I could distinguish the word employed by the Romans to express chick-pease [i.e. *cicera*].  The police required, that every loaf should bear a name, designating the kind of flour of which it was made.' (*Travels*, pp. 244–5.)

most curious Intelligence to be communicated as such to Dean Lyttle-ton [1] or any other of our Friends of the Antiquarian Society.

It is not surprising that Lowth should have made this request. Something of the value placed on travellers' accounts of Herculaneum can be seen from the frustrations of George Shelvocke, [2] Secretary to the Post Office, who visited Herculaneum in 1740 and claimed to be the first to write 'any particular Description' of it, in a letter to the Earl of Leicester, then Lord Lovel. [3] Shelvocke was probably right in his claim. 'The Matter contained in this Letter', he told the Secretary of the Spalding Society in 1750, [4] 'was so new here, that a great Number of written Copies were taken of it, & handed about, till two or three years ago', when it was printed, without his per-mission, in a 'Miscellaneous Work, where I could not have expected to find it'. There were, Shelvocke wrote, some errors in the printed version, and he had intended to send the Society 'a Fair Written and Corrected Copy of it', together with a more recent account sent to him 'from an English gentleman of great ability & curiosity'. To his great disappointment, he was unable to send either, for the 'Mis-cellaneous Work' was out of print and the later account, which he had 'communicated to a Great Hand, upon the first receipt of it, &, upon Inquiry, it is not at present to be found'.

[1] Charles Lyttelton (1714–68). Dean of Exeter 1747, Bishop of Carlisle 1762; Fellow of Society of Antiquaries 1746, President 1765–8. His interest in antiquities led him first to the Royal Society: he became a Fellow in 1743 and communicated papers on fossils in 1748 and 1750. Lowth became a Fellow of the Royal Society in 1765 but was never either an Antiquary or a member of the Dilettanti Society.

[2] 1702–60; son of George Shelvocke, privateer and author of *A Voyage round the World* (1726); Secretary of the Post Office 1742–60.

[3] Thomas Coke (1695–1759, cr. Baron Lovel 1728, and Earl of Leicester 1744; Joint Postmaster-General 1733–59) was elected to the Royal Society in 1739 and to the Dilettanti Society in 1741, the same year as his son, who was proposed by Dashwood. Lovel did not communicate Shelvocke's letter to the Royal Society, but it is likely enough that he showed it to Dashwood and other members of the Dilettanti. Shelvocke himself was elected to the Royal Society in 1742.

[4] Spalding Society MSS. 15 Dec. 1750. Shelvocke was elected to the Spalding Society in 1745 and sent it the privilege of franking which the Royal Society had.

Lyttelton may well have received a copy of Lowth's letter, and may have handed it round privately, and Dashwood must surely have shown it to members of the Dilettanti Society. But Lyttelton did not communicate it to the Society of Antiquaries, which was not yet interested in Herculaneum, nor to the Royal Society, which was. Between 1740 and 1757 twenty letters about Herculaneum were communicated to the Royal Society and printed in its *Philosophical Transactions*. Half of these were letters written by private travellers like Lowth and Shelvocke, and the other half were written by Camillo Paderni, Keeper of the Museum at Herculaneum, to English correspondents. Only five of the twenty are earlier than 1750. Lowth's letter would certainly have been welcomed, as was one written a week later than his, on 2 May 1750, and read to the Society on 28 February 1751.[1] This letter, written by Mr. Freeman[2] to Lady Mary Capel, is longer and more detailed than any previously communicated to the Royal Society, and it describes, as Lowth does, the statue of Balbus and the loaf of bread,[3] each with its inscription.

Dashwood had, it seems, finished his own travels before Lowth wrote to him. His first visit abroad was to France, from January to September 1726. It seems that he later spent two periods of between one and two years each travelling on the Continent, from 1729 to

[1] *Philosophical Transactions, giving some Account of the Present Undertakings, Studies, and Labours, of the INGENIOUS in many considerable parts of the world*, vol. xlvii (1751), pp. 131–50.

[2] Perhaps Sambrooke Freeman (1720–82) of Fawley Court, Henley-on-Thames; traveller and collector; member of the Dilettanti Society 1748; M.P. Pontefract 1754–6, Bridport 1768–74. Langley notes that the gardens of Fawley Court were 'handsomely disposed and kept in great order. The rides . . . display the whole scenery of the vale, in which the windings of the Thames above Henley to Medmenham are singularly picturesque'; opposite was 'an island richly planted, on which there is a temple in good taste' (Thomas Langley, *History and Antiquities of the Hundred of Desborough and the Deanery of Wycombe, in Buckinghamshire* (1797), p. 195). The temple was built for Freeman in 1771 by James Wyatt.

[3] Cf. Freeman's explanation of the inscription on the loaf: '*SILIGO*, which signifies fine flour; of which the bread might be made, with the mixture of flour of chick-pease or vetch which I think the E CISER signifies' (*Philosophical Transactions*, vol. xlvii, p. 136).

1731 and from 1739 to 1741. Much of his time, on both occasions, was spent in Italy. In Rome, in 1731, he became acquainted with the Abbé Niccolini, and began a friendship which lasted until Niccolini died in 1769.[1] Niccolini visited England only once, between 1747 and 1749. It is reasonable to suppose that for part of this time he stayed either with Dashwood or with Westmorland: in 1762 and 1763 Niccolini referred, in letters to Dashwood, to his visit to England and to his friendship with Dashwood and his acquaintance with Westmorland and with Mereworth at this time.[2] Niccolini was elected a Fellow of the Royal Society in 1747. He was a man of intelligence and learning, a philosopher and a theologian. He was suspected of leanings towards Jansenism. According to Parson Etough's scurrilous account of Frederick, Prince of Wales, Niccolini was also a Jacobite.[3] There is no hint in his letters to Dashwood of any Jacobitism in the straightforward sense of liking for the Stuarts, but he was certainly a Jacobite in the curious sense in which the word was sometimes used round about 1760: that is, he shared Westmorland's view that George III's reign would be the beginning of a new era. Westmorland, of course, expressed this view publicly as well as privately, for example, when in 1760 as Chancellor of the University of Oxford he objected to certain phrases in the University's Address to the new king on the grounds that they were hypocritical and inaccurate praises of George II. He protested to the Vice-

[1] Many travellers in Italy praised Niccolini. One of those who asserted his liking for and knowledge of things English was John Earl of Cork and Orrery, who described him in 1754 as 'a man of great family, of excellent sense, thorough knowledge of books, persons, and things, and particularly obliging and attached to the English' (John Duncombe, *Letters from Italy in the years 1754 and 1755 by the late John Earl Of Corke and Orrery* (1773), p. 109). Another was Robert Adam, who in 1756 called him 'a prodigious sensible, clever man as ever I saw. No man knows the constitution of England better, no man was ever more respected than he was' (John Fleming, *Robert Adam and his Circle* (1962), p. 128).

[2] Dashwood MSS. B 11/4. Niccolini to Dashwood, 21 Nov. 1762 and 23 May 1763.

[3] 'So absurd was his [Frederick's] infatuation [for the Jacobites] that he contracted intimacys with and made the Pretender's Spys and Agents his familiar companions. This was the justly supposed character of Nicolini.' (*Free and Impartial Reflections*, pp. 63–64.)

Chancellor, Joseph Browne, Provost of The Queen's College, and refused to take part in presenting the Address.[1] More to the point, perhaps, as far as Dashwood's Jacobitism is concerned, was his presence in Rome in 1731 and again in 1741. Lady Mary Wortley Montagu believed in 1739 that Englishmen travelling in Italy could not prudently stay in Rome 'on whose account you may guess . . . it is very hard to avoid meeting a certain person [the Pretender]; and there are so many dirty little spies that write any lie that comes into their heads, that the doing it may be dangerous'.[2] Certainly Horace Mann seems to have told Horace Walpole something about Dashwood — perhaps an 'anti-Minister' remark — that upset him and that he chose to call Jacobite.

Given Dashwood's well-attested friendship with Niccolini, which was resumed during his second visit to Italy, it is surprising to find that, on 4 October 1739, Montesquieu wrote to Niccolini from Paris, commending Dashwood to him. 'Monsieur le Chevalier Dashwood est un homme de lettres que je vous présente, et je le présente à un homme de lettres; il vous estimera autant que le je fais, mais il ne vous aimera tant. Je vous prie de lui rendre le séjour de votre ville agréable.'[3] It is difficult to guess whether when Montesquieu wrote this he was unaware, or had forgotten, that Dashwood already knew Niccolini, and it seems impossible to establish either how well Montesquieu knew Dashwood or when he met him. There is no reason to suppose that Dashwood was out of England during the whole of Montesquieu's visit to it, between October 1729 and August 1731, though he must have been in Italy for much of this time. Very little is known about Montesquieu's acquaintances in England, or about where he stayed, and the journal he kept has disappeared. It is not unlikely that he met Westmorland, though the likelihood can only

---

[1] Dashwood MSS. C 6. 9 Nov. 1760. The Jacobite Dr. William King, however, who at this time lived with Westmorland, went up to London and assisted in the presentation. King (1685–1763) was Principal of St. Mary Hall 1718–63. Three of the occasions on which he was said to have flourished his 'Jacobitism' were his oration at the opening of the new Radcliffe Library in 1749, his support for the Tories in the Oxfordshire election of 1754, his speech at the installation of Westmorland as Chancellor in 1759.

[2] *Letters and Works*, ii. 44–45 (To Mr. Wortley Montagu, 10 Sept. 1739).   [3] *Correspondence* (ed. F. Gebelin), i. 346.

rest on a certain number of possible — but entirely supposititious — connections. Bolingbroke, for example, who knew Montesquieu, left France in April 1725 with his second wife, Marie Claire de Marésilley, who later corresponded with Lady Westmorland. Admiral Forbes, with whom Dashwood went to St. Petersburg in 1733, knew Montesquieu.[1] Montesquieu's son, Jean-Baptiste de Secondat, came to England and was elected a Fellow of the Royal Society in December 1744, eighteen months before Dashwood's election, and his grandson, Charles Louis de Secondat, lived and died at Bridge Hill House near Canterbury in Kent, and about thirty miles from Mereworth. It is, of course, not impossible that Dashwood met Montesquieu during his visit to France in 1726. Montesquieu, director of the Academy of Bordeaux from November 1725 to November 1726, was at that time thinking of selling his house in Bordeaux and settling in Paris, and was particularly interested in English ways of government and anxious to meet English visitors.[2]

Nothing more of any importance is known about Dashwood's second stay in Italy. He is known to have visited Leghorn as well as Rome and Florence. Horace Walpole several times mentioned his presence in Florence; Lady Mary Wortley Montagu said she 'knew him' there, and that he helped to find her a lodging. It is likely that he went to Herculaneum, as Horace Walpole did, but there is no evidence for or against this. He seems to have returned to England in the summer of 1741.

The exception to these unsolved questions and lack of firm evidence is Dashwood's visit to St. Petersburg in 1733, for of this he himself wrote a diary, filling seventy-three quite closely written pages of an exercise book.[3] It is described in a list, dated 1816, of six books 'to be returned to the Library of Sir John Dashwood-King', as 'Travels of Sir F. Dashwood. MSS.'. Dashwood travelled to Russia with George, Baron Forbes,[4] Envoy Extraordinary to the court of St.

---

[1] *Le Spicilège* (ed. A. Masson, Flammarion, 1944), pp. 163–4.

[2] See, for example, *Memoirs of Michael Clancy, M.D., containing his Observations on many countries in Europe* (Dublin, 1750), ii. 19 et seq.

[3] Dashwood MSS. B 12/1. I have published the Diary in *The Slavonic and East European Review* (1959), xxxviii. 194–222.

[4] 1685–1765. Forbes succeeded as third Earl of Granard in 1734. He served in the army under Argyll (1707) and was later a naval commander and

Petersburg, whose negotiations resulted in the Anglo-Russian treaty of 1734, Russia's first commercial treaty with a European power. They left England on 10 May, sailed across the North Sea round the coast of Jutland and through the Sound to Copenhagen, where they stayed from 30 May to 2 June. They then crossed the Baltic and sailed up the Gulf of Finland to Kronstadt, and from there travelled overland to St. Petersburg, which they reached on 10 June. Forbes stayed until May of the following year and Dashwood returned alone, leaving St. Petersburg on 30 June, calling at Danzig, the island of Bornholm, staying a few days in Copenhagen, and landing at Lowestoft on 4 August.

The content of the diary leaves no doubt that Dashwood would have been interested in the sort of information that Lowth gave him about Berlin and Italy. But it shows much more than this. It reveals an intelligent, alert, and discriminating traveller, concerned to look at pictures and buildings certainly, but also deeply interested in the way of life of the people he was visiting, their methods of government, their armies, their finances. Moreover, it reveals perseverance and hard work. Dashwood collected a remarkable amount of detailed information in a short time. His descriptions of St. Petersburg and Copenhagen are first-hand and not taken from books. They have, moreover, a permanent value, for there is not in English any other description of St. Petersburg as it was just after the end of Peter the Great's reign, and there is no other known contemporary English account of Copenhagen after the great fire of 1731.[1]

One puzzle remains. In 1764–5 Dashwood's godson, Frank Skipwith, made an interesting addition to his Tour of Europe. He visited

diplomat: Governor of Minorca 1716–18, of Leeward Islands 1729–30, mission to Vienna 1719. He was M.P. for Queenborough 1723–7 and for Ayr burghs 1741–7. He was a member of the committee appointed in March 1742 to inquire into Walpole's conduct, opposed the employment of Hanoverian troops Nov. 1743, moved for a committee to inquire into naval management April 1744.

[1] Dashwood MSS. I/1 contains the manuscript 'A Particulaire Accoumpt of our Voyage to Denmarke' written by Arthur Capel, first Earl of Essex, ambassador to Denmark in 1670. Lady Mary Capel, who married Forbes's younger son John in 1758, was his great granddaughter.

Athens, from thence went to Delos, and other Islands of the Archie-
pelago, went over to the Asiatick side, and visited Ephesus, Smyrna,
& the twelve Ionian Cities, from thence to the reputed spot, where
Troy once stood, and then cross'd over to the place of residence of the
Grand Signior.—when he left Constantinople he travers'd Moldavia, &
Wallachia on his way to Warsaw, where the King then was, where great
civilities are shown to the English, by that wise & benevolent Prince;
from thence to Berlin, and then to the German Capitol; there he was to
continue but a few days, and then set out on his Rout towards Venice.[1]

His father, who thought this a 'very judicious, & instructive' tour,
told Dashwood he could not 'forbear thinking but that your Lordship had a hand in the planning of it, as it so much resembles the Tour
you once made yourself'. There is no other surviving reference to
this tour of Dashwood's, and Skipwith gives no idea of when it took
place. It must also have been useful in planning the expedition sent
by the Dilettanti Society to Asia Minor in June 1764. Frank Skipwith left England at about the same time as the Dilettanti expedition.
He travelled with two companions. They were in Siena and Rome
in the autumn of 1764 and went to Asia Minor with Dr. Turnbull,
'a very worthy physician, who had lived many years at Smyrna, and
was highly esteemed there by the Europeans in general'.[2] They
reached Smyrna in August 1765, just in time to exchange visits with
the Dilettanti expedition before it left.[3]

It is, of course, very natural that Dashwood should have visited
Greece and Asia Minor. Nothing tangible remains of his interest
in Turkey except a few drawings that he made of Turkish mosques,
and some of the thirty-seven pictures of Turkish costume which,
according to the inventory drawn up after his death, he housed at
West Wycombe. But in any case it was interest in the Greeks and
their colonies, not in the Turks who had conquered them, that sent
travellers to Greece and Asia Minor, and most of the few who went

[1] Dashwood MSS. B 11/3. Francis Skipwith to Dashwood, 2 Aug.
[1766]. Skipwith wrote two more letters about his son's travels, on 5 Nov.
[1764] and 25 Feb. [1765]. All are dated with the day of the month but
not the year, and it is possible to put them in order only because of Frank
Skipwith's meeting with the Dilettanti expedition.

[2] *Travels in Asia Minor: or, An Account of a Tour made at the Expense of
the Society of Dilettanti*, by Richard Chandler, D.D., Fellow of Magdalen
College and of the Society of Antiquaries (1775), p. 277.     [3] Ibid.

there no doubt ignored the mosques.    Dashwood's interest in Greece
left very solid legacies, both in the encouragement given by the
Dilettanti Society to the examination and description of Greek ruins,
and in the encouragement he himself gave to the new neo-classical
Greek influence in English building.    Little is known of Dashwood's
activities in the five years between his Russian journey and his second
visit to Italy, and it seems probable that it was in these years that he
visited Greece and Asia Minor.

Travel was the inspiration of the Dilettanti Society, and Dashwood played the chief part in founding it.    It was founded in 1732,
the year between his first visit to Italy and his journey to Russia, with
the aim of promoting knowledge and understanding of classical art
and taste in England.    Its rules date from December 1734 and its
minutes from 1736.    Dashwood was an active member of the Society
for more than thirty-five years, and sat on nearly all its important
committees, often acting as chairman.[1]    In 1743 he was a member
of the committee set up to consider the possibility of providing the
Society with a permanent place of meeting, and a site in Cavendish
Square was bought in his name in 1747.    In 1751 he was chairman
of the committee which considered three plans submitted to it — one
of them Dashwood's own.    It was decided in 1753 to build on the
model of the Temple of Pola, but the project was abandoned.    In
1759 the site was sold and the proceeds invested in the names of
Dashwood and Sir George Gray, the Society's treasurer.    When the
scheme was revived in the 1760s Dashwood was a member of the
committee which recommended a site on the Green Park side of
Piccadilly, and it was he who presented a petition to the king to
'allot a proper piece of ground' in the Park.    The proposal was to
build 'an exact copy of an Antique Temple . . . the first example of
this kind in His Majesty's Dominions'.    This plan, too, was abandoned, and the Society settled in the 'Star and Garter' tavern in Pall
Mall, perhaps in a room permanently rented, and spent its money on
other things.    Dashwood was also a member of the committees set
up to discuss the promotion of a public Academy of Arts, and in 1761
he put forward a scheme for a public gallery of casts.

Dashwood played a prominent part in what was perhaps the

[1] Dilettanti Society Minute Books and Committee Book (now deposited
with the Society of Antiquaries), passim.

Society's greatest achievement: the encouragement and assistance given to the scholarly recording of classical remains in Greece and in Asia Minor. James Stuart and Nicholas Revett went to Athens from Venice in 1751 for the purpose of implementing their *Proposals for publishing an accurate description of the Antiquities of Athens, &c.* (1748). Before they left Venice the Dilettanti Society elected them as members, on the recommendation of Sir James Gray, then British Resident, and decided to subscribe towards the cost of publishing their findings. Their work,[1] published in 1762, presented the first accurate and detailed drawings of Greek ruins, and heralded the Greek influence in English architecture. The Preface, which described 'the motives of the authors', was 'a sort of history of the arts of design, and a comparative view of the merits of the Grecian and Roman architecture'.[2] This comparative view was also a call to action. It urged, as the Abbé Laungier, the great theorist of early neo-classicism, had done in France in 1753,[3] that not Roman but Greek architecture should be regarded as the standard of excellence in building, for Greece 'is the Place where the most beautiful edifices were erected, and where the purest and most elegant Examples of ancient Architecture are to be discovered'.[4] Architects had paid much attention to the 'ruined edifices of Rome', and these had been 'drawn and engraved by skilful Artists', but

> Athens, the Mother of elegance and politeness, whose magnificence scarce yielded to that of Rome, and who for the beauties of her style must be allowed to surpass her; has been almost entirely neglected. So that unless exact Copies of them be speedily made, all her beauteous Fabricks, her Temples, her Palaces, now in Ruins, will drop into Oblivion. The reason indeed, why those Antiquities have hitherto

---

[1] *The Antiquities of Athens measured and delineated, by James Stuart, F.R.S. and F.S.A., and Nicholas Revett, Architects and Painters*, vol. i. The Dilettanti Society assisted with the publication of later volumes.

[2] *Annual Register* (1763), p. 247.

[3] *Essai sur l'architecture* (Paris, 1753). It was followed in 1758 by *Les Ruines des plus beaux monuments de la Grèce*, by J. D. Le Roy, who had visited Greece with the same object as Stuart and Revett. His work, however, was less careful and thorough, and they corrected 'numerous and important mistakes' in it. Their own work was translated into French and was accepted as superior to Le Roy's.

[4] *Antiquities of Athens*, i, p. v.

been neglected, is obvious. Greece, since the revival of the Arts, has been in the possession of Barbarians.[1]

The purpose Stuart and Revett had set themselves was to add to the existing

Collections [of Antiquities of Rome] some Examples drawn from the Antiquities of Greece. . . . It even seemed that a performance of this kind might contribute to the improvement of the Art itself, which at present appears to be founded on too partial and too scanty a system of ancient Examples.[2]

The book, and its message, had something of the effect its authors hoped for. The Dilettanti Society decided to send a similar expedition to Asia Minor 'in order to collect Informations, and to make observations, relative to the Ancient State of those countries, and to such Monuments of Antiquity as are still remaining'.[3] Dashwood was chairman of the committee set up to organise the expedition. Richard Chandler, historian, Revett, and William Pars, painter, were chosen as its members. The committee drew up detailed instructions for them, made financial arrangements, and provided them with letters of introduction to consul Hayes at Smyrna, to other local officials, and to the Turkey company. The instructions included an injunction to keep a journal 'of Every day's Occurrences and Observations, representing Things exactly in the light they strike you, in the plainest Manner, and without any regard to Style or Language, except that of being intelligible'. The expedition sailed in June 1764, made Smyrna its headquarters from September 1764 to August 1765, stayed at Athens until June 1766, and arrived back in England in November 1766. From the drawings and plans they sent and brought back the Society published, in 1769, the first volume of *Ionian Antiquities*, which they dedicated to George III. In 1775 Chandler published the first volume of the journal he had kept.[4] He

1 Ibid., footnote, printing the *Proposals*.     2 Ibid., p. i.
3 Dilettanti Society Minute Books and Committee Book, Mar.–May 1764.
4 *Travels in Asia Minor*. Chandler was the chief member and treasurer of the expedition. He had already published, in 1774, *Inscriptiones Antiquae*, compiled from the drawings and inscriptions which the Society had decided not to use in its own publication, and in 1776 he published the second volume of his journal as *Travels in Greece*. These also were dedicated to the Dilettanti Society.

dedicated it to the Society and prefaced it with 'the Instructions of the Committee of Dilettanti, which the Author has the leave of the Society to lay before the Public'. 'We altogether agree with him', wrote the reviewer in the *Annual Register*, 'in the praise they deserve . . . the Society of Dilettanti in a manner exculpate our times from the imputation of sordid and selfish enjoyments: they do credit to their rank and fortune, when their patronage and liberality are employed in a noble attention to arts and letters'.[1]

Interest in English antiquities, which had no comparable message, was left to the Society of Antiquaries in London, which was revived in 1717 and incorporated by royal charter in 1751, and to its brother societies in other parts of the country. The Dilettanti Society was more exclusive and richer than the Society of Antiquaries, and its members were on the whole more eminent and more aristocratic, and perhaps this was why Horace Walpole, who became a Fellow of the Society of Antiquaries in 1753 but was never elected to the Dilettanti Society, did not like them. However, he fell out with the Antiquaries too, for the very things that might have been said to have distinguished them from the Dilettanti: their lack of 'taste', their pomposity, and their undiscriminating enthusiasm for old things. Walpole was, of course, not alone in ridiculing those 'who hold everything worth preserving, merely because it has been preserved'. Sir John Cullum, who was one of them, was indignant to find that the author of the *Dictionary of the Terms used by the Canting Crew*, 'a most impudent rascal', defined an Antiquary as

> a curious critick in old coins, stones, and inscriptions, in worm-eaten records and antient manuscripts; also one that affects and blindly doats on relicks, ruins, old customs, phrases, and fashions.[2]

Dr. Johnson laughed at Antiquaries in *The Rambler*. The *Annual Register* in 1771 reprinted from the *Town and Country Magazine* the story of the Society's learned deliberations about the 'antique description' on a stone found in a village in Northumberland, until

> alas! *vanitas vanitatum, omnia vanitas!* how is this aerial structure, raised by the united knowledge of that venerable body, shaken to its foundation, by the oral tradition of an old grey-bearded schoolmaster

---

[1] *Annual Register* (1775), p. 238.
[2] Nichols, *Literary Anecdotes*, viii. 68.

of the village! whose memory unluckily informed him, when the affair became public, that this invaluable inscription was neither more nor less than — *keep on this side*, an instance of the benevolence of some good-hearted cottager, to warn the traveller of his danger, and prevent him from riding into the quagmire . . . the inelegance of the sculpture [due] to the excentricity of the untutored hand which had engraved it.

The great Samuel Pegge's paper on Dick Whittington in December 1771, which 'deny'd his cat', provoked Samuel Foote to lay the third act of his comedy *The Nabob* in the rooms of the Society.[1] No doubt Pegge's paper on the Turkey

> deriving it from the E. Indies denying it in Africa, and Guinea; called Turkey from its rarity — as French beans in Kent are called Turkey beans[2]

was also laughed at.

Of course the members of the Society of Antiquaries was not as pettifogging and absurd as Horace Walpole painted them; nor did their learning exclude taste, any more than the Dilettanti Society's taste excluded learning. But most of the members of the Dilettanti Society would have agreed with him. There were amongst them Fellows of the Royal Society and of the Society of Arts, but, until towards the end of the eighteenth century, hardly any Antiquaries. A few became Antiquaries after the Society began to publish *Archeologica, or Miscellaneous Tracts relating to Antiquity*, in 1770, and in the nineteenth century the number who belonged to both Societies increased. Dashwood was one of the first to do so.[3] He was elected a Fellow of the Society of Antiquaries on 1 June 1769, a few months after the Society had received the books and manuscripts left to it by

[1] It was after Foote's ridicule of 'the learned Society in Chancery Lane, sitting, as they really did, on Whittington and his Cat' that Walpole resigned, in Apr. 1773. He had already 'washed his hands' of the Society in Jan. 1771, after Robert Master's critical paper on his *Historic Doubts on the Life and Reign of Richard III*.

[2] Bodleian Library, Top. MSS. C London, 2, f. 89. 19 Dec. 1771.

[3] I have only found four who preceded him: Andrew Mitchell (Dilettanti 1736, Antiquary *c.* 1746); Edward Wortley Montagu (Dilettanti 1749, Antiquary 1761); James Stuart (Dilettanti 1751, Antiquary 1758); Charles Lennox, third Duke of Richmond (Antiquary *c.* 1745, Dilettanti 1765).

its President, Charles Lyttelton — to whom Dashwood had presumably communicated Lowth's information about Herculaneum in 1750 — and a few months before James Stuart read his paper on Ionian Antiquities.[1]

The most prominent brother-society of the Society of Antiquaries in London was the Society of Gentlemen at Spalding. It was founded by Maurice Johnson, of the Inner Temple, steward of Spalding and other manors in Lincolnshire, a member of the group of London antiquaries who succeeded in reviving the London Society in 1717. Johnson went to Spalding in 1709, and at once formed a group of 'men of sense and letters' who met 'at a coffee-house to pass away an hour in literary conversation, and reading some new publications'.[2] In 1712 the group was formally constituted as a 'Society of Gentlemen, for the supporting of mutual benevolence, and their improvement in the liberal sciences and in polite learning'. It corresponded with the London Society and until 1753 regularly sent copies of its minutes to London. Many of its members, including Johnson, William Stukeley, Roger Gale, William Bogdani, were members of the London Society. The Spalding Society was wider in its interests, and dealt, in Johnson's words, with 'all arts and sciences, and exclude nothing from our conversation but politics, which would throw us all into confusion and disorder'.[3] Dashwood was connected in one way or another with many members of the Spalding Society.[4] Westmorland belonged to it, as did Francis Fane of Fulbeck, Dashwood's cousin. Stephen Lyon, a Huguenot refugee, rector of Mereworth and Spalding, who had travelled with Westmorland and possibly with Dashwood, was a founder-member. Sir Richard Ellys, whose widow Dashwood married in 1745, became a member in 1729. Dr. John Mitchell, who called Ellys his patron and who acted as his librarian and secretary, and perhaps doctor, was a member, and so was his brother Dr. Robert Mitchell of Guildford, pupil of the famous Leyden physician Herman Boerhaave, Fellow of the Royal Society. Dashwood knew Ellys and his wife, and the Mitchells, in the 1730s,

[1] Bodl. Top. MSS. C, London, 2, f. 79. 18 Jan. 1770.
[2] Nichols, *Literary Anecdotes*, vi. 5.  [3] Ibid. 7.
[4] Nichols gives a list (ibid. 69–120). See also W. Pickering, *The Gentlemen's Society at Spalding: its Origin and Progress* (Pickering, 1851), reprinted 1960 on the occasion of the Society's 250th anniversary.

perhaps through the Fanes of Fulbeck or through his other cousin Samuel Dashwood of Well Vale. In 1741 John Mitchell commissioned Robert Trevor,[1] then secretary to the embassy at The Hague, to buy rare books for Ellys in Holland, and it seems that Trevor performed the same service for Dashwood. Ellys's library and, apparently, these particular books, were the subject of a paper, 'Sir Richard Ellys's library and some curiosities lately come in there',[2] read to the Gentlemen's Society at Peterborough in 1742. Ellys's books in general seem also to have inspired the Latin 'lyrick amusement' that the elder Horace Walpole composed in the summer of 1741.[3] Edward Walpole of Dunston, the poet, was a 'worthy, learned and Beneficent Member' of the Spalding Society. Peter Davall, who made the calculations for Dashwood's militia bill in 1745, became a member in 1753. Charles Lyttelton was a member. Samuel Wesley, rector of Epworth, became a member in 1723, and his son, usher at Westminster, in 1729. Two surveyors concerned in the draining of the Witham fens, Humphrey Smith and John Grundy, were members, and Grundy read several papers on the navigation of the Witham and other rivers. Captain John Perry,

---

[1] 1706–83, fourth Baron Trevor; joint Postmaster-General 1763–5; son of Thomas, first Baron Trevor, who was grandson of Sir John Trevor (d. 1673) and his wife Ruth, daughter and co-heir of John Hampden; succeeded to the Bucks. estates and took the name of Hampden 1754; created Viscount Hampden 1776. (John Hampden was also great-grandfather of Sir Richard Ellys and great-great-grandfather of John and George Hobart, second and third Earls of Buckinghamshire.)

[2] Nichols, *Literary Anecdotes*, vi. 138.

[3] Walpole's letter of 31 July 1741 (Dashwood MSS. I 1/2) makes various corrections in his 'lyrick amusement'. Two of them (*Hobartium* and *libros*) are clues to its subject-matter. The poem itself has disappeared. Charles Hanbury-Williams's poem 'Peter and my Lord Quidam' (*Works, with notes by the younger Horace Walpole* (ed. E. Jeffery (1822) pp. 37–49) describes how Ellys was courted for his 'vast wealth', unsuccessfully, by the elder Horace Walpole and by Richard Hampden, Ellys's brother-in-law. Horace Walpole's footnote refers to Ellys's 'very expensive library', and states that his uncle 'wrote a Latin ode to him [Ellys] to flatter his pretensions, gave his portrait to Sir Richard, and had Sir Richard's in his own Library — in vain'. There can I think be no doubt that this Latin ode was the 'lyrick amusement', and that Walpole's letter correcting it was written to Ellys.

who built canals and drained marshes for Peter the Great, and published his *State of Russia* in 1716, belonged to the Spalding Society from 1730 to his death in 1732. All these had some connection either with Dashwood personally or with his activities.

It is therefore at first sight surprising that Dashwood does not appear in any of the lists of those who attended the Society's meetings.[1] But, just as one of the reasons why he did not join the Antiquaries until 1769 must have been that his membership of the Dilettanti Society seemed to make this unnecessary, so it is very likely that his reason for not belonging to the Spalding Society was that he belonged to another Lincolnshire society. This was the Lincoln Club, which met at the Green Man Inn, about five miles from Nocton. The Lincoln Club was perhaps more congenial, as well as nearer to Nocton, which Dashwood visited regularly after his marriage in 1745. It was one of a group of perhaps a dozen clubs and societies formed in and near Lincolnshire in the first half of the eighteenth century. Most of them were probably in origin, as Spalding was, literary societies, and some but perhaps not all developed strong antiquarian tastes. The Gentlemen's Society at Peterborough, for example, was an offshoot of the Spalding Society, founded by Timothy Neve, Master of Spalding Grammar School, in 1722. Like Spalding, it corresponded with the London Society of Antiquaries. Boston had its society. Three successive societies were formed at Stamford, one by Maurice Johnson in 1721, and two by Stukeley, but all withered soon. 'I endeavoured twice', Stukely wrote in March 1745, 'to erect a truly literary society at Stamford under the name of the Brazen Nose Society, but *in vain*.' Stukeley, the 'Arch-Druid of our age', also helped in 1729 to establish a society at Ancaster, which he considered a suitable place because there was good accommodation and 'besides, tis a roman castle seated in the very bosom of the most delightful heath imaginable'.[2] Nothing is known about the proceedings or the fortunes of the Ancaster society. The Lincoln Club

---

[1] After 1755, when Johnson died, minutes were kept regularly until 1758, and then lapsed for seventy years. So, although I can find no trace of Dashwood's name in the Society's minute books, lists, or manuscripts, I think one might say that it is not entirely impossible that he became a member after 1758. But it is very unlikely.

[2] Spalding Society, MSS. correspondence.

shares with it the distinction of being situated, not in a town, but in the middle of a heath. The Green Man was however more remote than Ancaster, which is after all only five miles from Grantham: it was in the middle of Lincoln Heath, three miles from the nearest village, Blankney, ten miles from Lincoln and about the same from Sleaford. It was known in the eighteenth century as the 'Half Way House' or 'Greenman'. The Club was founded in 1741. It was a literary club, consisting of 'the most distinguished men of the county'. It met in a building erected by John Chaplin of Blankney some yards away from the inn, and probably connected with it by some sort of passage. On the ground floor was a long 'club-room'. In this room, which had a tall Venetian window at one end, were 'the busts of the principal members, with their armorial ensigns'.[1] Only two of these are known: Chaplin and Dashwood. Chaplin belonged to an old Lincolnshire family, originally of Tathwell near Louth. His mother was the sister of Thomas Archer of Umberslade, Warwickshire, the first recorded president of the Dilettanti Society; he was himself elected to it in 1750. He was not a member either of the London Antiquaries or of the Spalding Society. He had travelled. Blankney Hall was a Palladian mansion. Thomas Archer the architect, who also married a Chaplin, may have done some building at Blankney, as it is supposed that he did at Well Vale House, not far from Tathwell, which was built by James Bateman in 1725 and added to by Samuel Dashwood, his son-in-law, in the 1760s. This is not much, but, with Dashwood's membership, it is just enough to suggest that the Lincoln Club was rather different from the societies formed on the Spalding model, and even that it may have been more like the Dilettanti than the Antiquaries.

Dashwood's membership of the Lincoln Club may well suffice to explain why he did not join the Spalding Society, but his membership of the Dilettanti Society was not the only reason why he should not have wished to join the Antiquaries until 1769. He had been a Fellow of the Royal Society since June 1746. There was, in the eighteenth century, a much greater common membership between

1 T. Allen, *History of the County of Lincoln* (1834), ii. 261. The building is now a private house and the club-room is divided into two. The house was used by the Army during the Second World War, and the busts survived, though mutilated, until the end of it.

the Dilettanti Society and the Royal Society, and between the Society of Antiquaries and the Royal Society, than there was between the Dilettanti and the Antiquaries. The Royal Society was still catholic in its concerns. Its interest in antiquities increased under the presidency of Sir Hans Sloane, 1727–44, and, even more, under Martin Folkes,[1] who was President 1744–52, and James West, who was Treasurer 1736–68 and President 1768–72. Before 1800, the Royal Society's *Philosophical Transactions* contain 120 papers on the subject of antiquities. These include not only papers on coins, urns, and inscriptions, but also fourteen papers between 1740 and 1757 on discoveries at Herculaneum, and others on such things as Palmyra, antiquities in Greece, catacombs at Rome and Naples, the date of Homer's poems, Edward Wortley Montagu's papers on the route taken by the Israelites out of Egypt and on Pompey's pillar (1766 and 1767). There was therefore good reason for Dilettanti and Antiquaries to wish to be Fellows of the Royal Society, and for antiquaries to be Fellows of the Royal Society without belonging to either of the other Societies, but less reason for an overlap between Dilettanti and Antiquaries. Towards the end of the century the Royal Society became more specialised, and its overlapping membership with the Antiquaries and with the Dilettanti began to decrease.

Benjamin Franklin, who was elected a Fellow of the Royal Society in 1756, became a Fellow of the Society of Antiquaries in 1773. He and Dashwood were both early members of the Society for the Encouragement of Arts, Manufactures, and Commerce, founded in 1754 by William Shipley, brother of Franklin's friend Jonathan Shipley, Dean of Winchester in 1760 and Bishop of St. Asaph in 1769. Here, Dashwood was also in contact with David Hartley.[2] The interest which they are known to have shared was the prevention

---

[1] Folkes was Vice-President of the Society of Antiquaries 1737–50 and President 1750–4.

[2] 1730–1813, son of David Hartley the philosopher; friend of Sir George Savile and regarded by him and Rockingham as an expert on finance; July 1765 refused Rockingham's offer of post of Secretary to the Treasury but gave him advice on revenue matters; M.P. Hull 1774–80 and 1782–4; spoke frequently on finance and on America; he made his first motion for conciliation on 25 Mar. 1775 and, after 1776, urged conciliation based on the recognition of American independence; corresponded with Franklin through-

of fire, and this was also one of Franklin's interests. Franklin and Dashwood had other things in common, as did Franklin and Hartley, who was a Rockinghamite, a friend of George Savile, and, in the 1770s, a supporter of the American colonies in their quarrel with England. It is not known whether Dashwood and Hartley had other things in common. Hartley was a financial expert. His scornful dismissal of Grenville's claim that his 1764 budget had 'imposed no new burdens on the people' — a claim which Hartley believed covered up a multitude of financial omissions — spared Dashwood and even compared him favourably with Grenville. 'Nothing has been done this year,' Hartley wrote, 'during the administration of our very laborious Chancellor of the Exchequer, but what always comes of course in the routine of office, and was very successfully accomplished the last year, by a gentleman who never pretended to any great skill in the finances.'[1] He opposed the Stamp Act, which Dashwood supported, but it seems probable that Dashwood's ideas on America after 1769 were congenial to Hartley as they clearly were to Franklin. Although there is unfortunately no evidence about the content of the 'Plan of Reconciliation' that Dashwood drew up in the summer of 1770, Franklin was 'persuaded that, so far as the Consent of America is requisite, it must succeed'.[2] It therefore seems unlikely that Hartley, whose own series of 'Plans' began with his motion of March 1775, should not have approved Dashwood's.

The prevention of fires, and of the spreading of fires, was a grave problem throughout the eighteenth century, in England and elsewhere. There was no Great Fire in London after 1666, but there were several dangerous outbreaks, and nearly all the European capitals

out the war; sent as British representative to peace negotiations 1782; his pamphlets include *The Budget, Inscribed to the Man who thinks himself Minister* (1764); *The State of the Nation* (1765) (an answer to *Remarks on 'The Budget'*); *Letters on the American War* (1778).

[1] *The Budget*, p. 5. One of Hartley's charges against Grenville was that his budget took from the Sinking Fund a sum larger than the surplus that would accrue to it, and he absolved Dashwood from this charge (see *The State of the Nation*, pp. 27–31). He made no mention of the cider tax, but he had strongly attacked the jurisdiction of the Excise Commissioners in *The Right to Appeal to Juries* (1763).

[2] American Philosophical Society, Franklin Papers, 54–60, 127. Franklin to Dashwood, 26 July 1770.

had more than one. Hartley made his invention of 'a method of securing Buildings and Ships against the Calamities of fire' in 1773, and was authorised to make experiments to test its 'practicability and utility'. In May 1774 he obtained a parliamentary grant of £2,500 towards the cost of such experiments. The method, for buildings, was simply to lay thin fire-plates, made of iron, between the floors and ceiling, above and below the wooden joists. For ordinary houses it was sufficient to lay the plates under the floors. This could be done when the houses were being built, and could be applied to old houses 'by taking up, and relaying the floors'. Hartley's most famous experiments were six public ones, when he repeatedly set fire to a three-storied house specially built for the purpose on Wimbledon Common, and proved that the fire did not spread. These experiments were conducted before audiences which included the Royal Family, members of the government, the lord mayor and corporation of the City of London, and special committees of builders and others concerned in the construction of houses. After the third one, on 2 September 1776, the lord mayor, John Sawbridge, laid the foundation-stone of a pillar erected 'one hundred and ten years after the Fire of London, on the anniversary of that dreadful event, in memory of an invention for securing buildings against fire'.[1] Hartley was given the freedom of the City of London, and in 1777 he obtained an Act of Parliament guaranteeing him the 'sole Use and Property' of his invention for thirty-one years. Before Hartley staged the public experiments, he had conducted a number of private ones. The three he considered most important were one at West Wycombe on 9 July 1774, which may well have been the first, and two at the house of his half-brother Winchcombe Henry Hartley, at Bucklebury in Berkshire, on 29 April and 18 May 1775. Hartley wrote an account of the West Wycombe experiment,[2] and accounts were published both in local newspapers and in the *Annual Register* for 1774.[3] Nevertheless, though Hartley's first draft[4] of *An account of some experiments made with the Fire-Plates*, 1776, includes the West Wycombe experiment, the printed pamphlet does not. Instead of 'I have selected three out of the number. . . . The first was tried at

[1] *Annual Register* (1776), pp. 191, 244–8.
[2] Berkshire Record Office, Hartley-Russell MSS. D/EHy.
[3] Pp. 136–7.          [4] Hartley–Russell MSS. D/EHy.

Lord Despencer's at West Wycombe, the others at Bucklebury', the printed version runs: 'I have selected two out of the number, which were tried at *Bucklebury*'.

The omission is understandable enough, as a bit of vanity not foreign to Hartley's character. Nevertheless, it hides not only the fact that Dashwood's interest in the prevention of fire was of long standing, but also the fact that he used copper for this purpose, and the probability that the fire-plates he used in the 1770s were all made not of iron, but of copper. Nor does Hartley mention this in his second pamphlet, *An Account of the Invention and Use of Fire-Plates*,[1] published in 1785, which asserts the superiority of copper over iron for the manufacture of fire-plates.

There was a fire in West Wycombe village in 1756, which destroyed several houses. In 1765 a fire in Dashwood's house destroyed two rooms in the old part of the house.[2] It seems that Dashwood had considered the use of copper for roofing, as a precaution against fire, even before this, and was in touch with George Pengree, a copper merchant, and John Tucker, who were building a house at Temple Mill, near Hurley. In October 1762 Dashwood bought some sheets of copper from Pengree, thicker and 'much stronger' than those used at Temple.[3] It is not clear how much of the roof of his house Dashwood covered. Some time before 1770 he covered 'a long piazza, or gallery' with copper sheet roofing. This was, Franklin said, 'one of the few instances only' in England of the use of copper to cover houses. He quoted it in 1770, in writing to Michael Hillegras, merchant, and Samuel Rhoads, architect of the Pennsylvania Hospital and other public buildings in Philadelphia, about 'the safety of our town'. 'It appears to me of great importance', he wrote to Rhoads, 'to build our dwelling-houses, if we can, in a manner more secure from danger by fire. . . . It is . . . partly in hope that by turning your attention to the point, some methods of greater security in our future building may be thought of and promoted by you, whose judgement I know has deservedly great weight with our fellow-citizens.' Franklin enclosed a description of the method of laying the copper sheets, made by an 'ingenious friend, who is what they

---

1 The date on the title-page is 1 Aug. 1785.
2 Dashwood MSS. B 11/3. Skipwith to Dashwood, 23 Feb. [1765].
3 Ibid. B 12/6. Pengree to Dashwood, 24 Oct. 1762.

call here a civil engineer', and quoted Dashwood's opinion that the estimate of cost was too high.[1]

One of the ways in which Hartley sought to extend the use of his fire-plates was by recommending them to public servants at home and abroad. One of these was Sir James Wright, British Resident in Venice. Wright bought some in 1774, for his house near Woodford in Essex, but in November 1778 he wrote to Hartley saying that one of the rooms where the fire-plates had been installed had developed dry rot in the rafters and the floors, and the plates had rusted. His workmen blamed the fire-plates for 'the introduction of the dry-rot'. He asked Hartley to visit him and provide him with 'Arguments in Vindication of your Ingenious Invention'.[2] Hartley may have done so, but whatever happened Wright seems to have transferred his main enthusiasm to another invention, Mr. Cook's artificial slate. He wrote eight pages of glowing praises about it to Dashwood, 'recommending it warmly to your Lordship's protection, who I know is always ready to patronise the Invention of ingenious men with so much Generosity and Assiduity'. It was made of 'ground black flint, sand, marle, glass and lime united together with oakam, which is reduced to a pulp . . . emerged in a boiling Composition of Linseed Oil, Lithorge, lead and other Ingredients, the sheets of slate are then put into a drying stove, pass through a variety of Pressing by Screens and Cylinders and then hardened for use'. It had two great recommendations: it was 'proof against Fire' and 'more beautiful and cheaper than any other solid Covering'.[3]

When Hartley wrote his second pamphlet, in 1785, he clearly felt bound to answer Wright's complaints. The answer to the 'objection of dry rot — which we now impute to the want of the circulation of air', was simply, Hartley wrote, that 'we do not know the real cause of it . . . it remains precisely as it was before the invention of the fire-plates, it is not an evil newly accrued since that invention, and therefore is not imputable to it. It will probably happen in such cases, and from such causes as would have produced it unconnected with fire-plates, and not in any other. It is entirely independent of them.'[4]

[1] The correspondence was printed in the *Annual Register* (1793), i. 326–329.

[2] Hartley–Russell MSS. D/EHy.     [3] Dashwood MSS. B 12/6.

[4] *An Account of the Invention and Use of Fire-Plates*, p. 19.

This was not very convincing, but perhaps all that could be said. The answer to the 'objection of rust' — also unconvincing — was that iron fire-plates would not rust if they were painted. 'But if anyone should be so scrupulous as still to be unsatisfied . . . , it is to be observed, that the principle and specification of the invention . . . is not confined to plates of iron, but extends generally to the application of plates of any metal to the several parts of buildings, so as to prevent the access of fire and the current of air. Accordingly fire-plates are now made of copper, rolled to a proper thinness, as well as of iron plates painted. . . . And thus the objection of rust is compleatly and finally answered.' [1] This is Hartley's first reference to copper fire-plates. Clearly he now thought them superior to iron ones. They were, he contended, altogether more suitable than iron for 'houses that are already built', because they could be applied without taking up and relaying the floor-boards. They could be 'laid upon any flooring boards without disturbing them, and, after that, a thin sheathing of deal may be laid upon them'. [2] They were, moreover, peculiarly adapted 'for security against fire at sea', for 'iron fire-plates, although painted, could not be expected to stand proof against the constant soaking and corrosion of salt water'. [3] Finally, 'copper fire-plates may likewise be applied for coverings to houses, and may be adapted in such manner as to constitute fire-proof roofs upon the principle, and in the same mode as fire-plates are applied to floors of houses against fire. Copper fire-plates being rolled much thiner [sic] than ordinary sheets of copper, the expence of such roofs may be reduced to a very moderate sum. They require slighter timbers, and therefore much less expensive framework than common roofs. The copper will always retain its intrinsic value. These considerations will more than counterbalance any additional expence, and the quality of resisting fire is super-added.' [4]

Hartley was, in fact, converted to copper. Dashwood's part in this conversion is unlikely ever to be known, but at least his example was there from the first. In August 1787 one of Hartley's correspondents wondered whether 'Dr. Franklin has introduced them [your Fire-Plates] to America, whose accidents from Fire are more frequent (perhaps on Account of the Shingle Roofs) than even in England.' [5]

1 Ibid., pp. 15–16.  2 Ibid., p. 22.  3 Ibid., p. 17.  4 Ibid., p. 23.
5 Hartley–Russell MSS. D/EHy. N (?) Strachey to Hartley.

The letter might have elicited the reply that Franklin had recommended something very like them to America seventeen years before.

In September 1771, three years before his experiment with fireplates at West Wycombe, Dashwood had arranged a 'jubilee' there, opening the gardens to the public for three days, to celebrate the completion of the Greek Ionic west portico of the house, which was designed by Revett and was one of the earliest examples of the new Greek influence in English architecture. It was modelled on a reconstruction of the Temple of Dionysus, or Bacchus, at Teos, about twenty miles from Smyrna. In the second century B.C., when the Temple was probably built, Teos was the principal seat of Dionysiac worship in Ionia, and renowned for its musical and dramatic festivals. The Dilettanti Society expedition had visited the site of the Temple in 1765.[1] They reported that 'the disorder in which this ruin lies, is so great, that no fragment of a column, or portion of the Cell, is found in its original place'. Nevertheless, using Vitruvius's description, they made drawings and plans, for 'the curious Reader will, it is hoped, derive some pleasure and satisfaction from seeing this Temple restored'.[2] What Dashwood achieved at West Wycombe was then not just a vague resemblance to a classical temple. 'The temple of Bacchus at Teos', Chandler wrote

was one of the most celebrated structures in Ionia. The remains of it have been engraved at the expence of the Society of Dilettanti, and published, with its history in the *Ionian Antiquities*; and a beautiful Portico has been erected at the seat of the Rt. Hon. Lord Le Despenser, near High-Wykeham, under the inspection of Mr Revett, in which the exact proportions of the order are observed.[3]

---

[1] In Feb. 1767 the Dilettanti Society selected three of 'the most curious and interesting subjects as the first specimen of the intended work [on Ionian Antiquities]' and Revett was asked to prepare them for engraving. One of the three was the Temple of Bacchus at Teos (Dilettanti Society Committee Book, 7 and 14 Feb. 1767). In Jan. 1770 Dashwood, for the Society, presented the book to George III (ibid. 14 Jan. 1770). See *Ionian Antiquities*, i (1769), 1–12, and plates. (For the 1862 excavation, see ibid. iv (1881), 35–39, and plates, and for discussion of the temple and Vitruvius see D. S. Robertson, *Handbook of Greek and Roman Architecture* (1945), 154, 333.)

[2] *Ionian Antiquities*, i. 6.    [3] *Travels in Asia Minor*, p. 98.

Dashwood had started his building at West Wycombe, and the landscaping of the gardens which set the scene for the pageant of 1771, more than twenty years before, probably soon after his marriage in 1745. Indeed, in 1748 it was thought that he was 'going to build a Steep at Wycombe, and pull down his present House'.[1] Although he did not do this, he transformed his father's plain brick house by building a double colonnade on to the south front, the original main entrance, and porticos on the east and west sides, and stuccoing the whole. Inside, he remodelled and redecorated the rooms. The park was landscaped, given a lake by blocking the waters of the tiny river Wye, and embellished with statues, busts, urns, and trees sent from Italy, many by the dealers Lefroy and Charron of Leghorn, some by Thomas Hyam and Son, and others by Isaac Jamineau, British Consul at Naples. The final plans of the house were included in the 1771 edition of *Vitruvius Britannicus*, under the name of John Donowell, and were exhibited by him. It is clear, however, that the work was done in stages, over more than twenty years, and not all by Donowell, and that Dashwood himself had a hand in it. The names of some who worked on the house and buildings in the park are known, though it is not always clear what each one did. Robert Adam, who built the library for Dashwood's London house, 18 Hanover Square, designed the stables and offices at West Wycombe, and may have done more than this; Henry Cheere designed the beautiful mahogany staircase and was responsible for other woodwork; Joseph Borgnis and his son painted ceilings with classical scenes taken from Italian paintings. William Hannen who decorated some ceilings, painted a number of pictures of the house and park at different stages of the alterations, and he and John Tinney produced the series of paintings and engravings begun in 1754. Revett designed the west portico and the small temple standing near it, the Temple of Flora and the temple or Music Room on the island in the lake. He is said to have designed also the east Doric portico. This seems to have been finished before 1754, four years before Stuart's Doric temple at Hagley, and it is not impossible that Revett designed it before his first visit to Greece. He seems also to have supervised some building in 1780.[2]

[1] *Verney Letters*, ii. 242 (Lord Fermanagh to Earl Verney, 13 Sept. 1748). [2] Kent Record Office, (Fane MSS.) U 282, A 8.

The house which emerged in 1771 might have been one of Palladio's lighter productions, not boldly transported, as Mereworth was, but lightened still further and simplified by the Greek influence, and imaginatively adapted to a corner of the English countryside which, except in climate, is not dissimilar from the little hills round Florence. In the park, the happy mixture of Greek temples, Roman urns and statues, and English landscape gardening, made what Franklin called 'a paradise'. Thomas Langley, who was not uncritical of parts of the house, had no doubts about the gardens, though he agreed with Repton's opinion that they laboured under a profusion of ornament, 'which the false taste of the last age' required, admirable in themselves but not proportioned to each other.[1] But this was only a superficial defect, and could easily be remedied. 'The character of the gardens & scenery of West Wycombe park', Langley wrote, 'is beauty . . . and will long remain a monument of Lord le Despencer's taste & judgment of landscape scenery.'[2]

[1] *Observations on the Theory and Practice of Landscape Gardening* (1803), p. 5. One of the examples which Repton gives of inattention to the 'necessity of observing scale or comparative proportion' is a 'figure of a man in a brown coat and broad-brimmed hat . . . much larger than the natural proportion of a man'. This was the lead statue of William Penn, erected on 'the summit of a saw-mill in the park', which Franklin admired and recommended the Pennsylvania Hospital to copy (Franklin to Charles Moore, 5 Feb. 1775. This letter is now in the Pennsylvania Hospital Archives: I am grateful to Miss Gertrude Hess, Assistant Librarian, American Philosophical Society, for obtaining a copy for me). Dashwood-King got rid of the statue — perhaps because of Repton's strictures — and it was bought some time before 1803 by John Penn of Stoke Poges, who shipped it to Pennsylvania in 1804. It still stands on the lawn in front of the Pine Street entrance to the Hospital. The statue holds in the left hand a scroll on which is inscribed, in gold letters, part of the charter of privileges granted by Penn to Pennsylvania in 1700 — the promise of freedom from molestation to all who believe in 'one Almighty God'. Franklin wrote to Dashwood about this inscription on 14 Apr. 1774 (letter originally deposited in Bodleian Library but now removed).

[2] While writing his description of the house and park Langley made 'frequent applications' to Sir John Dashwood-King, whom he feared 'will be wearied with my importunities', and references to Repton, who restored the gardens 1796–9 and published his *Sketches and Hints on Landscape Gardening* in 1796 (Langley to Dashwood-King, 2 Dec. 1795. Dashwood

5. Dashwood's drawing of a (? winged) child on a young sea-bull, found —
almost certainly during his first visit to Italy — at Antium.  It may well have
come from one of Nero's buildings there (cf. Seneca, *Hippolytus*, 1013–45,
elaborating Euripides)

6. Temple of Bacchus at Teos, 1764

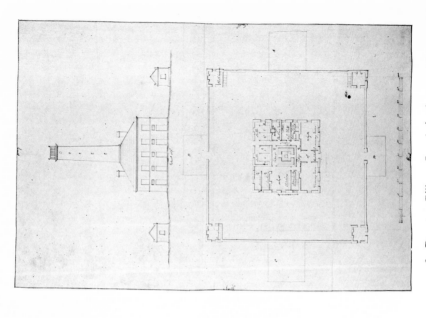

8. Dunston Pillar: Lumby's plan, c. 1770

7. Dunston Pillar

The church at West Wycombe stood on the hill behind the village and opposite the park. In 1763 Dashwood had the church rebuilt, except for the tower and nave. The tower was heightened, and a golden ball, made of copper, superimposed. The inside was decorated and refurnished, an organ was installed, a new bell hung. The church seems to have been much in need of repair, and in 1760, in gratitude to Dashwood for his promise to repair it, the parishioners had undertaken to keep it in good order and not 'to bury within its walls'. In 1763–4, with the legacy left him by Dodington in 1762, Dashwood built a hexagonal flint mausoleum, on the hill at the east side of the church. The site was skilfully chosen, so that the traveller along the last straight stretch of the London road from High Wycombe saw, and still sees, the church tower, topped with its golden ball, rising above the mausoleum and seeming one building with it. The church was opened on 3 July 1763. The *Gentleman's Magazine*, admiring the 'fine new organ . . . the font of inimitable workman-ship', and the other ornaments, concluded that 'on the whole . . . it is reckoned to be the most beautiful country church in all England'. Sir John Cullum, who visited West Wycombe in January 1782, told Richard Gough that he was 'much pleased with the modern church and adjoining mausoleum', and surprised that no engraving of the mausoleum had been made, 'for I see none is mentioned in your "Topography", and so I suppose none is extant. The furniture of the Church is a pattern of elegance and propriety; and, to add to the rarity of all this, it was done at the sole expence of the late Lord le Despencer.'[1] The architect of the mausoleum was the younger John Bastard of Blandford, and much of the stonework was done by Banister Watts, who built the column at the east end of the village in 1752. This was erected to commemorate the completion of the new road, on which Dashwood had employed the poor of Wycombe, in accordance with the scheme for voluntary public works proposed in his Poor Relief bill of 1747.

One of the builders who seems to have done some work at West Wycombe was Luffham Atterbury, who in the 1770s was employed

MSS. F 5/22 — enclosure missing). Bodley MS. Eng. misc. C 107, ff. 73–74*v*. (undated and unsigned) is in Langley's hand and must be the draft description he enclosed with his letter of 2 Dec. 1795.

[1] Nichols, *Literary Anecdotes*, vii. 683–4.

by Dashwood at Mereworth rectory and at Hall Place, near Bexley, where Dashwood's sister, Lady Austen, lived. Atterbury devoted his leisure to music, became musician-in-ordinary to George III, and composed many glees and catches. In August 1775 Atterbury's oratorio *Goliath*, which had been performed once only at the Haymarket Theatre in May 1773, was performed in West Wycombe[1] church at the ceremony held to commemorate Paul Whitehead, who left his body to a London hospital and his heart to Dashwood, and to place the heart in an urn in the mausoleum. Atterbury also conducted the music played as the procession moved through the park. Some of this was composed for the occasion by Dr. Samuel Arnold, whose oratorio *The Prodigal Son* had also been first performed in 1773, on the occasion of the installation of North as Chancellor of Oxford University.

Two pieces of Dashwood's building remain: Dunston Pillar on Lincoln Heath, and Medmenham Abbey near Marlow in Buckinghamshire. Dunston Pillar was built in 1751, Medmenham Abbey restored at about the same time. I believe that date is not the only connection between them.

Dunston Pillar, eight and a half miles south-east of Lincoln city and two and a half miles westwards from the village of Dunston, is easier to describe because there is no Dunston myth. It was a tall quadrangular column built of stone, ninety-two feet high, rising to a flat balustraded top, which was reached by a spiral inside staircase. On the top stood a large octagonal lantern, fifteen and a half feet high. It was built to serve as a lighthouse, and this it was called: 'the only land light-house ever raised'.[2] It was much needed. The heath was unenclosed, covered with furze and bracken, and the roads across it, based largely on the track of the old Ermine Street from Lincoln to Stamford, by-passing Grantham, and a rough track from Lincoln to Sleaford, were unfenced, ill repaired, and not clearly marked. The Lincoln to Sleaford track ran about three miles from the four small villages of Nocton, Dunston, Metheringham, and Blankney, and on it, two miles north of the Green Man, the light-

---

[1] *Grove's Dictionary of Music and Musicians* (5th ed., 1954). The *Whitehall Evening Post*'s account of the ceremony (reprinted in *Annual Register* (1775), pp. 59–61) states that this was a 'new Oratorio'.

[2] *Journal of Agricultural Society* (1843).

house was built. There can be no doubt of its usefulness: 'it was of great utility'[1] is a phrase found in gazetteers and topographical descriptions of Lincolnshire until the middle of the nineteenth century. The lantern was lighted regularly until 1788, when 'the inconveniences that this building was intended to remedy'[2] no longer existed. The road from Lincoln to Sleaford, and the road between the villages,[3] had been widened and repaired, much of the land had been enclosed, divided into fields and put under cultivation, especially in the late 1770s, and the first steps had been taken towards transforming 'this sterile district . . . [into] one of the most beautifully farmed parts of Lincolnshire'.[4] When Arthur Young visited Lincoln Heath in 1799 he found 'a large range which formerly was covered with heath, gorse &c and yielding, in fact, little or no produce, converted, by inclosure, to profitable arable farms . . . and a very extensive country, all studded with new farm houses, barns, offices, and every appearance of thriving industry.'[5] The lantern was still lighted occasionally until it crashed down in the bad storms of 1809. It was then replaced by a large statue of George III, fourteen feet high.[6] The Pillar remained 'as a monument of the benevolence and public spirit of the person who caused it to be erected'.[7]

The Pillar was more than a lighthouse, for it was made the centre

---

[1] See, for example, G. A. Cooke, *Topographical Description of Lincolnshire,* [*c.* 1798]; Allen, op cit.; William White, *History Gazetteer and Directory of Lincolnshire* (1842); *Illustrated London News* (Apr. 1859).

[2] *Gentleman's Magazine* (1795), p. 561.

[3] The first step towards this was the bill passed in 1756 for improving the roads from Lincoln to Sleaford. Dashwood was added to the committee which considered the bill (*Commons Journals,* xxvii. 510, 536, 548).

[4] Ripon in the debate on the repeal of the corn laws on 25 May 1846 (*Parliamentary Debates,* 3rd series, lxxxvi. 1098). Frederick John Robinson, first Earl of Ripon, married in 1814 Sarah Albinia Louisa, daughter of Robert Hobart, fourth Earl of Buckinghamshire (1760–1816), and after 1816 lived at Nocton.

[5] *General View of the Agriculture of the County of Lincoln* (1799), p. 78.

[6] Allen, op. cit. ii. 262.

[7] The statue, made of coade stone, remained in place until the Second World War, when it and part of the Pillar were taken down as a precaution against aircraft. What is left of the column is now no higher than the trees surrounding it, and hardly visible from the road. The staircase has disappeared.

of Pleasure Gardens. Round it was a square walled garden, less than an acre in extent, within a larger enclosure of heathland. There was an opening or gateway in each side of the wall, and a little stone pavilion at each corner. There were plantations outside the walls, and a bowling green just beyond the opening on the north side of the square. The pavilion at the north-east corner was at some stage converted into assembly-rooms by the addition, within the square, of a dining-room and other rooms on two floors. The Pleasure Gardens were greatly admired. It seems likely that members of the Lincoln Club were among their regular visitors. William Wroughton, vicar of Welbourne, who had been vicar of West Wycombe from 1756 to 1766, described the Gardens soon after he came to Lincolnshire as 'the Vaux Hall of this part of the world. The Bowling Green is the best and kept in the best Order I have ever seen, and the plantations are all in a very thriving state and will in a few years be the Paradise of Lincolnshire.'[1] The Pillar Grounds were celebrated enough to be mentioned, in 1836, in *Lincolnshire Views*, though they had then ceased to be Pleasure Gardens, leaving only the plantations, which made them seem like parkland. After explaining that the Pillar was originally a 'lighthouse — in the centre of wild open heath, of great extent', the author wrote:

> There are four little buildings surrounding the pillar, at equal distances, which were used many years for the accomodation of parties resorting thither for amusement — tea-parties — playing at bowls, quoits, &c. An inhabitant of Lincoln remembers, about fifty years ago, seeing as many as sixteen or eighteen carriages there at one time.[2]

Dashwood visited Lincolnshire regularly in the 1750s, staying at Nocton. In the 1760s and afterwards he went less often, for obvious reasons: his holding of government office, his succession to Mereworth and other Kentish property of the Earl of Westmorland in 1762, his wife's constant illness after 1763. In 1766 Dashwood and his wife signed an agreement with George Hobart[3] giving him

[1] Dashwood MSS. B 19. Wroughton to Dashwood, 15 Aug. 1766.
[2] *Lincolnshire in 1836: displayed in a series of Nearly One Hundred Engravings* (John Saunders, jun., 1836).
[3] 1732–1804; M.P. St. Ives 1754–61, Beeralston 1761–80; son of John Hobart, first Earl of Buckinghamshire (1694–1756), and younger brother of John, second Earl (ambassador to Russia 1762–5), whom he

possession of Nocton, which would be his after Lady Dashwood's death, in return for the payment to her of an annuity for her life. Hobart had just returned from acting as secretary to his brother's embassy in St. Petersburg, and wished to settle down. He went to live at Nocton immediately. Dashwood lost the house he had had for twenty-one years, and was left with Dunston Pillar and the property he owned in Dunston village.

In Dashwood's absences from Lincolnshire, before and after 1766, the 'Governance of the Pillar' was left to Dr. Francis Willis, rector of Wapping, son of one of the chaplains of Lincoln Cathedral. Since 1749 Willis had lived, rent-free, in the manor-house at Dunston which Dashwood owned, and was supposed to act as a sort of deputy for him, looking after his property and his interests in general. One of these interests was to buy land in Dunston, in order that ultimately it might be enclosed and put under cultivation. Willis, however, had interests of his own, which conflicted with Dashwood's. He practised as a doctor, unqualified until 1759, specialising particularly in the treatment of mental illness. His patients were accommodated in the manor-house, to which he made extensive alterations and additions, costing him, he said, at least £1,200. He also made some use of the pavilions and grounds at the Pillar 'for his business', and made alterations there too. In November 1770 he proposed to Dashwood that he should 'take the Pillar off your hands', on a 999-year lease, and 'turn architect'. When Dashwood refused the lease, Willis pressed him to sell the manor-house with about seventeen acres of land. He rejected Dashwood's offer of a lease of the manor-house, for as long as Willis lived, at a peppercorn rent. He tried to force Dashwood's hand, buying for himself some Dunston freeholds which he knew Dashwood wanted and offering to sell them if Dashwood agreed to his proposals. This was a piece of real blackmail, for, unless Dashwood agreed, he was prevented from enclosing. 'There are', he wrote in May 1773, 'doubtless many who inclose not haveing the Lordship to themselves, but I will not.'[1]

succeeded as third Earl in 1793. The first Earl was grandson of Sir John Hobart (d. 1683) and his wife Mary, daughter and co-heir of John Hampden; Mary's brother Richard was grandfather of Sir Richard Ellys.

[1] Dashwood MSS. B 19. Nor did he: Dunston was not enclosed until after his death.

It seems that in the late 1760s, after George Hobart went to live at Nocton, Dashwood thought of building 'a little house' near the Pillar, intending to use this on his short visits to Lincolnshire, rather than 'disturb' Willis at the manor-house. There is, in the Dashwood papers, a drawing[1] which could just possibly have been thought at first sight to represent Dashwood's proposed 'little house' but is almost certainly Willis's plan for the conversion of the Pillar after he had obtained his 999-year lease. It shows a square house, fifty-six feet long and two stories high, encasing the foot of the Pillar and rising half-way up it. The drawing was made by William Lumby, Surveyor and Clerk of the Works at Lincoln Cathedral in the 1770s. He undertook the alteration of several buildings in and near Lincoln and superintended the works at the Infirmary, which Willis visited. Lumby was said to be 'of a very ingenious turn of mind, mild and gentle'. His Pillar House is certainly ingenious; but it is an architectural monstrosity which Dashwood was hardly likely to have approved of.[2]

After a battery of long irrelevant letters from Willis, who was known in Dunston for his 'Volubility in Argument', complaining that Dashwood did not understand the difficulty of providing a family of five sons with somewhere to 'lay their heads', and 'accommodating a Family not easily accommodated', or the hardship of 'laying out money upon another's estate', Willis was given notice to quit in 1775. As he made no move to do so he was threatened with lega proceedings and ejectment in 1776. He evaded this by an agreement, which he did not keep, to leave 'peaceably and Quietly', and 'without committing any manner of spoil or Waste'. He took a large house at Greatford, near Stamford, and applied for a license[3]

---

[1] Dashwood MSS. E 1. The plan has no explanation or date. It was sent to Sir John Dashwood-King by his agent Parkinson but the covering letter has disappeared.

[2] Dashwood perhaps built the extension to the north-east pavilion and used this as his 'little house'. A plan of the Pillar grounds, dated 1793, shows the extension but gives no indication of when it was made (see p. 122).

[3] This was necessary under the 1774 Act for the Better Regulation of Private Madhouses, which established a system of annual license and inspection. The prevalence of abuses in private madhouses had been discussed in the Commons in Feb. 1763 (*Parl. Hist.* xv. 1283–90), but the proposal to

'for keeping the same for the Reception of insane patients', but he did not leave Dunston until 1778. At Greatford Willis continued his practice so successfully that he was summoned to Kew when George III fell ill and was feared insane in 1788.[1] There he became Pitt's ally in his duel with Fox over the Regency question.[2] All George's regular doctors agreed that he would probably recover, but Willis was 'more sanguine' than they were, and this was his great recommendation to Pitt. Willis and two of his sons were housed at Kew until George recovered. One may surmise that he would have recovered without Willis. He was called in again, in spite of George's protests, in 1801, after treating the Queen of Portugal, unsuccessfully, in 1792. In 1773 Dashwood said, correctly, that Willis had 'got his fortune in my house'; he multiplied it after treating George III and died at Greatford in 1807, at the age of ninety, rich and celebrated, with 'the largest [private asylum] in the Kingdom',[3] with his family well provided for and one of his five sons, Robert, physician-in-ordinary to the king.

It seems possible that, after Willis's departure from Dunston in 1778, and Dashwood's death in 1781, the Pillar Grounds suffered a period of neglect, and that, after the enclosure award of 1793, they were put in order again by Sir John Dashwood-King, son of

regulate them had apparently been dropped. It was revived on 1 Feb. 1772 by Thomas Townshend (ibid. xvii. 696).

[1] Willis was recommended by Mrs. Harcourt, wife of Col. William Harcourt, an equerry whose appointment as groom of the bedchamber by Pitt in 1766 had so upset Newcastle (see p. 70). She was Mary, daughter of Rev. William Danby of Swinton, Yorks., and widow of Thomas Lockhart; Willis had treated her mother.

[2] See, for example, *Annual Register* (1798), p. 107. 'Mr. Pitt treated the opinion of Dr. Warren . . . as if it had been dictated by a partiality to the rising administration [i.e. Fox's] . . . in return Dr. Willis . . . was represented as a tool to save the designs of Mr. Pitt's faction.' The 'Report of the Committee appointed to examine the Physicians who have attended his Majesty during his Illness, touching the State of his Majesty's Health' is printed in ibid., pp. 287–96. The most recent discussion of the nature of the king's illness, by Drs. A. Macalpine and R. Hunter, is in *British Medical Journal*, Jan. 1966.

[3] His monument, by Nollekens, is in Greatford church. See Sir George Clark, *A History of the Royal College of Physicians of London* (Oxford, 1966), pp. 582–3, for others who made their fortunes in this way.

Dashwood's half-brother, who a few years later employed Repton to restore the West Wycombe gardens. It was, one must suppose, partly because the grounds were neglected that the indefatigable traveller George Byng, who visited Dunston in June 1791, recorded neither pleasure gardens, bowling green, nor plantations, and that he did not even notice the pavilions. Nor did Byng see any utility in the Pillar; it seemed to him a folly, pointless and silly. It was, he wrote:

> built by the late Sir F. Dashwood, one of those gentlemen, who fancy-ing themselves architects, erect the horridest piles around them, and for others, who will be misled! Of what use, nature, or taste, is this odious obelisk? It can incur only ridicule! The original fancy was (I have heard) to form a lighthouse for the guide of stray travellers; and to make his Lordships 'Light so shine before men'. This is like all his Ldships other buildings, all a waste of stone! [1]

Byng's humourless tirade against the Pillar was clearly explained less by the neglected state of the Pillar grounds than by his dislike of other things that Dashwood built. West Wycombe Byng condemned as 'a bourgeois business, with his pepper & salt boxes & buildings'.[2] As he had a taste for gothic, this dislike was natural enough. More unexpectedly, he censured Dashwood for a piece of building with which, as far as I know, no other evidence connects him. This was the 'New Bridge over the Cherwell, usually called Magdalen Bridge'[3] in Oxford, built under the Oxford Mileways Act of 1771. It was opened in October 1777 but the 'Ballustrate on the South Side' was not finished until 1782. Byng describes it as 'ugly, narrow, new'.[4] His strictures are less interesting than his statement that Dashwood

[1] *Torrington Diaries* (ed. C. B. Andrews (1934), ii. 344 (and plate)).

[2] Ibid. i. 118.     [3] Jackson's *Oxford Journal*, 11 Oct. 1777.

[4] His opinion was not shared by the Oxford improver Edward Tatham, who planned a new bridge himself but had 'candour enough to own that Mr. Gwynn's has the superiority in construction, and will be executed at less expense' (*Oxonia Explicata & Ornata: Proposals for Disengaging and Beautifying the University and City of Oxford* (1773), p. 20), nor by Sir John Peshall, who praised the 'most elegant Stone Bridge, designed by the ingenious Architect Mr Gwynn' (*Antient and Present State of the City of Oxford. The whole chiefly collected by Anthony à Wood, with additions* (1773), p. 293). But James Dallaway, while recognising the difficulty of spanning two rivers, thought the bridge not a success, criticising in particular the 'double columns' as 'useless, for they add nothing to the support'

'guided' the bridge. Its architect was John Gwyn, friend of Dr. Johnson, who, with Boswell, accompanied Gwyn to Oxford in 1776 and tried to help him when he got into financial difficulties in 1777. Gwyn was a native of Shrewsbury. In the 1770s he built the English bridge in Shrewsbury and the Atcham bridge over the Severn near Shrewsbury, the bridge in Worcester, and the House of Industry and the New Markets in Oxford. In London, where he spent most of his life, his main concern was not with building but with planning and writing. He did however submit a plan, which was not chosen,[1] for the new bridge across the Thames at Blackfriars. The bill to authorise the building of this bridge was introduced into the Commons on 3 May 1758,[2] and Dashwood was a member of the committee to which it was referred. Even if this introduced Gwyn to Dashwood — and he may, like Dr. Johnson, have preferred Gwyn's plan to Mylne's — it was Gwyn's writing and ideas that particularly commended him to Dashwood. Gwyn's great work, *London and Westminster Improved*, was published in 1766. It gave great encouragement to the movement for planning, paving, and general improvement of London streets and squares, the building and repairing of bridges, and the embankment of the Thames.[3] This was one of Dashwood's long-standing interests. He was a member of one of the very earliest Commons committees on the improvement of London, the 1744 Committee to consider an Act 'for the better Enlightening

(*Anecdotes of the Arts in England* (1800), p. 122), and John Chambers quoted without dissent the opinion that the bridge 'has little to recommend it' (*Biographical Illustrations of Worcestershire* (1820), p. 504). Both Dallaway and Chambers thought Worcester Bridge the best that Gwyn built.

[1] Johnson wrote in the *Daily Gazetteer* (Dec. 1759) in support of Gwyn's design for Blackfriars Bridge against that of his successful rival Robert Mylne. Gwyn planned a bridge with semicircular arches and a stone balustrade; Mylne's had elliptical arches and iron railings. The controversy in which Johnson took part hinged largely on these differences (see *Annual Register* (1759), pp. 146–9).

[2] *Commons Journals*, xxvii. 592.

[3] J. Summerson, *Georgian London*, states that Gwyn's book 'inaugurates the age of improvement', and notes that a large number of his suggestions were implemented within the next hundred years (revised edn., 1962, p. 122). 'Inaugurates' perhaps rather belittles the Acts passed between 1744 and 1764. There were about twenty of them.

of the Streets of the City of London'.[1] This was followed by his membership of the committee set up to consider proper ways of lighting and paving the city of Westminster in 1751,[2] and by his own bill 'for Paving, Cleansing, Enlightening, and keeping in Repair, the Street called *Pall Mall*, as an Experiment towards the Paving &c of the Streets of the City and Liberty of Westminster',[3] which was passed in June 1751. In all, Dashwood sat on fourteen committees before Gwyn's book was published, dealing not only with the paving, lighting, and cleansing of Westminster and the adjoining parishes, Lambeth, and the City of London, but also with such things as widening the passage over London Bridge,[4] improving the streets around Charing Cross,[5] planning a square at Deans Yard,[6] repairing and rebuilding Terrace Walk and other buildings adjoining the river.[7] He was, moreover, a member of the committee[8] which drafted the Act which Gwyn particularly praised, the 1762 Act for paving Westminster and adjoining parishes, extended in 1765 to those on the Surrey side of Westminster Bridge. What made this committee especially notable was the series of twelve Resolutions which it presented to the House, stating the reasons why 'the Squares, Streets, Lanes, and Alleys' were 'in general very ill-paved and cleansed',[9] and suggesting remedies which it thought would be more effectual than past ones.

Dashwood and Gwyn shared another interest: the promotion of an academy for the encouragement of painting, sculpture, and architecture. In 1749 Gwyn published *An Essay on Design: Including Proposals for Erecting a Public Academy*. He praised the French Royal Academies of Painting and Sculpture, and of Architecture, and pointed out 'the great Advantages that may be derived from Drawing, and a Knowledge of the Art of Design, to all Ranks and Professions of Men'. Among his arguments was one which must certainly have appealed to Dashwood and the Dilettanti Society:

The curious Traveller . . . cannot, without this Art, make those Improvements he goes in Pursuit of. . . . How very imperfect many

---

[1] *Commons Journals*, xxiv. 526.     [2] Ibid. xxvi. 214.
[3] Ibid. 214, 264, 285.     [4] Ibid. xxvii. 569.   7 Apr. 1756.
[5] Ibid. xxviii. 74.   9 Feb. 1758.
[6] Ibid. xxvii. 189.   21 Mar. 1755.     [7] Ibid. 551.   30 Mar. 1756.
[8] Ibid. xxix. 182.   18 Feb. 1762.     [9] Ibid. 283.   15 Mar. 1762.

of our Accounts of distant Countries are rendered by the Relators being unskilful in *Drawing*, and in the general principles of Surveying.[1]

Gwyn's aim was the foundation of a public Academy which should not only be a society of artists but should, like the French Academies, teach and improve public taste. He urged that the expense would not be great: 'What is annually given [from public funds] to preserve and continue the *Gothic* Taste in the old Repositary of Tombs at Westminster, would, if properly applied, be sufficient to raise among us the Taste of Rome and Athens'.[2] If the 'Taste and Interest of those in Power' was not yet enlightened enough to support a public Academy, a step towards it might be the foundation of 'an Academy supported by private and voluntary subscription', taking advantage of the prevailing 'Taste of subscribing to Hospitals and Infirmaries'.[3]

In February 1749, just before Gwyn's book was published, the Dilettanti Society made a similar plea for 'a public academy for the improvement of painting, sculpture, and architecture'. Dashwood was a member of the committee which made this recommendation to the Society and suggested a constitution.[4] The committee looked to the French Academies, as Gwyn did, and suggested that the Academy be composed of twenty-one elected members and a certain number of professors and students in each of the three branches. Gwyn was not a member of the Dilettanti Society, but he was a member of the Committee of Painters, Statuaries, Architects, etc., which was formed in 1753 to consider the formation of an Academy for the Improvement of the Arts in General. In February 1755 this Committee wrote to the Dilettanti Society asking for their help, as a body which had been 'long ago convinced of the necessity of such a plan', and the Dilettanti Society promised 'all the assistance that shall be in their power' when plans should have been matured. The Committee sent its plans in April. Gwyn signed the covering letter, which asked the Dilettanti Society to 'assist conjointly with us in directing and governing the Royal Academy . . . being persuaded that with your countenance and assistance we cannot fail to obtain the countenance and assistance of the public', and Dashwood was a member of the Dilettanti Society committee to consider the

[1] *Essay on Design*, p. 50.     [2] Ibid., p. 74.     [3] Ibid., p. 78.
[4] Dilettanti Society Minute Book and Committee Book, Feb. 1749, Feb.–May, 1755.

plans. There seems no doubt that negotiations broke down not because the Dilettanti wanted too much power[1] but because the Painters repented of their proposal for condominion. The engraver Robert Strange, a member of the Committee of Painters who attended the meetings between the two bodies, had no doubt where the blame lay:

> On the part of our intended benefactors, I observed that generosity and benevolence, which are peculiar to true greatness; but on the part of the majority of the leading artists, I was sorry to remark motives apparently limited to their own views and ambition to govern, diametrically opposite to the liberality with which we were treated. After various conferences, the *dilettante* finding they were to be allowed no share in the government of the academy, or in appropriating their own fund, the negotiation ended.[2]

In the same year the Committee approached the Society of Arts, of which Dashwood was a member and in whose Great Room Gwyn exhibited in 1760. Again the negotiations failed, perhaps for the same reason. After many vicissitudes, the Royal Academy at last emerged in 1768, the result of a secession of malcontents, of whom Gwyn was one, from the Incorporated Society of Artists. The Academy's constitution was similar to that proposed by Gwyn and the Dilettanti in 1749 in that it provided for teaching, and resembled the French Academies rather than the English Royal Society.[3] Gwyn was an original member; the first President, Sir Joshua Reynolds, had been a Dilettanti since 1764, and in 1774 the Dilettanti Society set aside a sum of money to be spent on sending Academy students to Italy or Greece.

There is, then, certain acquaintance and common interest between Dashwood and Gwyn. Byng's statement that Dashwood 'guided' Magdalen Bridge is therefore not at all improbable, though the shape of the guidance, and the way it happened, are guess-work.

Much less is known certainly about Medmenham than about

[1] J. F. Hodgson and F. A. Eaton, *The Royal Academy and its Members, 1768–1830* (1905), p. 9.

[2] *An Enquiry into the Rise and Establishment of the Royal Academy of Arts* (1775), pp. 62–63.

[3] The first Professor of Perspective was Samuel Wale, who, with Gwyn, designed a reredos for the church at Bledlow, three miles from West Wycombe.

Dunston Pillar, but on a very little fact, there has grown a vast super-structure, most of it so flimsy, fancy, and unsupported, that it cannot be dislodged. To set about exploding it would be to take it too seriously. Nevertheless, it cannot quite be ignored, for the tissue of scandal and gossip which has its main origin in Wilkes, Charles Churchill, the novel *Chrysal*, and the *Town and Country Magazine*, has incongruously been made to serve as serious evidence for an assessment of Dashwood's character and abilities. One can, however, try to explain Medmenham from scratch, as if the superstructure did not exist. Then, perhaps, one can suggest why it does.

There is at least one piece of evidence to link Dunston Pillar and Medmenham: John King of Ashby-de-la-Launde, writing to Dashwood in 1770, said that he was unable to go to Medmenham, and must content himself with Dunston Pillar. The parallel presents Medmenham as pleasure gardens or a country club on the banks of the Thames.

Medmenham is six miles from West Wycombe, on a stretch of the river, between Henley and Marlow, famous for its fishing and sailing and dotted with fish-weirs and boat-houses. The house was a converted Cistercian abbey, as was Bisham Abbey on the opposite bank, and in the early eighteenth century very little of the original abbey building remained. The house belonged to and was lived in by the Duffield family, from the sixteenth century to 1778.[1] It seems that Dashwood rented it from about 1750, and, probably with the help of the builders he employed at West Wycombe, repaired it and made it look more like an abbey. The result was described by Thomas Langley in 1797:

> The abbey-house, with its ivy-mantled roof and walls, forms a very picturesque object. The late addition of a ruined tower, cloyster, and other corresponding parts, is made with so much taste and propriety, that when time shall have worn off all traces of the rule and blunted its sharp edges; when the ivy shall have continued its embraces, and the mosses of various hues overspread the surface, some future writer will be disposed to class it with the more ancient pile. Within the cloyster a room is fitted up with the same good taste, and the

---

[1] It was sold in 1778 to Robert Sawyer of Heywood, Berkshire, in 1779 to John Morton, Chief Justice of Chester, and in 1786 to Robert Scott, M.P. Wootton Bassett 1774–80.

glare of light is judiciously excluded by the pleasing gloom of ancient stained glass.[1]

Dashwood's tenancy of the abbey-house lasted until his death. If he instituted a country club there, with some similarity to the gatherings at Dunston Pillar, it is unlikely to have had any purpose other than a convivial or recreational one. There seems no doubt that visitors to Medmenham sailed on the river, and fished. There was a boat-house in the abbey gardens and others on the aytes opposite to the abbey. The lord of the manors of Medmenham and Little Marlow was John Borlase Warren, who lived at Bockmer, behind Medmenham, and most of the fishing between Medmenham and Marlow was shared between Dashwood and Sir Thomas Stapleton, of Grey's Court, Henley, who owned land at Cookham and Bray in Berkshire, across the river from Medmenham. The idea that in the 1760s the club's activities were transferred to the golden ball above the church at West Wycombe, or to the caves formed by the excavation of chalk for the new road in 1751, is unsubstantiated. It is also absurd. These places would have been no substitute for Medmenham, nor would they have stilled the gossip which is supposed to be the reason for the alleged transfer. John King's reference to Medmenham in 1770 shows that it was still used then. John Wesley is said to have visited Medmenham in 1774 and Sir Joseph Banks, Fellow of the Royal Society from 1767 and a member of the Dilettanti Society from 1774, went there in 1776. In 1776 Dashwood rented Round Tar Island, one of the aytes in the river between Marlow and Cookham, for the purpose of fishing, and was negotiating for another when he died. Revett was doing some building there in 1780–1.

If there was a Medmenham group, and not just a series of visitors to Medmenham, its composition is conjectural, and it hardly seems worth while to compile a list of the politicians, men of letters, 'Jacobites', architects, painters, and others, who have been most frequently alleged to belong to it.[2] John Dashwood-King, Dashwood's half-

---

[1] *History and Antiquities of the Hundred of Desborough*, p. 343.

[2] This is not cowardice, but a conclusion reached after careful examination of the lists which have been offered. There is of course nothing like a contemporary list, only the mention of one or two names, followed by 'and others', by Wilkes and Horace Walpole, and the supposed key to *Chrysal*.

brother, was in some way associated with the lease, and so probably also was Stapleton. He was Dashwood's second cousin, and his wife, Mary Fane, was the daughter of Henry Fane of Wormsley, descended from the Fanes of Fulbeck. It seems clear that Dashwood took his friends and guests from West Wycombe to Medmenham to admire the gardens and to fish or sail on the river. If there was, apart from this, anything so formalised as a club, or a society, there may well have been some kind of ceremonial, and even some trappings borrowed from the Dilettanti.[1] The portrait of Dashwood dressed as a friar, now in St. James's Club, the Dilettanti Society's present home, was painted for the Society by George Knapton, and as it was painted in 1742 and as nearly all the twenty-three members he painted were in some costume not their own, it can hardly provide evidence of what was worn at Medmenham.[2] The motto inscribed over the door, 'Fay ce que voudras', is taken from Rabelais. It is the only Rule of the Abbey of Thelème, the imaginary abbey on the river Loire which was organised on principles diametrically opposed to those of

Believers in the Medmenham myth would be surprised to find how few names are mentioned: not more than eight altogether, and of course there is no real justification for putting them together. Those who appear from Dashwood's own papers to have been in some way connected with Medmenham (usually by less exuberant phrases than Wilkes's 'hope to indemnify myself there for the noise and nonsense here') are fewer still: Dashwood-King, Stapleton, John Tucker. One should perhaps add John King, and Wilkes himself who, so far as the evidence goes, visited Medmenham once, on 21 June 1762, and mentioned his projected visit twice, to Churchill on 15 June and to Dashwood on 17 June (Add MSS. 30878, f. 1; Egerton MS. 2136, f. 49).

[1] C. Harcourt-Smith, *The Society of Dilettanti, 1732–1932, Its Regalia and Pictures* (1932), thinks 'some flavour of Medmenham is perhaps faintly traceable in the proceedings of the more respectable Society'. This is, of course, a *reductio ad absurdum*, not only by date, but also by the complete absence of information about Medmenham proceedings.

[2] Horace Walpole, who visited Medmenham in 1763, said the Medmenhamites had a costume 'more like a waterman's than a monk's' (*Journal of Visits to Country Seats* (Walpole Society, 1928), p. 51). This would be a very reasonable dress for sailing and fishing, but is hardly likely to have been their normal dress. Walpole remarked their 'handsome pleasure-boat': this was kept in order until Dashwood's death.

all existing monasteries. The phrase does not, of course, mean 'do as you wish' in any ordinary sense. It is an exhortation to honourable conduct, and consideration for others, not by enslavement to rules but by self-discipline. Men and women were to be admitted equally to Thelème. Each member was to regulate his life not by hours, bells, and rules, but by his own judgement and discretion, and all were to be free to leave if they wished. The taking of the Medmenham device from Rabelais would quite reasonably suggest that there was, in Dashwood, a disposition to mock monkishness, and a sympathy with the idea that true virtue consists in self-discipline rather than in obedience to rules: this is no more anti-religious than many religious reformers have been.

Thelème was a vast palace, a great deal more magnificent than the abbey-house at Medmenham. Nevertheless, they had certain physical features in common, and one of them was shared with Dunston Pillar. Thelème was built on the banks of the Loire, Medmenham on the banks of the Thames, and, to quote Urquhart's English translation of 1653, a copy of which was in Dashwood's library: 'By the river-side was the fair pleasure-garden, and in the midst of that the glorious labyrinth. [There were] courts for tennis and football . . . the orchard full of all fruit-trees . . . the great park . . . butts and marks for shooting . . . the stables . . . the falconry.'

If this explains Medmenham as well as the evidence allows, it does not explain the gossip about Medmenham. This is easier to explain, for the key lies in chronology. The germ from which the gossip grew was part of the campaign of Wilkes and Churchill against first Bute's and then Grenville's ministry. The entry of Charles Churchill into politics, in association with Wilkes, came in May 1762, and the first number of the *North Briton* was published a week after Bute's appointment as First Lord of the Treasury and Dashwood's as Chancellor of the Exchequer. Number 43, which appeared on 26 March 1763, was devoted to denouncing that 'hydra of Excise', the cider tax, and to railing at Dashwood's incompetency. The print 'Secrets of the Convent', attributed to Churchill, appeared in April, with Wilkes's advertisement of it. Churchill's *The Conference*, which attacked Paul Whitehead, was published in May, and Wilkes's reference to the 'English Eleusian Mysteries' of Medmenham appeared in the *Public Advertiser* in June. Meanwhile, Bute

9. Sir Francis Dashwood, 15th Baron Le Despencer, in 1776
Attributed to Nathaniel Dance

Compiler

Doctor Franklin is desired to add,
alter, or diminish as he shall think
proper, any thing herein contained
[illegible] is by no means tenacious.
for besides the differing sentiments
of persons and well disposed persons in
Speculative points who in general
have a good opinion of our Church,
with well to her interest.

He is a sincere lover of social Worship,
deeply sensible of its usefulness to
Society, and he aims at doing some
service to religion, by proposing such
abbreviations and omissions in the
forms of [crossed out] that Worship retaining
every thing he thinks essential
as might if adopted procure a more
general attendance.

The author of the following
abridgment of the Liturgy of the
Church of England, thinks it but
decent and respectful to all (more
particularly to the reverend body of
Clergy who adorn the protestant
Religion by their good works preaching
and example) that he should humbly
offer some reasons for such an undertaking, he addresses himself to the
serious and discerning, he professes
himself to be a Protestant of the Church
of England, and holds in the highest
veneration the doctrines of Jesus Christ.

It has often been observed and
complained of that the morning and
Evening service as practised in the
Churches of England and elsewhere
are so long and filled with so many
repetitions, that the attention
suitable to so serious a duty becomes impracticable
[crossed out lines]
[illegible] of devotion slackened.

Many pious and devout persons
whose age or infirmity will not
suffer them to remain for hours
in a cold Church, more especially in
Winter season; and therefore are
obliged to forego the comfort they would
receive by their attendance on divine
service if by shortening the time the
would be relieved.

10. First page of manuscript Preface to *Abridgement of Book of
Common Prayer* (1773)

and Dashwood had resigned in April, and Wilkes had been arrested
and discharged on grounds of parliamentary privilege in May. Wilkes
was expelled from the House of Commons in January 1764. In
May 1764 Churchill's *The Candidate* was published. It is this that
contains the most frequently quoted reference to Medmenham,
Dashwood, and the cider tax, with Wilkes's note, 'Description of
Medmenham Abbey'.

There is much crudity but nothing very elaborate about any of the
hints here put forward about orgies, black magic, and mock-religious
ceremonies. But in 1765 Charles Johnstone added two volumes to
his picaresque novel *Chrysal, or The Adventures of a Guinea*, first
published in 1760, and these included an elaborate and detailed
description of activities of this kind. They were ascribed to a society
established by 'a person of flighty imagination' on an island 'in the
middle of a large lake upon his estate', where he 'erected a building
on the mode of the monasteries which he had seen in other countries,
and to make the resemblance complete, there was not a vice imputed
to the inhabitants of them for practising which he did not make provision in his'. Even in topographical situation, of course, this does
not fit Medmenham, and Thomas Langley had every reason to doubt
whether the 'anecdotes related in a publication of that day' did in
fact refer to Medmenham. Nevertheless, most of the so-called information about the organisation of Medmenham, and about its
practices, derives from *Chrysal*.[1]

After this, it is a relief to find that Horace Walpole, who was not
likely to let slip a good opportunity of spreading malicious stories,
implicitly discredits the Medmenham gossip by exposing its provenance
and its purpose. He mentions Knapton's picture of Dashwood 'in
the habit of St. Francis', and says that

> of later years Saint Francis had instituted a more select order [than the
> Dilettanti Society]. He and some chosen friends had hired the ruins
> of Medmenham Abbey, near Marlow, and refitted it in a conventual
> style. . . . Whatever their doctrines were, their practice was rigorously
> pagan. . . . Yet their follies would have escaped the eye of the public,
> if Lord Bute from this seminary of piety and wisdom had not selected a

---

1 Which was said by its most recent (1907) editor, E. A. Baker, without
any trace of humour, to be 'the best or the only authority' on what happened
at Medmenham.

Chancellor of the Exchequer. But politics had no sooner infused themselves among these rosy anchorites, than dissensions were kindled, and a false brother arose, who divulged the arcana, and exposed the good Prior, in order to ridicule him as Minister of the Finances.[1]

[1] Walpole, *George III*, i. 137–8.

# 5

## *Without Doors*

## (2)

### THE ABRIDGEMENT OF THE BOOK OF COMMON PRAYER

DASHWOOD'S *Abridgement of the Book of Common Prayer* [1] was printed in 1773, on his own press at West Wycombe, and sold by Wilkie in St. Paul's Churchyard. The making of the *Abridgement* is sufficient evidence of an interest in theological questions; its date, a year after the Feathers' Petition and a year before Lindsey's Prayer Book, makes the interest more specific, and gives Dashwood a place among eighteenth-century Prayer Book reformers; the fact that Franklin assisted him carried the influence of the *Abridgement* to America in the 1780s, and the American revision of the Prayer Book in its turn was cited by English reformers in 1789 and 1790. The setting provided by this sequence of events is so clear that one can, with some confidence, reconstruct something of Dashwood's attitude to current theological controversies, even though no correspondence has survived to explain it. There are, of course, clues. Dashwood was interested in the theological books in Sir Richard Ellys's library, and Lady Ellys shared her first husband's outlook in religion, which was both Presbyterian and Unitarian; he was friendly with Robert Lowth, 'that ornament of the Tory University of Oxford', who thought it 'of the utmost importance to the cause of true religion, that it be submitted to an open and impartial examination',[2] and, in the year that the *Abridgement* was published, himself

---

1 *Abridgement of the Book of Common Prayer, and Administration of the Sacraments, and other Rites and Ceremonies of the Church, According to the Use of The Church of England: together with the Psalter, or Psalms of David, Pointed as they are to be sung or said in Churches.* 8vo. It appears in the list of new publications in the *Gentleman's Magazine* for Oct. 1773. The phrase 'printed for Wilkie', has misled some commentators: it means of course that it was not printed *by* Wilkie but sold by him.

2 Visitation sermon at Durham, 27 July 1758. *Sermons and other Remains* (ed. P. Hall, 1834), p. 83.

revised the Thirty-Nine Articles; he was friendly with Talbot, who named the belief that 'as religion is of the utmost importance to every man, no person ought to suffer civil hardships for his religious persuasion' as one of the principles of real Whiggism. More tangible, perhaps, is the fact that in September 1774 Dashwood went, with Franklin, to the opening of Theophilus Lindsey's Unitarian chapel, which became one of the meeting-places for a group of liberal reformers, not all Unitarians, which included Joseph Priestley, Richard Price, John Jebb, Thomas Hollis, Gilbert Wakefield, and the Dukes of Grafton and Richmond. Lindsey singled Dashwood out as one who not only attended but understood the financial difficulties which faced an independent chapel: he 'subscribed handsomely towards indemnifying us for the expense of the chapel &c.'.[1]

The publication of Archdeacon Blackburne's *Confessional*[2] in 1766 heralded a fresh series of demands for reform of the Liturgy. Blackburne did not deny that the time had come to review the Liturgy, but he believed that the greater evil was the requirement of subscription to the Articles. This he denounced as 'unwarrantable interference with those rights of private judgement which are manifestly secured to every individual by the scriptural terms of Christian liberty and thereby contradicting the original principles of the Protestant Reformation'.[3] He considered that no Church had a right to impose subscription to 'human creeds and confessions' as a test of orthodoxy,

---

[1] T. Belsham, *Memorial of Theophilus Lindsey* (1812), 112. Lindsey to Jebb, 18 Apr. 1774. The first service was held on 17 Sept., in a room which had been used for book auctions. In 1777, out of contributions, the property was bought and remodelled into a chapel, which was opened on 29 Mar. 1778 (H. McLachlan, *Letters of Theophilus Lindsey* (1920), pp. 23 ff.). Dashwood was apparently the only peer who attended the first service.

[2] *The Confessional: or, a Full and Free Enquiry into the Right, Edification and Success of Establishing Systematical Confessions of Faith and Doctrines in Protestant Churches.* Francis Blackburne (1705–87), educated at Cambridge; rector of Richmond, Yorks 1739–87; archdeacon of Cleveland, 1750; well known for his liberal political and ecclesiastical views; friend of Edmund Law, Wyvill, Jebb, Thomas Hollis; opposed Stamp Act, and provision of bishops for America; contributed to *A Collection of Letters and Essays in favour of Public Liberty* 1774; edited *Memoirs of Thomas Hollis*; not a Unitarian.     [3] p. 50 (1770 edn.).

and thought that reformers should concentrate on removing this 'stumbling-block'. Not all reformers agreed with his emphasis. To those who objected not so much to subscription in itself as to the thing then subscribed to, the first need was to revise the Articles of faith and the Book of Common Prayer. Richard Watson,[1] for example, would himself have welcomed 'a total abolition of all Articles of Religion', believing that subscription was useless, since 'an uniformity of opinion [is], in all doubtful points, unattainable; and, in all others, unavoidable', but realised that 'many good and sensible men among the clergy' did not share his view. He therefore urged a reform of the Articles and of the Liturgy, and especially the removal from it of the Athanasian Creed. His argument for its removal set the tone for the 'temperate reform' which he championed all his life. He agreed with those who asserted the 'incomprehensibility of the [Athanasian] doctrine' but this was not his reason for wishing to remove it from the Liturgy. For, he wrote, 'we know the distinct provinces of faith and reason; we know that God will never require us to believe anything that is *contrary* to reason; and we are ready to believe anything that is *above* our reason, if it can be shown to come from him: we do not object to the doctrine of the Trinity because it is above our reason, and we cannot comprehend it; but we object to it, because we cannot find that it is either literally contained in any passage of the Holy Writ, or can by sound criticism be deduced from it'.[2]

Differences of emphasis were reflected in differences of opinion about the way to achieve reform. Blackburne advocated an approach

---

[1] 1737–1816. Fellow of Trinity College, Cambridge, 1760; Professor of Chemistry 1764; D.D., Regius Professor of Divinity 1771; Archdeacon of Ely 1779–82; Bishop of Llandaff 1782; made several chemical discoveries; supported Jebb's plan for university reform; urged reform of Liturgy and reforms in Church organisation; advocated parliamentary reform; supported Dunning's resolution; supported county petitioning movement and drew up scheme of association for county of Cambridge 1780; long friendship with Grafton; defended Christianity against Gibbon (1776) and against Paine (1796).

[2] 'Considerations on the Expediency of revising the Liturgy', 1790, *Miscellaneous Tracts* (1815), ii. 107–8. The pamphlet gives not only reasons for reform but an informed account of attempts to secure it.

to parliament,[1] and under his guidance an association was formed in July 1771, at the Feathers Tavern, to consider a petition to parliament for relief from the requirement of subscription. The Petition[2] adopted by the association was written by Blackburne, and was presented to the House of Commons on 6 February 1772 by Sir William Meredith,[3] of Henbury, Cheshire, member for Liverpool. The petitioners asked that 'they may be restored to their undoubted rights as Protestants of interpreting Scripture for themselves without being bound by any human explanation thereof'. According to William Belsham, a fair judge and not altogether sympathetic to the petitioners, Meredith was supported by 'various other members of the highest merit, talents and reputation', who argued that 'the Articles of the Church were well known to have been compiled at a period when the nation had scarcely emerged from the chaos of Popery — that they were dark, scholastic, unintelligible, and in many parts contradictory — that the doctrines maintained in them had been long ago discarded from the Creed of all rational Christians, and that it was undeniable that very few of the clergy could subscribe them without such salvos as would scarcely be deemed admissible in any other case'.[4]

Prominent among those who supported the Petition in the Com-

[1] *Proposal for Application to Parliament, in the matter of Subscription to the Liturgy and the 39 Articles, 1771.* Francis Stone, rector of Cold Norton, Essex, a Unitarian who kept his living until 1808, had suggested a petition to parliament in *A Short and Seasonable Application to the Public*, by Tyro Theologicus (1768).

[2] The Petition, 'from certain clergy men of the Church of England, and certain members of the professions of civil law and physic, and some others, who prayed for relief from the subscription to the 39 articles of faith', had nearly 250 signatories, 200 of them being clergy. It is printed in the *Annual Register* (1772), pp. 171–3.

[3] c. 1725–90; M.P. Wigan 1754–61 and Liverpool 1761–80; in 1750s called 'Tory', or 'Jacobite'; opposed Stamp Act Feb. 1765; lord of Admiralty 1765–6 (when Horace Walpole called him a 'converted Jacobite'); Comptroller of the Household 1774–7; after about 1775 opposed the government on America and in 1778 moved for repeal of Declaratory Act. His ideas on religious toleration (like his ideas on the reform of the criminal code) clearly had no connection with his political alignments, which in any case were not strong.    [4] *Memoirs*, i. 311–12.

mons were three independents: Thomas Pitt, who seconded the motion, and 'had heard no argument against the petition that would not impeach the Reformation'; [1] Sir George Savile, who wished to 'lay aside subscription to the Articles, and adopt the Scriptures in their room . . . [for] adhering to the Scriptures in opposition to human inventions and corruptions is the first principle of Protestantism'; [2] and John Sawbridge, the advocate of annual parliaments. Its most vehement opponent was Burke. After a long debate the motion to receive the Petition was defeated by 217 to 71.

One of the bishops, Edmund Law [3] of Carlisle, attended the Feathers Tavern meetings and welcomed the Petition, but in general it seems that the petitioners lost some sympathy because they chose to apply for remedy to the House of Commons and not to the bishops. Grafton, who thought that the Liturgy should be revised regularly, at stated intervals, and said he would 'ever lament, that they were not successful in their application to Parliament', [4] nevertheless saw that this method of seeking redress invited hostility. Watson, who also regretted the petitioners' failure, thought that they were attacking the wrong problem and approaching the wrong authority. As the author of *A Letter to a Bishop* wrote

> that branch of the Legislature, to which it [the Petition] was addrest, was perhaps not the most proper, from whence such a design should originate. With respect to the Bishops, on the contrary, every circumstance of their station makes us look up to them, as the proper and only fit persons to suggest and conduct any reasonable alterations in our Ecclesiastical Establishment. [5]

Nevertheless, application to the bishops, though less spectacular, proved no more successful. Watson, reminding them that the bishops

[1] *Parl. Hist.* xvii. 294.　　　　　　[2] Ibid. 290.

[3] Edmund Law, 1703–87; Master of Peterhouse, Cambridge 1756–68; Professor of Moral Philosophy 1764; Bishop of Carlisle 1768; his works include *Considerations on the State of the World with regard to the Theory of Religion* (1745) and *Considerations of the Propriety of requiring Subscription to Articles of Faith* (1774); he greatly admired Locke and edited his *Works* in 1777.

[4] *Autobiography and Political Correspondence of Augustus Henry third Duke of Grafton* (ed. W. R. Anson, 1898), pp. 267–9.

[5] *A Letter to a Bishop, occasioned by the late Petition to Parliament, for Relief in the Matter of Subscription* (1772), p. 49.

had revised the Articles in Elizabeth's reign, urged them not to wait until they were pushed into reform, but to take the initiative. 'It has injuriously been taken for granted', he wrote, 'that no blessings could come from the Bench, no reformation from the Prelacy, no good out of Galilee.'[1]   After the Petition was rejected, Watson begged the bishops to understand that its rejection was a reason for their undertaking reform of the Liturgy, not evidence that reform was not wanted. 'The eyes of the Laity, and Clergy, of England, and of Europe, are fixed, with impatient speculation, upon the Bench of Bishops.'[2]   In the same year a group of clergy, led by Beilby Porteus, afterwards Bishop of London, urged Archbishop Cornwallis to consider promoting a 'review of the Liturgy and Articles, in order to amend . . . those parts which all reasonable persons agreed stood in need of amendment'.  And, in 1773, Lowth went so far as to revise the Articles himself and teduce them 'by discharging the offending parts'. Cornwallis was believed to be not unsympathetic, but in February 1773 he replied to Porteous that he had consulted his colleagues and the opinion of the 'Bench in general' was 'that nothing can in prudence be done in the matter',[3] while Lowth's initiative had no more success than that of the compilers of reformed prayer books: he 'had the mortification to see his amendment and reductions set aside'.[4]

These failures were followed not only by an attack on subscription in both universities but also by an attempt to extend the degree of toleration accorded to Dissenters. In Cambridge the attack was strong. It was led by John Jebb

a man of learning and talents, though they were both so absorbed in controversy as to leave little among his writings of general use . . . a warm friend to the cause of America against England, an incessant advocate for annual parliaments and universal suffrage (these per-

[1] 'Letter to members of the Honourable the House of Commons, respecting the Petition for Relief in the Matter of Subscription, by a Christian Whig', 1772. *Miscellaneous Tracts*, ii. 29–30.
[2] 'A Second Letter . . . relating to the Subscription required of graduates in the Universities, by a Christian Whig.' Ibid. 48.
[3] R. Hodgson, *Works of Beilby Porteus*, (1811), i. 38, 40.
[4] Grafton's *Autobiography*, p. 269.

nicious engines for destroying the British constitution), a writer in newspapers, and a speaker in public meetings.[1]

Watson supported the movement in his second Letter from a Christian Whig, and it was so far successful that on 23 June 1772 the university voted to replace the requirement of subscription for bachelors of arts by a declaration: 'I, *A. B.*, declare that I am *bona fide* a member of the Church of England as by law established.' In Oxford, which Watson pretended to suppose 'pants for the same freedom', a similar amendment was proposed in Convocation in February 1773, but easily defeated. Relief to Dissenters was more in danger than the Feathers Petition had been of becoming a government–opposition issue, but the danger was averted. On 3 April 1772 Sir Henry Hoghton introduced and Savile seconded a bill 'for the enlargement of the Toleration Act'. George III urged North 'to oppose it personally at every Stage, which will gain You the Applause of the Established Church and every real friend of the Constitution'.[2] North, less indifferent to the claims of the Dissenters, chose not to take this advice, and the bill passed the Commons easily, though with a very small vote, by 70 to 9. In the Lords Richmond tried, from the other side, to induce Rockingham to support the bill and so gain the gratitude of 'that weighty Body of men the Dissenters' for the Whig opposition. He too failed and the bill was defeated by 102 to 29. Hoghton's second attempt, a year later, had a similar fate: the Commons passed his bill on 17 March 1773 by 69 to 16; the Lords rejected the motion to commit it, on 2 April, by 65 to 26. Dashwood was one of the twenty-six.[3]

[1] Nichols, *Literary Anecdotes*, i. 571–2. Jebb (1739–88) taught mathematics and was a Fellow of Peterhouse until he married in 1764; his plan for university reform was supported by Law, Watson, and Paley; he published *Letters on the Subject of Subscription to the Liturgy* in 1770; in 1775 he resigned his ecclesiastical preferments and devoted himself first to 'the study of physick' (which enabled him to practise as a doctor in London) and then to radical politics; he was active in the Society for Constitutional Information, a friend of Major Cartwright, an advocate of legal reform and prison reform.

[2] *Correspondence* (ed. Fortescue), ii. 334–5. (2 Apr. 1772.)

[3] *Parl. Hist.* xvii. 766, 786, 790; Debrett, *History*, vi. 277. This one would expect. But the fact that the names of the 26 are recorded is (given

There followed an exodus from the Church of a handful of men who were no longer willing to accept Blackburne's position: criticism of the Liturgy and the Articles but refusal to leave the Church even after it had refused to consider reform.[1] The seceders, naturally enough, were men who had positive objections to the Liturgy as well as principled dislike of subscription. One of them was Theophilus Lindsey, staunch supporter of the Petition, who resigned his living at Catterick in November 1773 and journeyed to London.[2] In the following year, on 17 September, Lindsey opened the first Unitarian chapel in England, in Essex Street in the Strand. This was the ceremony that Dashwood attended. On the next day Lindsey introduced his revised Prayer Book. Although its title was *Book of Common Prayer Reformed according to the Plan of the late Dr. Samuel Clarke*, Lindsey had clearly already advanced beyond Clarke's semi-Arianism. 'The Liturgy now offered to the public', he wrote in his Preface, 'is the Liturgy of the Church of England, with the amendments of Dr. Clarke, and such further alterations as were judged necessary, to render it unexceptionable with respect to the OBJECT of religious worship.'[3]

Dashwood's revised Prayer Book, published nearly a year earlier, has, like Lindsey's, a Preface giving his reasons for making the revision. Here there is compensation for the lack of correspondence explaining Dashwood's attitude, for one can see this Preface in the

the vagaries of those who reported eighteenth-century debates) merely a piece of luck and does not enhance the importance of the occasion. The list is no more significant than, for example, that of 1772, which is not recorded.

[1] There were two later debates on the question of relief from subscription: on 23 Feb. 1773 Meredith's motion for a Committee of the Whole House to consider the question of subscription at the universities was defeated by 159 to 67 (*Parl. Hist.* xvii. 722; Debrett, *History*, vi. 450–2), and on 5 May 1774 his motion for a Committee to consider the question of subscription by clergy of the Church of England had so little support that 'he declined dividing the House' (*Parl. Hist.* xvii. 1325–7).

[2] 1723–1808. Educated at Cambridge; vicar of Piddleton 1756, Catterick 1763; supported cause of America, parliamentary reform, law reform, anti-slavery movement; married Blackburne's stepdaughter; works include *Apology* (1774); *A Sequel to the Apology* (1775); *Historical View of the Unitarian Doctrine from the Reformation to the Present Time* (1783).

[3] p. iii.

making. There is a manuscript draft of it, in Dashwood's hand-writing, in the Dashwood papers now deposited in the Bodleian Library,[1] and this particular draft is the one that Dashwood showed to Franklin when he went to stay at West Wycombe in August 1773. At the top of the left side of the first page Dashwood wrote: 'Doctor Franklyn is desired to add, alter, or diminish as he shall think proper anything herein contained. LLD is by no means tenacious.' Franklin made his suggestions in pencil. There are not many of them, and they are concerned not with substance, but with wording and punctuation. There is only one phrase which, on Franklin's suggestion, Dashwood omitted altogether: the description of the Old Testament as 'a Jewish book very curious, perhaps more fit for the perusal of the learned than suited to the capacitys of the general illiterate part of Mankind'. The omission does not, of course, alter Dashwood's argument, that the Old Testament does not 'teach the doctrine of Christ' and is better read privately than as the First Lesson in church. Franklin was the author of only two small parts of the Preface, the comments on the Psalms and on the Catechism, and he wrote these because he was responsible for this part of the *Abridgement*.

Clearly, then, Franklin's part in Dashwood's Prayer Book was small. But Franklin's presence at West Wycombe in the summer of 1773 had an important and unexpected repercussion. In 1783, after the end of the war with England, it was necessary for the Episcopalian Church in America to delete from the Book of Common Prayer references to king, parliament, and other English institutions. Some churches had already done this, on their own initiative, during the war. Ecclesiastical conventions, consisting of laymen as well as clergy, were held in various states in 1784 and 1785. It seems that there was a widespread desire that the work of revision should not be confined to those modifications which were necessary for political reasons. On 19 June 1785 the King's Chapel, the oldest episcopal church in Boston, produced a revised Prayer Book,[2] which it hoped

---

[1] Dashwood MSS. B 12/2, endorsed 'Some heads for a Preface'. See Appendix III. Apart from the Preface, there are drafts of the forms of service for Confirmation, Matrimony, Burial of the Dead, Thanksgiving after Childbirth.

[2] *Liturgy collected principally from the Book of Common Prayer, for the use of the first Episcopal Church in Boston* (Boston, 1785).

might win general approval, based on Lindsey's 1774 Liturgy. In September 1785 the first General Convention of Protestant Episcopal Churches met in Philadelphia. A subcommittee, under Bishop William Smith of Maryland, was charged with the task of proposing not only such modifications to the Liturgy 'as shall render it consistent with the American revolution', but also 'such alterations as it may be desirable for the Convention to recommend to the consideration of the Church here represented'. Smith's aims were clear. He believed that 'many of the greatest, wisest, and best Divines of our Church . . . and among the Laity a multitude more' had desired 'some alterations and improvements' in the Prayer Book, and that the 'greatest and most important alterations and amendments were proposed at the Revolution, that great æra of liberty, when in 1689 Commissioners were appointed. . . .[1] upon another great revolution, about a hundred years after the former, all these proposed alterations and amendments were in our hands. . . . It is our duty, as it hath been our great endeavour in all the alterations proposed, to make the consciences of those easy who believe in the true principles of Christianity in general, and who, could they but be made easy on certain points in no way essential to Christianity itself, would rather become worshippers, as well as labourers, in that part of Christ's vineyard, in which we profess to worship and to labour, than any other.'[2] The result of the committee's work was the Proposed Book. The Convention ordered it to be printed,[3] and used it at the service held at its final

[1] The Commission (10 bishops and 20 other clergy) appointed by William III on 13 Sept. 1689 to 'prepare such alterations of the Liturgy and canons, and such proposal for the reformation of ecclesiastical courts, and to consider such other matters as might most conduce to the good order, and edification, and unity of the Church of England, and to the reconciling as much as possible of all differences'. For some of its proposals see Edward Cardwell, *A History of Conferences and other proceedings connected with the revision of the Book of Common Prayer, from the year 1558 to the year 1960* (1840), pp. 411–55.

[2] Horace W. Smith, *Life and Correspondence of Rev. William Smith* (Philadelphia, 1880), ii. 134–9.

[3] *Book of Common Prayer as Proposed to the Use of the Protestant Episcopal Church* (Philadelphia, 1786). It was printed in England by Debrett in 1789 and again in Peter Hall, *Reliquiae Liturgiae* (Bath, 1847), vol. 5. W. McGarvey, *Liturgiae Americanae* (Philadelphia, 1895), prints both the Proposed Book and the Prayer Book adopted in 1789.

meeting on 7 October. The question of its ratification was left for a later Convention.

The Proposed Book incorporated most of the suggestions of the 1689 Commission for shortening the Liturgy and avoiding repetitions, and also introduced certain theological changes. The Athanasian and Nicene Creeds were omitted; the phrase 'he descended into hell' was left out of the Apostles' Creed. The book was not intended to be Unitarian, and the prayers were not altered so as to be addressed only to the Father. The Preface, describing the purpose of the revision, states that 'it is humbly conceived that the doctrines of the Church of England are preserved entire, as being judged perfectly agreeable to the Gospel'. This is exactly the sentiment of Dashwood's Preface. But there is a sharp contrast with the King's Chapel Liturgy, whose authors believed, with Lindsey, that the Book of Common Prayer was 'essentially erroneous with regard to the object of prayer'. Although the Preface to the King's Chapel Liturgy expressed the hope that it 'is such that no Christian, it is supposed, can take offence at, or find his conscience wounded in repeating. The Trinitarian, the Unitarian, the Calvinist, the Arminian will read nothing in it which can give him any reasonable umbrage', it was not acceptable to the other Episcopal Churches. The publication of the Proposed Book, which did not 'expunge all disputable doctrines', made this clear, and after 1786 the King's Chapel was gradually isolated. Nevertheless, by the time of the General Convention of 1789 it had begun to seem that the Proposed Book, too, might lead not to comprehension, but to schism. Disapproval of its changes, especially the omission of two creeds, had been expressed not only in England,[1] but also in America, and several states,

---

[1] Nevertheless, as William Knox pointed out, although the English bishops expressed the hope that certain omissions would be reinstated, their decision to consecrate the American bishops was made *before* this was done (*Observations upon the Liturgy. With a Proposal for its Reform, upon the Principles of Christianity as professed and taught by the Church of England. By a Layman of the Church of England, late an Under Secretary of State* (London, Debrett, 1789), pp. 41 ff.). Knox (1732–1810) was agent in Great Britain for Georgia and East Florida until dismissed in 1765 for his pamphlets defending the Stamp Act; 1770–82 Under-Secretary of State for American Affairs.

including Maryland, New Jersey, and Pennsylvania, had refused to accept it. 'For the sake of accommodation', therefore, and more specifically for the sake of the unity of the American Church, the Proposed Book was abandoned. But the Prayer Book adopted in its stead in 1789 was a compromise, not a return to the English Book. The phrase 'he descended into hell' was put back into the Apostles' Creed, but the Athanasian Creed was not restored, and the Nicene Creed, though restored, was made optional.

There is no doubt that the framers of the Proposed Book knew and paid attention to Dashwood's *Abridgement*. On 17 June 1785 Granville Sharp,[1] who had for the last ten years worked for the introduction of episcopacy into America, and who was anxious that the American revision of the Prayer Book should not be regarded in England as unorthodox, asked Franklin for information about the *Abridgement*.[2]

> I have been informed, that, several years ago, you revised the Liturgy of the Church of England, with a view, by some few altera-tions, to promote the more general use of it; but I have never been

[1] 1735–1813; grandson of Archbishop John Sharp; clerk in Ordnance Office from 1758 to 1777 when he resigned because he disapproved of the government's policy towards America; his efforts at reconciliation were sup-ported by Richmond but not by Chatham who 'insisted on the sovereignty of England'; advocate of annual parliaments and parliamentary reform; prominent in movement for abolition of slavery. His publications include *Declaration of the People's Natural Rights to a Share in the Legislature*, 1774 (enlarged in 1775 and '*against the Attempts to tax America*' added to title; *Declaration of the People's Right to Annual Parliaments*, 1780. His *Plan to Reform the Representation of Great Britain* and *The Claims of the People of England* are printed in Oldfield, *History of the Boroughs*, i, pp. 162–98.

[2] Prince Hoare, *Memoirs of Granville Sharp, composed from his own Manuscripts* (1820), pp. 216–18. Franklin sent Granville Sharp a copy of the *Proposed Book* on 30 May 1786. 'You will be happy to hear', he wrote to his brother Dr. John Sharp on 15 July, 'that it is perfectly orthodox, and that "most of the amendments, or alterations, which had the sanction of the great divines of 1689, have been adopted". And they profess in the Preface — "It is far from the intention of this church to depart from the Church of England, any farther than local circumstances require; or to deviate in any thing essential to the true meaning of the Thirty nine Articles"' (ibid., pp. 228–9). It was lucky, perhaps, that Sharp's grandfather had been a member of the 1689 Commission.

able to see a Copy of the form you proposed. Our present public Service is certainly, upon the whole, much too long, as it is commonly used; so that a prudent revision of it, by the common consent of the Members of the Episcopal Church in America, might be very advantageous; though, for my own part, I conceive that the addition of one single rubric from the Gospel, would be amply sufficient to direct the revisers to the only corrections that seem to be necessary at present — I mean a general rule, illustrated by proper examples, references, and marks, to warn the officiating Ministers how they may avoid all useless repetitions and tautology in reading the service. . . . Such a prudent abridgement of the service, if it were done by common consent, to preserve order and uniformity, would afford great relief to the clergy, as well as to their congregations; and both would be better enabled to fix their attention to their duty during the service; because the human mind is not easily restrained for any long time together from wandering, or absence of thought; so that nothing can be more pernicious to devotion than *long prayers* and *needless repetitions*. This opinion is sufficiently justified by an injunction of our Lord himself respecting prayer; which, therefore, I purpose as the *one additional rubric* necessary to direct us in the use of our Liturgy viz. '*when ye pray, use not vain repetitions, as the heathens do; for they think they shall be saved for their much speaking*: be ye not, therefore, like unto them'.

The repetitions, and consequent unnecessary length, of our Church Service, are faults, however, which '*have crept in unawares*', and without design, by an inconsiderate use of several offices in immediate succession which seem to have originally intended for separate times of assembling. But in every other respect, the Liturgy of the Church of England is an excellent form.

Sharp's letter is interesting not only for his request, but also because his reason for advocating a 'prudent revision' of the Book of Common Prayer is very similar to one of Dashwood's, and expressed similarly: the harm caused by needless repetition and long prayers. Franklin's reply is interesting because it contains a precise statement of his contribution to the *Abridgement*. 'The Liturgy you mention', he wrote,

was an abridgment of the Prayers, made by a Noble Lord of my acquaintance, who requested me to help him by taking the rest of the Book, viz. the Catechism, and the reading and singing Psalms. These I abridged, by retaining of the Catechism only the two questions, *What is your duty to God? What is your duty to your neighbour?* with their answers. The Psalms were much contracted, by leaving out the repetitions (of which I found more than I could have imagined), and the imprecations, which appeared not to suit well the Christian doctrine of forgiveness of injuries, and doing good to enemies. The book was printed for Wilkie, in Paul's Churchyard, but never much noticed. Some were given away, very few sold, and I suppose the bulk became waste paper. In the prayers, so much was retrenched, that approbation could hardly be expected; but I think with you, a moderate abridgement might not only be useful, but generally acceptable.[1]

Perhaps Granville Sharp procured a copy of the *Abridgement* and sent it to Philadelphia. In any case, Franklin instructed his daughter, Mrs. Sarah Bache, to give a copy to Bishop William White, president of the Convention, and White and Smith both referred, in correspondence, to 'Franklin's Book'.

The Proposed Book played its part in the last flickering expression of a wish for reform in England. It was printed in England in 1789, at the instance of William Knox, just as it was on the point of being modified in America. In his *Observations on the Liturgy*, published in the same year, Knox argued, perhaps ingenuously, that the 'Consecration of Bishops to preside over and superintend the American Church in the use of it [the revised Book of Common Prayer]' was tantamount to its acceptance 'by the whole Illustrious bench of Bishops' as orthodox. He urged the adoption of the American reforms in England and believed this 'would do much towards the

---

[1] *Works of Benjamin Franklin* (ed. J. Sparks, 1840), x. 206–7 (5 July 1785). Franklin evidently did not think his part in the Preface important enough to mention. But Sparks thought otherwise, and, because his statement has been accepted, the Preface has been regarded ever since as evidence of Franklin's religious ideas. 'The *Preface*', Sparks wrote, 'is wholly from the pen of Dr. Franklin, and is evidently a studied composition. It is interesting and curious, as exhibiting his views, more fully than they are anywhere else to be found, on the subject of public worship, and the best forms to be adopted in conducting it.' After this comment Sparks prints the Preface (ibid., pp. 209–12). A. H. Smyth also prints the Preface, with a note '"the preface" exists in MS in an incomplete draft in A.P.S. [American Philosophical Society]. The part found in the draft is enclosed here in brackets.' (*Writings*, vi. 165, 168–70.) The manuscript — a very small part of the Preface — is A.P.S., Franklin papers, 50(2), 6. See Appendix III (*a*).

easing of tender consciences among us'.[1]  Watson returned to the charge in 1790, quoting Knox and using the American revision as evidence of the practicability of reform, and pointing out that although the Proposed Book had not been ratified, the Prayer Book which had been adopted instead was much closer to the Proposed Book than to the English Book of Common Prayer.

Dashwood's Prayer Book came into prominence again in America in the latter part of the nineteenth century, though it was of course not given that title.  In 1896 there was sold in Boston 'a rare old volume known as Franklin's Prayer-Book'.  This was the copy of the *Abridgement* which Franklin's daughter gave to Bishop White in 1785.  In 1897 there appeared in the *Pennsylvania Magazine of History and Biography* an article by R. M. Bache entitled 'The so-called Franklin Prayer Book'.  The purpose of the article was to prove Franklin's authorship of the Preface and to show its importance as evidence of his religious ideas.  Much of Bache's argument about authorship is easy to criticise.  On the title-page of one of the few surviving copies of the *Abridgement*, owned in 1855 by Bishop Stevens of Philadelphia, there is a manuscript note:

> This abridgement, together with the preface, was drawn up by Sir Francis Dashwood, Bart., Baron Le Dispencer, and given by him to Lord Mount Stuart[2] in 1775.  The book was printed in a private press of his own at West Wycombe, Bucks.

Bache quotes this note, but gives it less weight than a statement made in 1859 by Dr. T. H. Bache, Franklin's great grandson, 'I have heard that Mr Sparks first found the MS of the Preface in Franklin's handwriting.'[3]  Franklin's own description of his contribution to the

---

[1] *Observations upon the Liturgy*, pp. 41, 42.  Knox confessed (pp. 42–47) that he thought the Proposed Book could be improved: in particular, prayer should be directed 'to the Father alone'.

[2] John Stuart (1744–1814), eldest son of Bute; M.P. Bossiney 1766–76; member of Dilettanti Society 1766; first Baron Cardiff 1776; fourth Earl of Bute 1792; first Marquess of Bute 1796.

[3] This must be compared with Spark's editorial statement 'A large part of it [i.e. the Preface] is extant in Dr. Franklin's handwriting' (*Works*, x. 207) and with his private statement in 1837, that he had found a fragment of the Preface 'in Franklin's handwriting' (Bache, *Pennsylvania Magazine*, p. 225).  It seems that the 'fragment' was twice magnified, first by Sparks

*Abridgement* is not quoted. Nevertheless, it is perhaps unfair to confront Bache with straightforward criticism of this kind, for he rests his main argument for Franklin's authorship of the Preface not on facts, but on its style, and on its conformity with Franklin's general outlook and ideas. Paradoxically, this argument makes Bache's conclusion more interesting than it would be if he were right about the authorship of the Preface, for his conclusion is in fact, what it is far from being in intention, some sort of testimony to the similarity between Franklin's outlook and Dashwood's. Bache finds the Preface

> so Franklinian that no person familiar with the turn of thought and phrase of Franklin, than which no other style was ever more informed from outmost to inmost core with personality, can doubt the authorship of it in its entirety. Comparison of it with any of his writings touching ethical matter will prove that in it the family likeness is unmistakable. Part of it being found in his handwriting by Mr Sparks is, in the existing case of collaboration, only proof presumptive that he was its author, but the man revealed in the style is proof positive of the fact.

The Preface continues to be regarded as a valuable source for Franklin's religious ideas. J. M. Stifler, author of *The Religion of Benjamin Franklin*, published in 1925, regrets the paucity of evidence for Franklin's views on church organisation and public worship and finds the Preface 'especially interesting because of his frank expression of his attitude to the details of public worship'.[1] This view, like Bache's, is interesting because of the importance it accords to the Preface, which is printed as an Appendix to Stifler's book. Van Doren, who laughs at the friendship of Franklin 'the philosopher' and Dashwood 'the rake', takes the *Abridgement* less seriously, but has no doubt that Franklin wrote the Preface. He describes the *Abridgement* as having 'a preface by Franklin, who economically

himself and then by T. H. Bache, and that it is Smyth's 'incomplete draft'. If there had been two drafts — the 'fragment' and another — Sparks would surely have said so. In any case, the existence of a longer draft in Franklin's handwriting would not be, as Bache claims, 'proof presumptive' of Franklin's authorship.

[1] p. 69. Stifler does not mention either the 1785 Convention or the Proposed Book.

suggested that shorter services would save the time of both congregations and ministers'.[1] L. C. Jones finds the whole affair puzzling:

> These two men [he says] would seem the least likely in England to have set about a sincere effort to reform the ritual of the Church, yet they appear to have busied themselves with a revision of the *Book of Common Prayer* . . . their deism was of the same shade, and they had little difficulty in agreeing on what should be eliminated — for brevity was their watchword.[2]

In England Dashwood's *Abridgement* has fared differently but not more happily. Although its setting was England, not America, and although it was written at a time of controversy over the content of the Prayer Book and over the Articles, no one seems to have taken the straightforward view that a man who revised the Prayer Book at such a time was likely to be seriously interested in that controversy. The reason is, in part, the reverse of the reason for the attention paid to the *Abridgement*, and especially the Preface, in America. American historians have searched enthusiastically and assiduously for evidence of Franklin's religious ideas, English historians have not searched for evidence of Dashwood's. There are semi-facetious references[3] to the *Abridgement*, rather like those of L. C. Jones, but there are no serious ones, like those of Bache and Stifler, and no reference to current controversies. Thus, for example, the *Abridgement* is not mentioned by writers on the eighteenth-century Church, and is not included in the list of eighteenth-century revised Prayer Books compiled by Elliot Peaston.[4]

[1] *Benjamin Franklin* (New York, 1952), p. 438.

[2] *The Clubs of the Georgian Rakes* (Columbia University Press, 1942), p. 110. Jones does not mention the Preface, even to attribute it to Franklin. The authority he quotes for his statement is Van Doren.

[3] See, for example, R. Fuller's statement that Dashwood 'amused his leisure hours by an abridgment of the *Book of Common Prayer*, which he had printed for very private circulation in 1773' (*Hell Fire Francis* (1938), p. 240). The footnote states that Dashwood asked Franklin 'to assist him in his pious labours', and that the abridgement 'became the basis for the official Book of Common Prayer' in America. This is incongruous as well as inaccurate: mere common sense would suggest that the basis for anything so serious was serious itself.

[4] A. Elliot Peaston, *The Prayer Book Reform Movement in the XVIIIth Century* (Blackwell, 1940).

It deserves to be included. It could indeed be compared with William Hopkins's Liturgy[1] of 1763, and considered as one of the Prayer Books composed in response to the plea made by John Jones in 1750, that if Convocation did not revise the Liturgy, 'private persons . . . [should] humbly propose what they think proper . . . and even publish what they have drawn up, if they shall have just reason to believe it may be of Service to the Public'.[2] But the *Abridgement* is more than this, for it is clearly related to the renewed subscription controversy after 1766. Like most of the eighteenth-century revisions, the *Abridgement* introduced both utilitarian and theological changes. Among the utilitarian changes were the deletion of unnecessary repetitions, for example of the Lord's Prayer and the *Gloria Patri*, the merging of the three services read consecutively on Sunday into one service, the shortening of some prayers, the revision of the Lessons. Some of these changes had been urged by the Ecclesiastical Commission of 1689 and by Jones. Dashwood's theological changes were omissions, not innovations. The chief problem, of course, was the creeds and the doctrine of the Trinity. It was perfectly possible, as Watson said, to reject the Athanasian version of the Trinity without rejecting the idea of the Trinity itself. The 1689 Commission had considered taking the Athanasian Creed out of the Liturgy, but in the end had decided to leave it, 'lest the

[1] *The Liturgy of the Church of England, in its ordinary Service, Reduced nearer to the Standard of the Scripture. To which are prefixed, Reasons for the Proposed Alterations. Revised and published by the Author of the Appeal to the Common Sense of all Christian People, &c. and the Defence of it, or the Trinitarian Controversy reviewed* (London, 1763). Hopkins was vicar of Bolney, Sussex. His Preface begins with the fictitious statement that the Liturgy which follows 'was put into my hands in order to get it published to the world'. *An Appeal to the Common sense of all Christian people, more particularly the members of the Church of England, with regard to an important point of faith and practice imposed upon their consciences by Church authority* was published in 1754, *The Trinitarian Controversy* in 1760.

[2] *Free and Candid Disquisitions relating to the Church of England, and the means of advancing religion therein*, 2nd ed., 1750, p. 61. The note containing this passage is not in the 1st (1749) edition. Peaston notes ten liturgies published between 1749 and 1768; of these six refer to the Disquisitions. Four of the six were produced by Anglicans (op. cit., p. 6 and 'Chart of Liturgies').

wholly rejecting it should by unreasonable persons be imputed to them as Socinianism', and to recommend instead a rubric stating that the Creed's curses were intended only 'against those who deny the substance of the Christian religion in general'.[1]  Jones objected to the Athanasian Creed as not readily intelligible and therefore not 'truly useful and edifying to a congregation'; Hopkins objected to it as 'a gross corruption of Christian faith'. 'It may be observed of the truly learned and judicious Athanasian writers,' Hopkins wrote in the Preface to his Liturgy, 'that they generally evade entering into a particular discussion of worshipping the Holy Spirit in prayer, praise, or glory: and as for the gross worship of three persons and one God, it seems to be absolutely given up in point of argument, as they never make the least attempt to prove it from Scripture.'  Hopkins thought the main recommendation of his Liturgy was that 'so great a proportion of its devotional parts is directed to the One God and Father of all, in the name and thro' the mediation of Jesus Christ, this being an essential part of Christian worship, settled and determined by the divine appointment of Christ and his apostles'.  He omitted not only the Athanasian but also the Nicene Creed, because 'it contains some articles, expressed in obscure terms, not warranted by Scripture'.  In any case, quite apart from objections to these two creeds, Hopkins thought it desirable that the Church should have a single creed or statement of faith.  He retained the Apostles' Creed 'as being a plain summary of articles in which the whole Christian World are uniformly agreed'.  The only change he made in it was to omit, as most of the reformers did, the phrase '*He descended into hell*, as being misunderstood by the vulgar and illiterate'.  Dashwood, like Hopkins, left out the Athanasian and Nicene Creeds, and for similar reasons. The Apostles' Creed he very much shortened.  His version was: 'I believe in God the Father Almighty, Maker of Heaven and Earth: And in Jesus Christ his Son, our Lord. I believe in the Holy Ghost; the Forgiveness of Sins; and the Life everlasting. Amen.' This is neither Unitarian nor deistic.  Watson and Lowth would not have been the only ones to have agreed with Dashwood that it contained the 'more intelligible and more essential parts' of the Creed, and that it constituted a sufficient statement of Protestant belief.

[1] Cardwell, op. cit., p. 429.  Watson, quoting this phrase, underlines 'unreasonable' ('Considerations on the Expediency', *Misc. Tracts*, ii. 87).

The fundamental difference between Lindsey's Book of Common Prayer and Hopkins's Liturgy is one of purpose. Hopkins's aim was comprehension: he hoped that a liturgy reformed so as to exclude non-scriptural doctrines might be acceptable to some of the Dissenters. Lindsey had no such hope: his liturgy was Unitarian, not merely non-Athanasian, and intended 'to be made use of by a Society of like-minded Christians'.[1] He retained the Apostles' Creed, omitting 'holy Catholic Church' and 'communion of saints' on the grounds that they are of 'so low a date, and also obscure and of indeterminate meaning', omitting 'descended into hell', and replacing 'Holy Ghost' by 'Holy Spirit'. Most important, in the sentence 'I believe in God the Father Almighty' he inserted a comma after 'God', as Samuel Clarke had done, 'to denote that there is but *one God*, the Father'.[2] Dashwood shortened the Apostles' Creed more than Lindsey did, but his purpose was nearer to Hopkins than to Lindsey. He might doubt, as Hopkins did, the intelligibility of the Athanasian Trinity, and find no authority for it in Scripture, and, he might, with Watson, think the Trinity not one of the essentials of Christian belief, but he made no step towards Unitarianism. The omissions in Dashwood's *Abridgement* were made for the sake of intelligibility and shortening the service, not for the sake of positive dogma. He 'omitted but did not reject', as Bishop West said of the framers of the Proposed Book. He justified the removal of repetitions by reference to the New Testament: 'Our Lord gave us a short prayer as an example, and Censured the Heathen for thinking to be heard because of their much Speaking'. Hopkins made the same reference,[3] for the same purpose, and so did Granville Sharp in 1785. More important, Lowth did so in 1777, as proof that 'Christ is well pleased that our words be few'.[4]

Dashwood's statement of his own position was simple: 'He addresses himself to the serious and discerning. He professes himself to be a Protestant of the Church of England, and holds in the highest veneration the doctrines of Jesus Christ.' This is not unlike Hopkins's appeal to Protestants and 'rational Christians', and it is very like Watson's undogmatic Christianity.

---

[1] *Book of Common Prayer Reformed according to the Plan of the late Dr. Samuel Clarke* (London, 1774), p. v.     [2] Ibid., p. 18.
[3] *Liturgy*, pp. vii–viii.     [4] *Sermons and other Remains*, pp. 340–1.

Dashwood's *Abridgement*, in fact, though contemporary with Lindsey's Prayer Book is very different in purpose. Dashwood aimed at clarity, intelligibility, and conciseness, the elimination of statements not explicitly based on Scripture, and also, as Hopkins did, the excision of all remnants of Catholicism. His objection to the Athanasian Creed was Watson's not Lindsey's. He believed, as Watson and Lowth did, that the Liturgy rested on human not divine authority, and that it needed revision. Like Lowth before 1773, and Watson all his life, Dashwood thought that the bishops should undertake this; until they did, he hoped the *Abridgement* might be found useful. Dashwood's intention was to produce a Prayer Book more suitable than the existing Book of Common Prayer was for use in a Protestant Church of England. His definition of Protestantism perhaps resembles Watson's rather than Hopkins's or Blackburne's, standing not simply for anti-Catholicism but positively for liberty of conscience, toleration, reason, and common sense. Although one would not look for suggestions for practical church reform in a revised Prayer Book, it is characteristic of Dashwood that he should have made one. 'In regard to the inferior clergy', he wrote at the end of his Preface, 'it is indeed to be wished, that they were more equally provided for than by that odious and vexatious as well as unjust method of gathering Tithes in kind: which creates animosity and litigations, to the interruption of good harmony and respect which might otherwise exist between the Rectors and their parishioners.' It is not inappropriate to put this side by side with Watson's abortive attempt in 1782 to persuade Shelburne to undertake certain reforms in the organisation of the Church, including equalising the incomes and increasing the stipends of the inferior clergy, so that it should be possible to insist on the requirement of residence.[1]

[1] *Anecdotes of the Life of Richard Watson, Bishop of Llandaff, written by himself at different intervals and revised in 1814* (published by his son, 1817), pp. 96–102, 114–15.

# THE 1747 ADDRESS

[THERE are three drafts of this pamphlet in the Dashwood papers in the Bodleian Library (B 7/2). One is dated 9 June 1747; another gives the name of the bookseller, E. Amey, at Charing-Cross. Amey, who was not one of the well-known booksellers, also sold in 1747, *An Address to the Electors of Great Britain. In which the Constitution of England is considered and asserted; particularly the original Design, Nature, Privileges and Power of the House of Commons, as opposed to Ministerial Influence and Corruption. And the Independency of Parliaments earnestly recommended — By an Independent Elector.* There is a copy of both pamphlets in the British Museum.]

AN

ADDRESS

TO THE

GENTLEMEN, CLERGY, AND FREEHOLDERS

OF ALL THE

COUNTIES IN GREAT BRITAIN,

AND TO THE

MAYORS, JURATS, BAILIFFS, ALDERMEN, COMMON COUNCILMEN, and Burgesses of all the Cities, Towns-Corporate, and Boroughs throughout the said Kingdom of GREAT BRITAIN.

The following necessary and friendly Advice is humbly offered, by a CORDIAL ADMIRER of Truth and Liberty, and a Zealous Friend to this CONSTITUTION.

Gentlemen, Friends, and Countrymen,

SURE it requires very little Argument to convince Man of common Sense, that in this Country they have a constitutional, as well as a natural Right to be free. By Freedom, is not nor can be meant, that every Individual should act as he lists, and according as he is swayed by his own Passions, Vices, or Infirmities; but Freedom is a Right every Man has to do what he will with his own, conformable to Law; is a Right every Man has to be judged impartially by his Equals, and to have his Property secured to him and his Posterity. If Freedom therefore is thus founded in Justice, and justifiable by Reason and sound Sense, the Support and Preservation of it is certainly a Consideration of the highest Importance, when you come to reflect on the great Duty you owe to yourselves, to Posterity, and to Millions of your Fellow Subjects.

The Blessings that are derived from a well constituted Liberty, cannot possibly be continued to you and yours, if once the Majority of this Nation should become profligate and abandoned, devoid of all Sense of Honour, or Sense of Shame; when once each Particular shall consult only his own immediate paltry Convenience, then the Frame, the Spirit, the Beauty of this Constitution must moulder, wither, and decay, and all its Harmony be lost.

It is therefore equally honest and necessary to offer you this friendly Admonition, which the approaching Dissolution of this Parliament renders yet more seasonable, lest an over-late Conviction of the Indignities endured by a brave and free People from the Cabals of designing Ministers, and the Treachery of pretended Patriots, should leave you under the dreadful Dilemma of chusing either a tame Submission to tyrannical Power, or a fatal Struggle for the Preservation of your Liberty.

Then sure, you will (my Countrymen) as it is your Duty, give your honest Assistance to save your Country, by a sober, prudent Choice of your Representatives. If a violent and extraordinary ministerial Measure should be taken to dissolve the present Parliament, you will have once more (and perhaps but once) an Opportunity of declaring in a lawful Manner, whether you will or will not be free; and if you should be so unfortunate as to mis-judge in the Choice of your Representatives, (notwithstanding the Precaution, which I shall hereafter point out to you) and many of them (like Villains) should barter away your Liberties to gratify their Insolence or Revenge, their Avarice or Ambition; nevertheless I affirm, that those Electors, who shall act on the Principles of Liberty, though mistaken in their Choice, will have some Degree of Self-consolation, when they reflect, that the cruel Treason does not lie at their Doors.

The Dissolving of a Parliament, is always acknowledged and understood to be a violent Measure, merely Ministerial, and cannot be National, and bespeaks some extraordinary political Jobb to be put in Execution, that will not bear the Light, and must mean to declare, that it is not safe to suffer the Elections to take Place after the Secret is out. I will state to you a few Points, that, since the Commencement of the War, this Nation is further indebted upwards of Twenty Millions, and has spent upwards of forty-two, that we have exported out of this trading Country, upwards of twelve Millions to support a most impracticable, unsuccessful, expensive War on the Continent, and have lost above fourscore Thousand Men by Land and Sea. It is known by all, that the Marine is our natural Strength, which lately Admiral *Anson* and *Warren's* Conduct and Success evidently prove, but we have (nay we must have) neglected this national favourite Point, for the Sake of another favourite Point, the Land War. So that we have lost upwards of thirteen Hundred Ships, taken by the Enemy, together with *Madras*, our principal Settlement in the *East Indies*: And turn your *Eyes* upon the Continent, and you will find the *French* in possession of all *Flanders*.

A late memorable ungrateful Resignation of Employments, or rather Desertion of his Majesty's Service by a powerful Faction, in the midst of the late horrid Rebellion, grown formidable merely by a Series of Misconduct, supported by Expedients with as much false Ability as Want of Oeconomy; I say such an Outrage against the Honour, the Dignity, the known Prerogative of the Crown, just at that Juncture when the Constitution of *Great Britain* was reduced to so nice, so tremendous a Crisis, plainly demonstrates to what immoderate Lengths the Ungrateful and Ungenerous will run, when spur'd on by Pride, Revenge, Avarice, and Ambition. If such Men should find it impossible to continue a Continent War upon so unequal, so impracticable a Plan as the present, they may be induced, from the above righteous Motives, to consent to an infamous, dishonourable and scandalous Peace, such as may render it necessary to have an immediate new Courtly Parliament, to save their Heads who made it at least for Seven Years.

Suppose then the Parliament dissolved. You now only are permitted to chuse your Representatives once in Seven Years; but remember you once had a Right to judge of the Behaviour of your Representatives every three Years. That Parliament which you or your Fathers chose to represent the Commons of *Great Britain* for three Years only, assumed a Power not delegated to them by the Commons, to continue themselves for seven. Sure this ought to have alarmed the People, for it was an Act that Parliament could not, in common Justice and common Sense, have a Right to pass, particularly in regard to themselves; but, to Astonishment, so supine and careless, so little jealous have you been ever since, of that great Branch of your Liberty's being torn from you; I say, it is my Astonishment, that every County, City, Borough, and Town-corporate, have not, one and all, obliged those they chose to represent them in Parliament, solemnly to declare under their Hands and Seals, that they would grant no Supplies, or Aids of Money to the Crown whatever, let the Exigencies of Affairs be ever so great, unless that unjust, odious, destructive Act was previously repealed, which entitles Members to sit for seven Years in Parliament; and an Annual Parliament or a Triennial one established in its room. You have a Right to elect, it is true, but sure no Man pretends a Right to be elected;

Have not you a Right therefore to make Terms on behalf of your-selves and the Nation, with those you constitute and appoint to re-present you? Suppose (and it is with deep Concern I mention it) that some may be so wicked and profligate, even to Perjury, as to take Bribes from Candidates or their Agents for their Votes; one would wonder that even such Miscreants should be such senseless Fools, as not to have some Security for restoring to the Nation its declared constitutional Right of choosing Representatives frequently, and to the Constitution its Right of being defended by a well ordered and numer-ous Militia, which is the only safe internal Defence of this Country, and abolish in time of Peace that ante-constitutional Tool of Power, a Standing Army. Should you not likewise insist with your Repre-sentatives, that they should, previous to granting of Money, procure a more extensive Place Bill, at least to exclude all Officers of the Army under the Degree of Colonels of Regiments, from sitting in the House of Commons, and likewise all Sea-Officers under the Degree of Rear-Admiral? Will you not, in Justice to yourselves, in Compassion to your Country, as Lovers of Liberty, and as honest reasonable Men, insist with all those without Distinction, who offer you their Services to represent you in Parliament, that they shall (previous to their Elec-tions) sign and seal Duplicates, wherein they shall declare solemnly, that they will not adhere to, support, or put Confidence in, any Ad-ministration whatever, nor grant any Aids of Money to the Crown, until those just Rights and Demands of the People are procured, by the three abovementioned Acts of Parliament being obtained; namely, the Repeal of the Septennial Bill, which enables Men to represent the Commons of *Great Britain* for the unreasonable Term of Seven Years. An Act to constitute an effectual and numerous Militia throughout the Kingdom, and a further Place-Bill, at least to exclude Officers, as abovementioned.

Give me Leave to add, if you let slip this Opportunity, in all human Probability, this Nation will be certainly undone. We are all in the same Ship, we must all sink together. Think of the extravagant In-fluence an unconstitutional Number of Placemen sitting in the House of Commons may have, if directed by a dissolute, immoral, luxurious Ministry. Reflect on the Constitutional Right you have to defend yourselves by a Militia; and seriously ponder on the vexatious Influence, the monstrous Expence, the Idleness, the Debaucheries of a Standing Army in Time of Peace; and think with Horror that in seven Years Time a corrupt Set of Men may give up your Liberties for ever.

I have thus, in the Fulness of my Heart, ventured to address you. This Paper favours not of Faction, nor is it a Party Libel; but speaks melancholly alarming Truths. Insist (as you have an undoubted Right) on something like the following Declaration, to be signed and sealed by all your Representatives, or you will be bought, you will be sold, you will be undone. Let the Success of these my honest Endeavours prove as it will, I have done my Duty; and you cannot say, (my Countrymen) hereafter, that you had no Warning; now shew your Zeal for Liberty, exert your publick Spirit, give Proofs that you deserve to be free. Farewel.

## A
## DECLARATION

Which all honest Men will not refuse to sign, if required, and what all prudent Men will require to be signed by those who offer themselves as Candidates to serve in Parliament.

I A. B. who now offer myself as a Candidate to be elected to serve in Parliament for          do solemnly and cordially declare, upon my Honour and Conscience, that if I am chosen a Member to represent the          of          I will never adhere to, support, or put Confidence in any Administration, until an Act is obtained to repeal that Act which entitles every Member of the House of Commons to sit for seven Years in Parliament, and to constitute in its Room an Annual or a Triennial Parliament; a second Bill to establish a numerous and effectual Militia throughout the Kingdom, for the natural Security and Peace of these Realms; and a third, by which a greater Number of those who hold Places under the Government shall be rendered incapable of sitting in Parliament, than are at present excluded by any Laws now in Force. And I further protest and declare, that I will not give my Consent to, but strenuously oppose the passing of any Bills, that shall grant Aids of Money to the Crown, until these three abovementioned Bills are obtained and passed into Laws. And I declare by these Presents under my Hand and Seal, that I accept of my Seat in Parliament upon these Terms; and that I understand this to be the Intention of my Constituents; and if I do not persevere in endeavouring to obtain to my utmost the three above-mentioned National Bills, I voluntarily acknowledge, in this publick Manner, that I shall justly be deemed by all Mankind false to my Constituents, and a Traytor to my Country.

Signed and Sealed, &c.

FINIS

# STANHOPE'S DECLARATION, 1751

[T H I S Declaration was apparently drawn up in response to Dodington's attempts to form a united opposition. Dashwood wrote, at the top, 'This Declaration was composed by Earl Stanhope in April 1751', and endorsed it 'Declaration April 1751, not approved by Torys'. The Tories may well have disliked its philosophy of government, its assertion of natural rights, its hint of an association, and such phrases as 'Delegation of Power from the People to their Representatives in Parliament'. These things, combined with a reverence for the principles of the Revolution and a conviction that the times were corrupt and the constitution in danger, were 'true Whiggism' rather than Toryism. Of course the distinction is sometimes blurred, but the Declaration helps to make it.]

Whereas Government is a human Institution, which is or ought to be calculated purely and solely for securing and improving the civil Happiness of the People, on whose Acquiescence it is founded, with as little Abridgment of the natural Liberty inherent in Mankind as the salutory Purpose of their political Union will admit: And Whereas that civil Happiness, which forms the only object of right Government, cannot possibly subsist unless there be diffused through the several Ranks and Orders of the Community a certain Measure of Virtue and public Spirit accompanied with Wisdom and Authority united in the leading Parts, as well as[1] Docility and Confidence residing in the subordinate Members of the State; which necessary Ingredients of national Welfare are however in the Opinion of Us, whose Names are underwritten, most notoriously and lamentably reduced in this Nation below that Measure which may suffice to preserve it from inward Dissolution, without some Attempt to remedy so fatal a Decay: we therefore hold ourselves indispensibly bound by all the sacred Ties of Duty and Affection towards our native Country to exert our utmost Endeavours for averting the dreadful, but threatning Consequences of a Depravity so widely spread and so deeply rooted. For this Purpose We hereby intend to cherish in ourselves, and, as far as in us lies, rekindle in our Countrymen that noble Ardor which ought to fire every Briton for making Britain great and happy by contributing, each in his proper Sphere, to make its Natives good and honest. We cannot, without the most dejecting Sorrow and Seriousness of Heart, reflect on the State, into which we are already brought, or forebode the Misery into which we seem to be farther sinking through a Complication of divers unhappy

[1] 'as' inserted by Dashwood.

Causes, that co-operate to our final Ruin. Our Debts, our Taxes, our Vices, our Luxury, our Supineness, our Corruption, our endless Errors, all conspire to alarm each considerate Friend of his Country with Variety of anxious Fears. The Existence of these and the like Evils among Us, We presume, no candid Observor will deny, their Tendency no Man of Common Understanding can mistake, and their Expulsion, if attainable, no upright Heart can help desiring above all other Considerations. For We account it an eternal and unalterable Maxim, that, whatever may some times chance to be the Success of Profligate Individuals, the Sum of public Happiness or Misery in human Society will ever be proportion'd to the Prevalency of the good or evil Morals which constitute the total national Character. Actuated by this great Principle, we have, by way of Pledge, both to the Public and to each other, for the Sincerity of our Intentions, subscribed our Names to this Declaration on Matters highly importing the Welfare and good Government of this Kingdom, whose True Interest we conceive ourselves authorized by our Birth-Right as free Subjects to promote in every loyal Manner, which our Observations or reflections can suggest. We shall accordingly subjoin such Determinations, as having long and maturely weighed in our Minds, we are firmly resolv'd never to renounce, without passing in our own Estimation, and in that of every Briton, for Men whom no Promises can bind, and whom no Principles inspire.

### First

Because the declared Principles of the Revolution and the Act of Settlement was to rescue and preserve us from tyrannical Government and from Popish Superstition, we do sincerely promise that Allegiance to his Majesty and his Successors of the illustrious House of Hanover, which the laws in being and our own Oaths require of Us, being firmly resolv'd to maintain their Right and Title to the Crown, on the Principles of Liberty, in Subordination to which we conceive their Succession established.

### Second

Because we apprehend ourselves warranted by Reason and Experience as well as by the Spirit of the British Constitution, to think a Delegation of Power from the People to their Representatives in Parliament for so long a Term as seven years, not only dangerous on Account of the palpable Tendency thereof to loosen the proper Dependency of Deputies on their Principals, but pernicious likewise, by Reason of the manifest Increase of Bribery and Corruption, which naturaly attends a Contest for so important a Trust of that Continuance; we are fully determin'd to struggle, without Intermission, for obtaining a Law to render Parliaments for the future, if possible annual, or at least, triennial.

*Third*

Because one of the principal and obvious Ends, that our Constitution has propos'd by providing a Representative of the People in the House of Commons, is to inspect and rectify Abuses in the executive Part of Government, as also to determine impartially the Necessity and Expediency of the Supplies demanded by Ministers for supporting their Measures; with which beneficial Intent we conceive the Admission of great Numbers of Persons holding Offices under the Crown into the House of Commons, to be wholly inconsistent, (such Persons having a visible Interest in the Decisions there depending) we will strive, with unwearied Diligence, to obtain a Law, whereby the whole Number of Persons in Offices both civil and military capable of sitting and voting in that House, shall not exceed *Fifty* at the most.

*Fourth*

Because We are thoroughly convinced, that a Standing-Army maintained in time of Peace without the Addition of a numerous and well-disciplin'd Militia is, at best not barely dangerous, but absolutely repugnant to public Liberty, and if join'd with such a Militia is, at best, both expensive and unnecessary; We bind ourselves to persevere in labouring with all our Might to procure the immediate Establishment of a Militia so constituted as effectualy to answer all the Purposes of National Defence against foreign and intestine Enemies, in Order to the gradual Reduction and final Rejection of that most alarming and inadequate Expedient for protecting us, a Standing-Army.

*Fifth*

Because that Liberty of the Press, which so gloriously and happily distinguishes Great Britain from other Countries, is, in our Judgment, a Blessing so inestimable by its Tendency to preserve among us Liberty and Property, Sciences and Arts, and to convey Information upon the most interesting subjects into every Corner of the Kingdom, as to deserve our warmest Zeal for preserving it; and because no Abuses or Inconveniences, that may sometimes result from it, can be sufficient in any Degree to counterbalance its manifest Utility; We engage ourselves in the most solemn Manner to contend, even at the Hazard, if necessary, of our Lives and Fortunes, for the Defence of so essential a Right; at the same Time that we condemn and shall ever be ready to concur in punishing, any enormous Abuse thereof, which has been, or shall be actually committed against the Laws of the Land, or against the Rules of common Decency; and We are persuaded, that such Kind of Perversions of this great Privilege will become less and less frequent and hurtful, in Proportion as the Reformation we propose advances with Success.

And, in Order to demonstrate to the World, as far as Words and Actions can extend, that our Intention is not to accomplish a change of Men, but of Measures; We do solemnly promise and declare, that, if the Administration at present employed, or any other hereafter to be employ'd by his Majesty, shall at any Time so far take our common Country's true Interest to Heart, as effectually and bonâ fide to carry these our avowed public Designs into Execution on their Part, We on ours, will in consequence of so desirable an Event, afford them all the honest Support in our Power for enabling them without Struggle or Opposition, either open or conceal'd, to administer the public Affairs committed to their Charge, so long, and so far forth, as they shall continue acting with the same laudable Views, and this without any tacit or express Bargain for the Gratification of any one or more Persons of our own Number, with any Office, Trust, Honour, or Reward whatsoever; leaving, as is our Duty and Inclination, the Disposal of those Matters for the best Advantage of the Kingdom to his Majesty's Wisdom, in whose Hands the present Constitution of our Country has vested the same.

One Reflection may, on this Occasion, be properly offer'd to the Consideration of our Countrymen in general, which is, that, whatever Hypocrisy some former Events may have tempted many of them to suspect lurking under all Professions of this Kind, and whatever Confirmation our future Infidelity (If any shall exist on our Part) may hereafter add to such Surmises, it is nevertheless certain, that, provided that Zeal for the public Welfare, to the Revival whereof our Declaration has an avowed Tendency, shall so far prevail among Numbers of our Fellow-Subjects, as [1] to divert their principal Attention from our Persons and Characters, to the great objects We presume to set before them, and to render them ernest in the glorious Pursuit; nor all the Falsehood or Dissimulation we can possibly be guilty of, will be able to frustrate the Success of their vigorous and united Efforts in the Cause of their Country.

[1] 'as' inserted by Dashwood.

# PREFACE TO THE ABRIDGEMENT OF BOOK OF COMMON PRAYER, 1773

### (a) Dashwood's Draft

[THE draft is in Dashwood's hand. I have preserved the arrangement exactly, showing Franklin's suggestions, which he wrote in pencil, in bold type. Franklin's deletions and marginal marks are distinguished by dotted, as opposed to solid, lines).

In the Franklin papers in the American Philosophical Society there is a manuscript (50 (2), 6) in Franklin's handwriting, endorsed 'Part of the Preface to the Book of Common Prayer'. This is an extract of that part of the Preface which surrounds Franklin's own contributions to it, beginning at 'time to attend Divine Service on other than Sundays' (see p. 173 below), incorporating Franklin's comments on the Psalms, and ending half-way through his comments on the Catechism.[1] The extract also incorporates a linking paragraph (before the comments on the first Lesson) beginning 'These were general reasons for wishing and proposing an Abridgement', which is not in Dashwood's draft. This paragraph, together with Franklin's comments on the Psalms and Catechism, are printed below (pp. 182–3).

Franklin's extract must have been made after he had made his comments on Dashwood's draft, and the alterations to the extract must have been made after discussing those comments with Dashwood. Franklin's corrected manuscript does not correspond exactly either with Dashwood's amended draft, or with the final printed version. The differences from both are, however, only verbal, and are explicable if one assumes, as one must, that Franklin altered a word here and there as he copied, and that Dashwood made later drafts. For example, Franklin's 'We do not conceive' instead of 'We do not apprehend' (p. 174 below), appears in the printed version, and was presumably adopted by Dashwood in a later draft.

A comparison of Dashwood's draft and amendments with Franklin's extract and amendments suggests the following time-table:

1. When Franklin arrived at West Wycombe in August 1773 Dashwood handed him the draft Preface for suggestions. (Franklin had presumably agreed beforehand — perhaps in November 1772 during his fortnight's stay at West Wycombe — that he would contribute the Psalms and the Cate-

---

[1] With the words 'Capacities of Children as might'. The American Philosophical Society's Franklin papers contain a complete manuscript version of his comments on the Catechism (50 (2), 7).

chism to Dashwood's revised Prayer Book, and perhaps brought his version with him.)

2. Franklin pencilled suggestions on the draft and wrote his comments on the Psalms and Catechism.

3. Franklin made a fair copy from Dashwood's draft, incorporating his own suggestions, of that part of the Preface which included his own contributions. He inserted in this a linking paragraph which was presumably a joint production. (It is of course possible that he made a fair copy of the whole, and that the rest is lost, but one cannot assume the accidental survival of this particular part.)

4. Dashwood and Franklin discussed the draft and Franklin's comments.

5. Dashwood made another draft. (?)

6. Franklin altered his fair copy in accordance with the discussion. For example, Franklin's sentence 'As all agree that there is but one God . . .'. is pencilled into Dashwood's draft but was not accepted; it appears in Franklin's extract but is crossed out in favour of Dashwood's amendment.

7. Dashwood made a final printer's draft (not now extant), making one or two verbal alterations himself and adopting one or two of Franklin's.]

# SOME HEADS FOR A PREFACE

## Editor

The Author of the following
abridgment of the Liturgy of the
Church of England, thinks it but
decent and respectfull to all, (more
particularly to the reverend body of
Clergy who adorn the protestant
religion by their good works preaching
and example,) that he should humbly
offer some reasons for such an under-
-taking.     He addresses himself to the
serious and discerning, he professes
himself to be a Protestant of the Church
of England, and holds in the highest
veneration the doctrines of Jesus Christ.
It has often been observed and
complained of that the morning and
Evening Service as practiced in the

## Compilers

Doctor Franklyn is desired to add,
alter, or diminish as he shall think
proper anything herein contained.
LLD is by no means tenacious.
for besides the differing sentiments
many
of ⟨ pious and well disposed
some
persons in speculative points
who in general have a good
opinion of our Church ⟨
~~wish well to her interests~~.
He is a sincere lover of Social
Worship, deeply sensible of its usefulness
to society and he aims at doing
some service to religion, by
proposing such abbreviations
and omissions in the forms of
our Liturgy

170

Churches of England and elsewhere,
are so long and filled with so many
~~continued~~
repetitions, that the ~~due~~ attention
suitable to so serious duty, becomes impracticable
~~requisite upon so serious a matter~~
the mind wanders and the fervency
~~is led astray, and the necessary ferven~~
~~-cy~~ of devotion is slackened.
Moreover
Many pious and devout persons

whether    whose age or infirmitys will not
for hours
suffer them to remain ~~an hour or two~~
in a Cold Church, more especially in
the Winter season; ~~and therefore~~ are
& Edification
obliged to forego the comfort they would
receive by their attendance on divine
Service. These, by shortening the time
would be relieved.

~~that Worship~~ retaining every
thing he thinks essential
as might, (if adopted) procure a more
general attendance ∧

**continued Attention suitable
to so serious an Employment
becomes impracticable, the
Mind wanders, & the Fervency
of Devotion is slackened.
It is humbly submitted &c.
See overleaf.**

likewise
and whether

and
er - - - - - - - - -
The young and more giddy sort,

who have some principles of

religion instilled into them and who
                    a Belief   the
have been educated in notions of a

necessity of adoreing their Maker;
     probably
would ∧ more frequently as well as

chearfully attend divine service, if

they were not detained so long at any

one time.
    also
It is ∧ humbly submitted whether

during the same service it is necessary

to say the same prayer more than

once for we are taught God delight-

-eth not in long prayers
  also
Many well disposed Tradesmen

Shopkeepers Artificers and others whose

also the propriety of saying the same

prayer more than once in the same

Service is doubted, as the Service is

thereby lengthened without apparent

necessity and such lengthening may seem

to some included in our Lord's censure of the

heathen

**And whether such Repetitions**

**are not included in that Censure**

**of the Heathen, that they thought**

**to be heard for their much speaking**

and Christ himself gave us a short prayer of his own.

172

habitations are not remote from

Churches, could, and ^probably would find time

(more frequently at least) to attend

divine service ^on other than on Sundays

if the prayers were reduced into a

much narrower compass.    Formerly

there were three services performed

at different times in the day    usually

which three services are now

joined together in one . This may suit with the

conveniency of the person who is inconvenient and

officiates, but ^ too often tiresome.

to the congregation.

We have presumed upon this plan of

abridgment, to leave out what is called

**It is thought that**
as an example
our Lord gave us a short prayer of his
own, and Censured the Heathen for
thinking to be heard because of their
much speaking.

Therefore
If this Abridgment should meet with

acceptance

But the well-disposed Clergy who are
desirous
laudably disposed to encourage the frequency
may
of divine service, might promote so great

and good a purpose by repeating this

without so much fatigue to themselves as

Abridgment ^three times on a Sunday
at present
Suppose at nine o'clock, at Eleven

and at one in the evening and by preaching
of moderate length
no more Sermons than usual which

Sermons should be moral and short.

173

the first Lesson
called the first lesson. The Old
Testament is allowed ⋋ to be an
accurate and concise history ⋋ and as
such, may and ought to be read at
home. But we apprehend it doth not
teach the doctrine of Christ so much
to be revered by ⋋ all Christians.

It is a Jewish book very curious,
perhaps more fit for the perusal
of the learned than suited to the
capacitys of the general illiterate part
of Mankind.

do    ap
We cannot comprehend that it is
necessary for Christians to make use
of more than one Creed. Therefore in
omitted
this Abridgment are left out the Nicene

by all the Sects of Christianity,
of God's dealing with his people,

the new Testament is sufficient
and more suitable to    .all mankind
and of more immediate importance to    Christians

of
⋋ The Apostles Creed
and as    the father son and holy Ghost
in which
are confessedly and avowedly part of
the
our belief ⋋ therefore in the Litany it does
not appear necessary after so solemn a

174

that
and the Creed of St. Athanasius. ~~We~~
In
~~have taken the first part of what is~~
~~stiled the Apostles' Creed~~ as absolutely

necessary to Salvation, the repetition of

the Son and holy Ghost not necessary:
all agree
as they make but one God. only
For the same reason we have taken

the first verse of the Litany, the Litany
~~which~~
being very long so greatly abridged,

but we trust the very material

parts are inserted.

We humbly suppose the same service

contained in this Abridgment might

properly serve for all Saints days    feasts

and fasts, reading only the Epistle and

Gospel appropriated to each day.

Confession ~~of our belief~~ ~~read~~ to repeat again
the Father Son and holy Ghost as that
remaining
part of the Service is otherwise very
prolix.

~~and~~

We have retained the Parts
that are most intelligible
& most essential.
we
As ⋀ all agree that there
is but one God, the addressing
him in Parts or Persons is omitted
in the Litany as unnecessary.
And that Part of the Service being
otherwise very prolix, is greatly abridged
tho we trust the material Parts remain.

Doctr Franklyn's remarks on the psalms to be
here inserted.

Quere,  what Abridgment (if any) of the
Collects Epistles and Gospels
Epistles and Gospels remain.

175

**Communion**

Although the ~~Sacrament~~ is greatly

on account

abridged ~~by reason of~~ its great

length, nevertheless it is hoped and

that those      retained

believed all ~~material~~ parts are

and all that is necessary for

Salvation. .

**Which are material**

**& necessary**

Infant baptism in Churches being

performed during divine Service, would

add greatly to the length of that

service if it were not abridged.

We have ventured therefore to leave

out the less material parts.

The Confirmation is here shortened.

The Comination and all cursing of

mankind is (we think) proper to be

For the Catechism Vide Doctᵣ Franklyn

176

left out of this Abridgment.

The form of solemnization of Matri-
-mony is often by our own Clergy not
strictly complied with. We have

what appear to us
selected ⟨ the material parts, which we

humbly hope will be deemed sufficient.

The
Whether long prayers contained in the

service for the visitation of the sick
seem
are not so proper when the afflicted
very
person is so weak and in distress, is

a point of serious consideration.

The Order for the burial of the dead
is very solemn and moving, neverthe-
-less to preserve the health and lives
of the living this service ought particularly

best omitted in

abbreviated by the officiating
Minister at his Discretion.

it appeared to us that

shortened
to be abridged, being very long.

For

Numbers standing in the open air

with their Hats off, often in

tempestuous weather ¦¦ must render

¦¦ it dangerous to the attendants.
hope    that
We ~~have~~ therefore ~~ventured~~ to

it
submit our Abridgement of _that_
_will be approved by_
service to the consideration of the

rational and prudent.

during the Celebration,
of that Service, its great Length
is not only inconvenient, but
may be

The thanksgiving of Women after

Childbirth being (when it is read) part

of the Service of the day we have

also

in some measure abridged that.

Haveing thus very briefly stated our

own suggestions concerning this work

Having thus stated very briefly

reasons

178

we are to declare in pureness of

heart the rectitude of our intention.
        lessen
We mean not to debase or prevent

the practice of Religion but to

honor and promote it.

    excellency of our
We acknowledge the ∧ present Liturgy

to be excellent and we only object

to its length.  We have not presumed
        remaining
to alter a word in the text, not even
        for
to substitute, who instead of which
        and elsewhere
in the Lord's Prayer altho it would be

more correct.

    respect
We do not attack the character

of Bishops and other dignitaries of

our Church, or any of the inferior

suggested
our Motives & Views

in undertaking this Work,

and our manner of proceeding in

the prosecution of this Work

we hope to be believed when we

declare the rectitude of our intentions

and tho' we have shortened it

We respect the

and with regard to

179

Clergy. In regard to the latter, it is

indeed to be wished, that they were

more equally provided for than by that

odious and vexatious as well as unjust

method of gathering Tithes in kind:

which creates animositys and litigati-

-ons, to the interruption of good                that

harmony and respect which ~~would~~            might

otherwise exist between the Rectors

and their parishoners.

and thus

meaning

Conscious of our upright intentions

we submit this Abridgment to

the serious consideration of the prudent

and dispassionate and not to the

Enthusiasts and Bigots, being convinced

in our own breasts, that this shortened

the inferior
we wish

method of <u>Worship</u> would further occasion religion, increase unanimity, and a more frequent attendance on the

Worship of God.

## (b) *Additions to Dashwood's Draft*

[These are the three passages not contained in Dashwood's draft: Franklin's comments on the Psalms, his comments on the Catechism, and the linking paragraph which is included in the Franklin extract (in the A.P.S.) and in the printed Preface. Throughout the printed Preface, the punctuation is different from that in the manuscript, and capital letters, much used both by Dashwood and by Franklin, are almost eliminated. The few differences in wording between the printed Preface and the Franklin extract are indicated.

### (i) *Franklin's comments on the Psalms*
(p. v. of printed Preface; A.P.S., Franklin MSS. 50 (2), 6.)

The Psalms, being a collection of Odes, written by different persons, it hath happened that many of them are on the same subject, and repeat the same sentiments; such as those that complain of enemies and persecutors, call upon God for protection, express a confidence therein, and thank him for it when afforded. A very great part of the book consists of repetitions of this kind, which may therefore well bear abridgement. Other parts are merely historical, repeating the mention of facts more fully narrated in the previous books, and which, relating to the ancestors of the Jews, were more interesting to them than to us. Other parts are *local* and allude to places of which we have no knowledge, and therefore do not affect us. Others are *personal*, relating to the particular circumstances of David or Solomon, as kings; and can therefore seldom be rehearsed with any propriety by Christians. Others imprecate, in the most bitter terms, the vengeance of God on our Adversaries, contrary to the spirit of Christianity, which commands us to love our enemies and to pray for those that hate us, [and despitefully use us].[1] For these reasons it is to be wished, that the same liberty were, by the governors of our Church, allowed to the minister with regard to the *reading psalms*, as is taken by the clerk, with regard to those that are to be sung, in directing the parts that he may judge most suitable to be read at the time, from the present circumstances of the congregation, or the tenor of his sermon, by saying, Let us *read* such and such parts of the Psalms named. Until this is done, our Abridgement, it is hoped will be found to contain what may be most generally proper to be joined in by an assembly of Christian people. The Psalms are still apportioned to the days of the month, as heretofore, though the several parts for each day are generally a full third shorter.

### (ii) *Franklin's comments on the Catechism*
(p. vi. of printed Preface; A.P.S. Franklin MSS. 50 (2), 7.)

The Catechism, as a compendium of systematic theology, which learned divines have written folio volumes to explain, and which therefore, it may

---

[1] Not in Franklin extract.

be presumed, they thought scarce intelligible without such expositions; is, perhaps, taken altogether, not so well adapted to the capacities of children as might be wished. Only those plain answers, therefore, which express our duty towards God, and our duty towards our neighbour, are retained here. The rest is recommended to their reading and serious consideration, when more years shall have ripened their understanding.

(iii) *The linking paragraph*
    (p. iv. of printed Preface; A.P.S., Franklin MSS. 50 (2), 6.)

These were general reasons for wishing and proposing an Abridgement. In attempting it we do not presume to dictate to a single Christian: we are sensible there is a proper authority in the rulers of the Church for ordering such matters; and whenever the time shall come when it may be thought not unseasonable to revise our Liturgy, there is no doubt but every suitable improvement will be made, under the care and direction of so much learning wisdom, and piety, in one body of men collected. Such a work as this must then be much better executed. In the mean time, this humble performance may serve to shew the practicability of shortening the service [near][1] one half, without the omission of what is essentially necessary: and we hope, moreover, that the book may be [occasionally] of some use to families, or private assemblies of Christians.

To give now some account of particulars. We have presumed upon this plan of Abridgement to leave out the first Lesson. . . .

[1] Not in printed Preface.

## (a) On Cyder

[THIS note is in the same clerk's hand as several of the estimates preserved among the Dashwood MSS. in the Bodleian Library, and there is no indication of its author. The phrase underlined was added by Dashwood. Although the sentiments are like Bindley's, his memoranda and letters are longer and more eloquent than this, and they are usually endorsed by Dashwood (e.g. 'Bindley on Wine'). The author's local knowledge suggests that he may have been the 'Exciseman from Hereford' who, according to Dowdeswell, together with 'Clerks in Office, . . . and a Man who had been a Distiller [Bindley]', advised Dashwood on the cider tax (*An Address to such of the Electors of Great Britain as are Not Makers of Cyder and Perry* (1763), p. 13). The most obvious candidate for the title 'Exciseman from Hereford' would, of course, be the Collector, Robert Stayner, who died in April 1763. Nevertheless, I think a more likely candidate is William Symons, Supervisor in 1758 and Collector from 1766. Symons was known to the Excise Office, for his technical manual *The Practical Gager: or the Young Gager's Assistant. containing Those Things which are actually practised, and which are also absolutely necessary to be Known and understood by every Person that is employed as a Gager or Officer in the Revenue of the Excise* was 'dedicated (by permission) to the honourable Commissioners of the Excise'. It was first published in 1758 and ran through many editions in the next seventy years. It is unlikely (for official reasons) that Symons belonged to the well-known Herefordshire family of that name, but it is possible that he was connected with John Symons of London who bought The Mynde, Hereford, in 1740 and was M.P. for Hereford City 1754–63.]

## On Cyder

Private Growers of Cyder to compound for Cyder drank in their own Family. *as any Compounder for Malt*

Such Persons selling Cyder to private Persons shou'd be charged with 4<sup>s</sup> or 5<sup>s</sup> pr Hogshead Duty

Whatever Duty is intended to be charged on Cyder must be imposed on the Grower or Maker, & not on the first Buyer, because the Difficulty of the Officers finding the Cyder to charge is when remov'd from the Makers.

There was a Duty of 4<sup>s</sup> pr Hogshead paid by the Private Consumer from 12 Anne to 17th Geo<sup>ls</sup> II<sup>dl</sup> — It prov'd indeffectual because it was not laid on the Grower.

If Cyder is of small Value in Plentifull Years, the better those who drink only Cyder can afford to pay a Duty

No Private Gentleman need be visited by an Excise Man, unless he sells his Cyder, but may be permitted to compound on giving in a List under their hands of the Numbers in their Family.

Many Gentlemen & Farmers (the Major Part in Worcestershire or Herefordshire) submit to be survey'd by an Officer for the making of Malt, rather than Compound because they use so much Cyder, as to make the Consumption of their Malt not worth their compounding for.

The Duty on ev'ry Barrell containing 36 Gallons of Strong Beer within the Bills of Mortality & 34 Gallons out of the Bills of Mortality is 8 shillings

A Barrell of Ale within the Bills of Mortality is allowed to contain no more than 32 Gallons & pays — 8ˢ–

Sixty three Gallons Wine Measure is an Hogshead of Cyder & nine Gallons of Ale Measure is equall to Eleven Wine Measure.

The Tradesman to brew good small Beer use 2 Bushells to the Barrell & one Barrell & half is equal to an Hogshead of Cyder Measure — the Hops used to that Quantity is about 1 pound

A Barrell of small Beer brew'd from  
      2 Bushell's  
Malt which is 3/6 the Bushell is        7  0  
One pᵈ of Hops on an Avarage         9  
                                    7  9

½ Barrell Do  
to make the Hogshead        3  10  
                                  11  7

is equal in Quantity to  
    the Hogshead of Cyder.

### (b) Bindley on Wine

There is no Branch of Trade (on which a large Branch of the Revenue depends) that demands more Consideration and Regulation than Foreign Wines. The Profit to the Retailers & intermediate Dealers between the Merchant Importer and Vitner is immense, even provided they did not mix & adulterate the same, as will appear by the following Calculation —

A Pipe of Neat Oporto Wine is to be bought on the Quay of London for £28. However say £30. This sold at 2ˢ per bottle by the Vintner produces £57.12s even allowing his Bottle to hold Measure. . . .

The above alone wou'd Point out a Justifiable reason for an encreas'd Duty, to come out of the enormous Profits of the Dealers in Wine without the Consumer's paying anything more for it. But the Misfortune wou'd be,

that the higher the Price of foreign Wine was made, the Greater the Tempta-
wou'd be for the Dealers in it to mix it with a Commodity of less value.
—— 4$^f$ pr Ton on Wine wou'd produce a great sum of Money & being
somewhat less than 1$^s$ pr Quart might certainly be expected to come out of
the Wine Dealers Profits. But whilst the facility to mix with Sweets &
Cyder is so great, the Revenue can never rely on the real Produce of any new
Levy on Wine. To Excise it at present might be impolitic, I hope the following simple Regulations may answer the same End. I must first beg leave to
observe in order to enforce the Necessity of Administrations taking the Wine
Trade into Consideration, That on my Knowledge I aver a single Wine
Merchant in this City makes 100 Pipes of Raisin Wine pr Annum; & never
sells any under that Denomination, but sends it to his foreign Vaults & from
thence distributes it all over the Kingdom in half hhds & Pipes at the Price
& under the Character of Foreign Wine, & the Consumers pay for it as
beleiving it Foreign Wine; & the Revenue in this single Instance loses from
£1000 to £1500 pr. Ann. — For as it appears that Neat Wine affords a
very large profit at 2$^s$ the Bottle, if the above had not been mix'd there wou'd
have been no Necessity to raise the Price on the Public consequently the
Consumption by no Means endagered —— The foregoing Instance is when
y$^e$ Raisin Wine or Sweets has been charged with that Duty. But 'tis too
frequently the Case that Dealers in foreign Wines make Raisin and other
British Wines without paying any Duty at all, which they have a right to do
as the Law stands at present, the Duty becoming chargeable only on the
Sale of them under their own Denomination & therefore being mix'd with
Foreign Wines are not under the Cognizance of the Officers of the Excise
— One of my fix'd Datas is, that every Commodity liable to Excise on Sale,
shou'd in some Degree be subject to the like if made by Persons for their
own Use, who have Advantages over their Neighbours, & can make that at
Home, which others are forced not only to buy with the Traders accumulated
Profit on that Duty — Malt & Candles have long pointed out the Modes of
attaining this without infringing on the Privacy or Liberty of the Gentleman
by being subject to the Survey of Officers. And this is by way of Composition which as in the propos'd Case for private Brewery I must wish to see
extended to Every exciseable Article, for the Security of Traders & the
Revenue and for the sake of a Just Liquidation of all Taxes

sign'd

JOHN BINDLEY

### Proposed

That every Person Dealing in Foreign Wine be obliged to take out the
Present Wine Licence without any regard being paid to the Quantity in
which they sell their Wine — That over every Vault or Warehouse in which
Foreign Wine is deposited for sale, the Name of the Dealer & Foreign Wine

be wrote & enforced to be kept legible — In order to prevent Private Dealer in Wine without Licence.

That the Duty on F. Wine be the same at all $y^e$ Ports in Engl$^d$. without Distinction whether impos'd by a Merchant or Retailer That every Person delivering Raisin Wine, Cyder, Sweets (or the other Commodities which shall be mention'd as fit to mix w.$^{th}$ F. Wine) to any Person dealing in Foreign Wines without first producing a Notice to the Excise Officer who surveys the said Dealers in Sweets & (For Dealers in British Wines are at present under the Survey of Excise) shall forfeit 10$^s$ for every Gallon — The same on the Receiver without Notice — That all Raisin Wines &c &c Brought into the Possession of ev'ry Dealer in foreign Wine shall be charged with the same Duty as is paid on the Importation of Oporto Wine — Provided only that Victuallers who sell F. Wine may be permitted on previous Notice giv'n to $y^e$ Excise Officer to receive Cyder for sale as Cyder in their Houses, & on farther declaring on Oath before the Justices of the Peace (or Comm$^r$ of Excise in Town) that the same is bona fide to be sold either wholesale or Retail as Cyder, & not to be mix'd with or sold as Wine — On Refusal of s.$^d$ Oath Duty of Wine is to be charged, And on receiving it into Custody without previous Notice Penalties are to be inflicted on s.$^d$ Victualler — No Dealer in F. Wine cou'd by $y^e$ above means receive into his Custody British Wine, nor shou'd he be permitted to sell it for the sake of $y^e$ Revenue & $y^e$ Person who paying a Foreign Price is impos'd on — For Raisin Wine Sweets &c Every Person selling or Dealing in Raisin Wine, or what must be distinguish'd under $y^e$ Gen$^l$ Denomination of British Wines be subject to a Licence Yearly for that Purpose at the rate of 20$^s$ only & oblig'd to write their Names & British Wines as in the former Case. And all private Persons making their own Wines be subject to a small Composition.

# DASHWOOD AND THE MILITIA

DASHWOOD'S part in the rescue of the militia from its period of neglect has not hitherto been known. The 1756 militia bill, with the amendments made in committee, was ordered to be printed on 9 April (*Commons Journals*, xxvii. 577) and can be found in *House of Commons Papers, 1731–1800. Bills*, vol. ii, no. 84 (in the House of Commons Library and in the British Museum; microprint in the Bodleian Linrary). The principles of the bill — a fixed quota for each county, raised by lot, officers chosen by Lords Lieutenant and their Deputies, payment out of money raised by taxation — were a departure from the 1662 Act and became the basis of all future territorial militia organisation. But it seems that these principles were first mooted not in 1756 but in 1745, by Dashwood. Two facts seem to prove that the incomplete draft bill in the Dashwood MSS. was the bill introduced into the Commons in February 1746: the figures in Dashwood's draft (of county quotas, etc.) are the same as those supplied to him by Peter Davall on 14 December 1745 (Dashwood MSS. B 8/1/1a, 8/2/15a and 15b, 8/1/3); two of Davall's memoranda — 'Estimate of the Amount of the Annual Pay of a Militia . . .' and 'Explanation of the Estimate . . .' — accord exactly (except for punctuation and capital letters) with two printed in *House of Commons Papers, 1731–1800. Accounts and Papers*, vol. i. no. 1, and endorsed 'Proposal for a Militia'. The 'Proposal' bears no date, and the volume which it begins is misleadingly dated 1749/50–1777.

## *Explanation of the Estimate for the Militia*

The first Column contains the names of the several Countys of England & Wales, including the Citys and Towns within those Countys tho' they may be Countys themselves. Except in the Cases of London and Westminster, each of which are distinguished from the County of Middlesex, and within Westminster are included the Inns of Court Palaces etc. And of Bristol w.ch is distinguish'd from the County of Somerset.

The 2.d Column contains the number of men to be raised by each County supposing the whole Kingdom to raise about 100,000 Men. But as sometimes a Man or at most two is added in some Countys to make the whole number of men exactly divisible by the number of Regiments. The whole number of men in this Case happens to be 100,007.

The 3.d & 4.th Columns contain the number of Regiments to be raised in each County, and the number of men in each Regiment, which latter no where exceeds 780 or is so little as 500; except in the smaller Countys whose whole number of men falls short of that number. In which Case wherever the number of men exceeds 100 which happens in all the Countys but two they are called a Regiment. And as to those two Countys viz. Anglesea & Cardigan. The first raising 82 men is divided into two independent Companys, and the latter which raises only 69, constitutes one such Company.

The fifth Column contains the number of Companys in each Regiment which is calculated to make each Company consist as near as may be of 50 Men. So as always to exceed 47 and to be less than 53 except in the smaller Countys above mentioned.

The 6th Column contains the number of Companys in each county arising by the multiplication of the number of Companys in each Regiment by the number of Regiments in each County. The use of this Column is to facilitate the calculation of the expence of each County as will presently appear.

The 7th Column contains the number of Commission'd and Non Commission'd Officers Drums etc. in each County and arises by the Multiplication of the number of Companys in each County by the number 9. As each Company is (besides private men) to consist of 1 Captain 1 Lieutenant 1 Ensign 2 Serjeants 2 Corporals and 2 Drums in all 9 Supernumeraries (except in the Case of the Company belonging to Cardigan which consisting of 69 men has 3 Serjeants and 3 Corporals.) The use of this is to shew how many Supernumeraries there are besides the 100,007 private men, which here amount to 18,083 viz 9 times 2009 the number of Companies and 2 more for the additional Serjeant and Corporal, and makes the whole Militia on this Plan to consist of 118,090 Men.

The 8th Column contains the expence of each County, which is computed thus. It is proposed that the ordinary days of Exercise for the Militia shall be 32 Sundays, to begin on the 4.th Sunday in February in every year or such other Sundays or Holydays as shall be most convenient; for each of which 32 days each private man is to receive six pence, in all 16.8 per Annum. Besides which it is proposed there shall be 4 days of general Muster Review and Exercise for each of which days each man is to receive one shilling which added to the 16.8 for the 32 ordinary days makes each mans pay per Ann to be just 20.8 or 1.£

The expence of Officers is thus computed. All above Lieutenant are supposed to be Gentlemen who will receive no pay.

|  | s | d |
|---|---|---|
| A Lieutenants pay on ordinary days is proposed to be . . . . | 4. | 0. |
| An Ensigns . . . . . . . . . . . . . . . . . . . | 3. | 0. |
| Two Serjeants 1.8 each . . . . . . . . . . . . . . | 2. | 0. |
| Two Corporals 9.d each . . . . . . . . . . . . . . | 1. | 6. |
| Two Drums 9.d each . . . . . . . . . . . . . . . | 1. | 6. |
| Total pay of Officers per Diem . . . . . . . . . | 0. 12. | 0. |

ESTIMATE of the Amount of the Annual pay of a Militia to consist for the whole Kingdom of England of 100,007 Private Men, and 18,083, Commission'd and non Commission'd Officers Drums etc. to be divided into 175 Regiments and 3 Independent Companies, each man to receive such pay and for such time as is more particularly explain'd in another Paper: And of the number of private men, number of Regiments, Companies, and Officers to be raised in and the Annual expence of each County. And likewise of the annual Sums which would be raised in each County by a Land-Tax at five pence in the Pound in proportion to the present Land Tax at 4s. And of the Surplus of such Tax in each County above the Annual pay of the Militia.

| 1. | 2. | 3. | 4. | 5. | 6. | 7. | 8. | 9. | 10. |
|---|---|---|---|---|---|---|---|---|---|
| *Names of Counties* | *Number of Men to be raised in each County* | *No. of Regim$^{ts}$ in each County* | *Number of Men in each Regiment* | *No. of Companys in each Regiment* | *No. of Companys in each County* | *No. of Officers in each County* | *Annual charge of each County* | *Sums w$^{ch}$ a Land Tax at 5d. in the £ wo$^{d}$. produce in each County* | *Surplus in each County* |
| BEDFORD | 1436 | 2 | 718 | 14 | 28 | 252 | 2108 0 0 | 2974 9 0½ | 866 9 0½ |
| BERKS. | 2052 | 3 | 684 | 14 | 42 | 378 | 3060 0 0 | 4254 12 3¼ | 1194 12 3¼ |
| BUCKS. | 2368 | 4 | 592 | 12 | 48 | 432 | 3520 0 0 | 4910 13 8¼ | 1390 13 8¼ |
| CAMBRIDGE | 1644 | 3 | 548 | 11 | 33 | 297 | 2436 0 0 | 3409 13 3 | 973 13 3 |
| CHESTER | 1438 | 2 | 719 | 14 | 28 | 252 | 2110 0 0 | 2979 1 10 | 869 1 10 |
| CORNWALL | 1605 | 3 | 535 | 11 | 33 | 297 | 2397 0 0 | 3327 8 0 | 930 8 0 |
| CUMBERLAND | 187 | 1 | 187 | 4 | 4 | 36 | 283 0 0 | 386 17 3½ | 103 17 3½ |
| DERBY | 1212 | 2 | 606 | 12 | 24 | 216 | 1788 0 0 | 2509 15 10 | 721 15 10 |
| DEVON | 4151 | 7 | 593 | 12 | 84 | 757 | 6167 0 0 | 8602 8 3 | 2435 8 3 |
| DORSET | 1662 | 3 | 554 | 11 | 33 | 297 | 2454 0 0 | 3445 16 5¼ | 991 16 5¼ |
| DURHAM | 533 | 1 | 533 | 11 | 11 | 99 | 797 0 0 | 1103 18 6¾ | 306 18 6¾ |
| YORK | 4600 | 8 | 575 | 12 | 96 | 864 | 6904 0 0 | 9532 13 6½ | 2628 13 6½ |
| ESSEX | 4492 | 8 | {4 of 561<br>{4 of 562 | 11 | 88 | 792 | 6604 0 0 | 9311 17 6¾ | 2707 17 6¾ |
| GLOUCESTER | 2380 | 4 | 595 | 12 | 48 | 432 | 3532 0 0 | 4931 3 0¼ | 1399 3 0¼ |
| HEREFORD | 1026 | 2 | 513 | 10 | 20 | 180 | 1506 0 0 | 2125 19 5¼ | 619 19 5¼ |
| HERTFORD | 2130 | 3 | 710 | | 42 | 378 | 3138 0 0 | 4413 13 2 | 1275 13 2 |
| HUNTINGDON | 780 | 1 | 780 | 15 | 15 | 135 | 1140 0 0 | 1614 5 11¼ | 474 5 11¼ |
| KENT | 4151 | 7 | 593 | 12 | 84 | 756 | 6167 0 0 | 8599 5 10½ | 2432 5 10½ |
| LANCASTER | 1056 | 2 | 528 | 11 | 22 | 198 | 1584 0 0 | 2186 8 7 | 602 8 7 |
| LEICESTER | 1746 | 3 | 582 | 12 | 36 | 324 | 2610 0 0 | 3619 19 4 | 1009 19 4 |
| LINCOLN | 3612 | 6 | 602 | 12 | 72 | 648 | 5340 0 0 | 7491 18 5 | 2151 18 5 |

| | | | | | | | | | |
|---|---|---|---|---|---|---|---|---|---|
| London | 6200 | 10 | 620 | 12 | 120 | 1080 | 9080 0 0 | 12854 1 11½ | 3774 1 11½ |
| Westminster | 4780 | 8 | 4 of 598 | 12 | 96 | 864 | 7084 0 0 | 9910 17 6 | 2826 17 6 |
| Middlesex | 5400 | 9 | 600 | 12 | 108 | 972 | 7992 0 0 | 11208 12 0½ | 3216 12 0½ |
| Monmouth | 493 | 1 | 493 | 10 | 10 | 90 | 733 0 0 | 1022 2 4 | 289 2 4 |
| Norfolk | 4240 | 8 | 530 | 11 | 88 | 792 | 6352 0 0 | 8781 19 1¼ | 2429 19 1¼ |
| Northampton | 2400 | 4 | 600 | 12 | 48 | 432 | 3552 0 0 | 4970 1 0½ | 1418 1 0½ |
| Northumberland | 730 | 1 | 730 | 15 | 15 | 135 | 1090 0 0 | 1515 10 1½ | 425 10 1½ |
| Nottingham | 1370 | 2 | 685 | 14 | 28 | 252 | 2042 0 0 | 2841 6 1¼ | 799 6 1¼ |
| Oxon. | 1950 | 3 | 650 | 13 | 39 | 351 | 2886 0 0 | 4036 13 3½ | 1150 13 3½ |
| Rutland | 277 | 1 | 277 | 6 | 6 | 54 | 421 0 0 | 575 10 9¾ | 154 10 9¾ |
| Salop | 1460 | 2 | 730 | 5 | 30 | 270 | 2180 0 0 | 3026 15 4 | 846 15 4 |
| Bristol | 371 | 1 | 371 | 8 | 8 | 72 | 563 0 0 | 769 19 0¼ | 206 19 0¼ |
| Somerset | 3270 | 6 | 541 | 11 | 66 | 594 | 4854 0 0 | 6779 6 9 | 1925 6 9 |
| Southampton | 2760 | 4 | 690 | 14 | 56 | 504 | 4104 0 0 | 5724 19 3½ | 1620 19 3½ |
| Stafford | 1362 | 2 | 681 | 14 | 28 | 252 | 2034 0 0 | 2825 2 4¾ | 791 2 4¾ |
| Suffolk | 3696 | 6 | 619 | 12 | 72 | 648 | 5424 0 0 | 7656 17 9¾ | 2232 17 9¾ |
| Surrey | 3324 | 6 | 554 | 11 | 66 | 594 | 4908 0 0 | 6888 17 0½ | 1980 17 0½ |
| Sussex | 3020 | 5 | 604 | 12 | 60 | 540 | 4460 0 0 | 6264 8 9½ | 1804 8 9½ |
| Warwick | 1998 | 3 | 666 | 13 | 39 | 351 | 2934 0 0 | 4144 15 2¾ | 1210 15 2¾ |
| Worcester | 1686 | 3 | 562 | 11 | 33 | 297 | 2478 0 0 | 3498 2 2½ | 1020 2 2½ |
| Wilts. | 2596 | 4 | 649 | 13 | 52 | 468 | 3844 0 0 | 5380 19 7 | 1536 19 7 |
| Westmoreland | 153 | 1 | 153 | 3 | 3 | 27 | 225 0 0 | 317 4 1½ | 92 4 1½ |
| Anglesea | 82 | 0 | 0 | 0 | 2 | 18 | 130 0 0 | 170 2 11 | 40 2 11 |
| Brecon | 153 | 1 | 153 | 3 | 3 | 27 | 225 0 0 | 317 18 1½ | 92 18 1½ |
| Cardigan | 69 | 0 | 0 | 0 | 1 | 11 | 96 10 0 | 143 0 0 | 46 10 0 |
| Carmarthen | 220 | 1 | 220 | 4 | 4 | 36 | 316 0 0 | 455 4 5 | 139 4 5 |
| Carnarvon | 117 | 1 | 117 | 3 | 3 | 27 | 189 0 0 | 243 9 4½ | 54 9 4½ |
| Denbigh | 342 | 1 | 342 | 7 | 7 | 63 | 510 0 0 | 708 6 8 | 198 6 8 |
| Flint | 117 | 1 | 117 | 3 | 3 | 27 | 189 0 0 | 241 2 7¼ | 52 2 7¼ |
| Glamorgan | 398 | 1 | 398 | 8 | 8 | 72 | 590 0 0 | 823 11 10 | 233 11 10 |
| Merioneth | 123 | 1 | 123 | 3 | 3 | 27 | 195 0 0 | 253 8 4 | 58 8 4 |
| Montgomery | 294 | 1 | 294 | 6 | 6 | 54 | 438 0 0 | 609 13 7 | 171 13 7 |
| Pembroke | 160 | 1 | 160 | 4 | 4 | 36 | 256 0 0 | 330 9 11 | 74 9 11 |
| Radnor | 135 | 1 | 135 | 3 | 3 | 27 | 207 0 0 | 280 8 11½ | 73 8 11½ |
| | 100,007 | 175 | | | 2009 | 18083 | 148,226 10 0 | 207,302 17 1½ | 59,076 7 1½ |

Which for 32 Ordinary days comes to . . . . . . . . . . 19. 4. 0.
And for 4 days at double pay viz £1. 4. 0 per
Diem comes to . . . . . . . . . . . . . . . } 4. 16. 0.

Total of the pay of the Officers of
each Company per Ann.

24. 0. 0.

So that to compute the Annual charge of each county the number of Companys must be multiplied by 24 and to the product must be added the number of private men; and the Sum will give the number of pounds which will be the annual expence of each County. And accordingly if the whole number of Companys in the Kingdom viz. 2009 be multiply'd by 24 it will produce £48,216 to which adding £3. 10. 0. the annual charge of the additional Corporal and Serjeant in Cardigan & 100,007 for the annual expence of the private men the Sum is £148,226. 10. which is the sum of the annual charges of each particular County put together.

The 9.th Column contains the annual Sum which each County would raise by a Land Tax at 5.d in the pound in proportion to the present Land Tax at 4.s which is given for £1,990,111. 10. 3. Notwithstanding care has been taken to compute the particular assessments in each County as near as possible, yet the Sum total of these falls short by a few shillings of the total tax at 5.d in the pound which amounts to £207,303. 5. 7¾. This Error in the total is unavoidable, without more labour than is requisite in this Case, where it may be asserted that the particular Errors are extremely trifling and inconsiderable.

The 10.th Column contains the Surplusses which the 5 penny Tax produces in each County above the Charge of the Militia. which may be applied to the providing Arms Clothes etc. The total of these Surplusses amounts to upwards of £59000 which in a few years will be sufficient for the purposes above mentioned, and then the Tax may be reduced to 4.d in the pound which will produce in the whole £165,842: 12. 6¼ and as the Annual pay of the Militia amounts only to £148,226. 10 there will be an annual Surplus of £17,616: 2: 6¼ for Clothes etc.

# THE EXCISEMAN'S CREED

[T HIS small piece of satire (Dashwood MSS. B 7/2) was written by some-one well informed on the organisation of the Excise collection, with its hierarchy of collectors, supervisors, and gaugers. Each collector made a round of his collection, and each supervisor drew up accounts of production in his division, once every six weeks. Central control was exercised by 'general orders' sent by the Commissioners to the collectors, and by the requirement imposed on supervisors to keep elaborate and detailed diaries recording, for every hour of every day, his activities and those of the gaugers. The completed diaries were sent in to the Board, where they were kept by the Clerk of Diaries, and the Commissioners used them as the basis for pro-motion, punishment, or other appropriate action. Entrants to the Excise service were required to possess a certain minimum standard of education, including the 'art of arithmetic', and began their official career with a period of training in the 'art of guaging'.

The 'Creed' is written in Dashwood's hand. It seems likely either that he composed it himself, or that he copied and kept it because its association of the mystery of the Excise collection with the mystery of the Athanasian creed appealed to him. It is the sort of skit that might well have been in-spired by a sentence written by Daniel Whitby (1638–1726, Bishop of Salisbury 1668) and quoted by Watson because Whitby's 'piety and learn-ing are above all question': 'This doctrine that the Father, Son, and Holy Ghost, are of one and the same individual and numerical essence, seems to burlesque the Scriptures, or give them an uncouth and absurd sense, from the beginning of the Gospel to the end of the Epistles' (*Miscellaneous Tracts*, ii. 80–81).]

Proper Rules and instructions, without which
no Man can be an Exciseman.

Whosoever will be an Exciseman it is necessary, before all things, that he learn the art of Arithmetick

Which art unless he does well understand, without doubt he shall be no Exciseman, and the art of Arithmetick is this: to know how to multiply.

The (1) is a figure the (2) is a figure and the (3) is a figure the (1) is a number the (2) is a number and the (3) is a number, and yet not three — desunt plurima. For likewise as we are compelled by the Rules of Arith-metick to acknowledge every figure by itself to have Signification & Power so we are forbidden by the Rules of right reason, to say each of them have three Significations or three powers. The one is abstracted from none, neither depending nor produced, the (2) is of the one alone, not made nor depending, but produced, the three (3) is of the one and the two neither made nor depending but divided. So there is a figure of (3) not XXX desunt nonnulla.

Furthermore it is necessary for the preservation of his place that he believe rightly the authority of his Supervisor, for his right interest is that he believe and Confess, that his Supervisor the servant of the Commissioners, as being obliged to return his accounts, perfect Master and perfect Man of unconscionable soul and frail flesh subsisting, equal to the Commissioners as touching the respect which is showed to him, and inferior to the Commissioners as touching the profits and Salary. who although he be Master and Man, he has not two Customs Supervisors. One not by Confusion of his place but by Virtue of his authority.

for as the Seal and Sign Manuall perfect his Warrant deputation or commission to his Guaging the Vessels & inspecting the Exciseman's books made his Superior

Who travells thro' thick and thin and Suffers much from heat for Our Salvation from additional Taxes, thro' deficiency in the funds by Corruption & inadvertency.

Who thrice in seven days goes his rounds, and once in six weeks meets the Collector who shall judge between the Exciseman and the Victualler — At whose coming the Exciseman shall bring in their Accounts and the Victualler their Money. And they who make prompt payment and the exciseman whose accounts are just shall be well treated, but they who are tardy in paying their money, shall be cast into Goal. And the Excisemen whose books are blotted or their Accounts unjustifiable shall be turned out of their places. These are the Rules which except a man do follow & believe faithfully he cannot be an Exciseman. Honour be to the Commissioners fatigue to the Supervisors and bribery to the Excisemen As it was in the beginning when Taxes were laid upon Malt is now and ever till our debts are paid Amen.

# CHIEF MINISTERIAL CHANGES
# FEBRUARY 1742 TO FEBRUARY 1782

| | Jan. 1742 Walpole's Administration | Feb. 1742 | Aug. 1743 |
|---|---|---|---|
| Lord Chancellor | Hardwicke (1st Bn.; 1st Earl of, 1754) | ... | ... |
| Lord President | Wilmington (1st Earl of) | Harrington | ... |
| Lord Privy Seal | Hervey (2nd Bn.) | July. Gower (2nd Bn.; 1st Earl, 1746) | Dec. Cholmondeley (3rd Earl of) |
| First Lord of Treasury | Sir Robert Walpole | Wilmington | Pelham |
| Chancellor of Exchequer | Sir Robert Walpole | Samuel Sandys (1st Bn., 1743) | Dec. Pelham |
| First Lord of Admiralty | Sir Charles Wager | Winchilsea (8th Earl of, and 3rd of Nottingham) | ... |
| Secretaries of State: South | Newcastle (1st Duke of) | ... | ... |
| North | Harrington (1st Bn.; 1st Earl of, 1742) | Carteret (2nd Bn.; Earl Granville, 1744) | ... |
| Colonies | | | |
| Secretary at War | Sir William Yonge | ... | ... |
| Paymaster of Forces | Henry Pelham | 1743. Thomas Winnington | ... |
| Treasurer of Navy | Arthur Onslow | Thomas Clutterbuck Dec. Wager | Dec. Sir John Rushout |
| First Lord of Trade | Monson (1st Bn.) | ... | ... |
| Postmasters-General | Lovel (1st Bn.; 1st Earl of Leicester, 1744) Sir John Eyles | ... | ... |
| Attorney-General | Sir Dudley Ryder | ... | ... |
| Solicitor-General | Sir John Strange | Nov. William Murray (1st Bn. Mansfield, 1756; 1st Earl of, 1776) | ... |

| Nov. 1744 Broad Bottom Administration | 10 Feb. 1746 Granville–Bath | 14 Feb. 1746 Pelham | Mar. 1754 Newcastle |
|---|---|---|---|
| ... | ... | ... | ... |
| Jan.'45. Dorset (6th Earl of; 1st Duke of) | ... | June '51. Granville | ... |
| Dec. Gower | Carlisle (4th Earl of) | Gower | Jan. '55. Marlborough (3rd Duke of) Nov. Gower (2nd Earl) |
| ... | Bath (1st Earl of) | Pelham | Newcastle |
| ... | ... | ... | Legge Nov. '55. Sir George Lyttelton (1st Bn., 1756) |
| Bedford (4th Duke of) | Winchilsea | Bedford Feb. '48. Sandwich (4th Earl of) June '51. Anson (1st Bn.) | ... |
| ... | } Granville | Newcastle Feb. '48. Bedford June '51. Holdernesse (4th Earl of) | Sir Thomas Robinson (1st Bn. Grantham, 1761) Sept. '55. Fox |
| Harrington | | Harrington Oct. Chesterfield (4th Earl of) Feb. '48. Newcastle | Holdernesse |
| ... | ... | July. Henry Fox (1st Bn. Holland, 1763) | Nov. '55. Barrington (2nd Visc (Irish)) |
| ... | ... | May. William Pitt (1st Earl of Chatham, 1766) | Nov. '55 Darlington (1st Earl of) Thomas Hay, commonly called Viscount Dupplin (8th Earl of Kinnoull, 1758) |
| Dec. George Bubb Dodington | ... | May '49. Henry Bilson Legge | April. George Grenville Dec. '55. Dodington |
| ... | ... | 1748. Halifax (2nd Earl of) | ... |
| Sir Everard Fawkener | ... | ... | ... |
| ... | ... | ... | Murray |
| April '45. Sir Richard Lloyd | ... | ... | ... |

| | Nov. 1756<br>*Pitt* | *June* 1757<br>*Pitt–Newcastle*<br>*coalition* | Mar. 1761<br>*Bute–Newcastle* |
|---|---|---|---|
| *Lord Chancellor* | In commission | Jan. '61. Henley | ... |
| *Lord President* | ... | ... | ... |
| *Lord Privy Seal* | ... | Temple | Bedford |
| *First Lord of Treasury* | Devonshire<br>(4th Duke of) | Newcastle | ... |
| *Chancellor of Exchequer* | Legge<br>April '57 Mansfield | Legge | Barrington |
| *First Lord of Admiralty* | Temple (2nd Earl)<br>April '57. Winchilsea | Anson | ... |
| *Secretaries of State:* South | Pitt<br>April '57. Holdernesse | Pitt | Oct. Egremont (2nd Earl of) |
| North | ... | ... | Bute (3rd Earl of (Scottish)) |
| Colonies | | | |
| *Secretary at War* | ... | ... | Charles Townshend |
| *Paymaster of Forces* | ... | Fox | ... |
| *Treasurer of Navy* | Grenville | ... | ... |
| *First Lord of Trade* | ... | ... | Sandys |
| *Postmasters-General* | ... | 1759<br>{Besborough (2nd Earl of)<br>Robert Hampden<br>(4th Bn. Trevor,<br>1764; 1st Viscount<br>Hampden, 1776) | ... |
| *Attorney-General* | Sir Robert Henley<br>(1st Bn., 1760; 1st<br>Earl of Northington,<br>1764) | Sir Charles Pratt<br>(1st Bn. Camden,<br>1765) | Jan. '62. Yorke |
| *Solicitor-General* | Charles Yorke | ... | Dec. '61. Sir Fletcher<br>Norton (1st Bn.<br>Grantley, 1782) |

| May 1762<br>*Bute* | April 1763<br>*Grenville* | July 1765<br>*Rockingham* | July 1766<br>*Chatham* |
|---|---|---|---|
| ... | ... | ... | Camden |
| ... | Sept. Bedford | Winchilsea | Northington |
| ... | Marlborough (4th Duke of) | Newcastle | Chatham |
| Bute | Grenville | Rockingham (2nd Marquis of) | Grafton |
| Sir Francis Dashwood (15th Bn. Le Despencer, 1763) | Grenville | William Dowdeswell | Townshend |
| Halifax Oct. '62. Grenville | Sandwich Sept. Egmont | ... | Sept. Sir Charles Saunders. Dec. Sir Edward Hawke (1st Bn. 1776) |
| ... | Sept. Halifax | Henry Seymour Conway. May '66. Richmond (8th Duke of) | Shelburne |
| Grenville Oct. Halifax | ... | Grafton (3rd Duke of) May '66. Conway | ... |
| Welbore Ellis | ... | Barrington | ... |
| ... | ... | Townshend | { Frederick North (commonly called Lord North) George Cooke |
| June '62. Barrington | ... | Howe (4th Viscount (Irish); 1st Earl, 1782) | ... |
| March '63. Townshend | Shelburne (2nd Earl of (Irish)). Sept. Hillsborough (1st Earl of (Irish)) | Dartmouth (2nd Earl of (Irish)) | Hillsborough. Dec. Robert Nugent (1st Visct. Clare (Irish) 1767; 1st Earl Nugent (Irish) 1776) |
| Nov. Egmont (2nd Earl of (Irish)) | Sept. Hyde (1st Bn.; 1st Earl of Clarendon, 1776) | { Besborough Grantham | Dec. { Le Despencer Hillsborough |
| ... | Dec. '63. Norton | Yorke | de Grey |
| ... | Nov. William de Grey | ... | Sir John Willes |

| | Dec. 1767 Grafton | Jan. 1770 North | Changes in North's administration to Feb. 1782 |
|---|---|---|---|
| *Lord Chancellor* | ... | Yorke (d. Jan. 1770) Jan. In commission | Jan. '71. Apsley (1st Bt.; 2nd Earl Bathurst 1775). 1778, Thurlow |
| *Lord President* | Gower | ... | Nov. '79. Bathurst |
| *Lord Privy Seal* | Nov. '68. Bristol (2nd Earl of) | Halifax | Jan. '71. Suffolk (12th Earl of, and 5th of Berkshire) May. Grafton. 1775. Dartmouth |
| *First Lord of Treasury* | Grafton | North | ... |
| *Chancellor of Exchequer* | North | ... | ... |
| *First Lord of Admiralty* | ... | ... | Jan. '71. Sandwich |
| *Secretaries of State:* South | Oct. '68. Weymouth (3rd Viscount) | Dec. Rochford | Nov. '75. Weymouth Nov. '79. Hillsborough |
| North | Jan. '68. Hillsborough Oct. '68. Rochford (4th Earl of) | Dec. Sandwich | Jan. '71. Halifax June. Suffolk Oct. '79. Stormont (7th Viscount (Scottish)) |
| Colonies | Jan. '68. Hillsborough | ... | 1772. Dartmouth 1775. Lord George Germain (1st Viscount Sackville 1782) Feb. '82. Ellis |
| *Secretary at War* | ... | ... | 1778. Charles Jenkinson |
| *Paymaster of Forces* | Cooke Thomas Townshend } 1768. Richard Rigby | ... | ... |
| *Treasurer of Navy* | ... | Sir Gilbert Elliot | 1775. Ellis |
| *First Lord of Trade* | Jan. '68. Hillsborough | ... | 1772. Dartmouth 1775. Germain 1779. Carlisle (5th Earl of) Dec. '80. Grantham (2nd Bn.) |
| *Postmasters-General* | Jan. '68. Sandwich | Dec. '70. H. F. Thynne | Jan. '82. Barrington |
| *Attorney-General* | ... | ... | Jan. '71. Thurlow 1778. Alexander Wedderburn 1780. James Wallace |
| *Solicitor-General* | John Dunning (1st Bn. Ashburton, 1782) | Edward Thurlow (1st Bn., 1770) | Jan. '71. Wedderburn 1778. Wallace 1780. James Mansfield |

# Index

Adam, Robert, 96, 117
*Address to the Electors of Great Britain, An* (1747), 2–3, 159
Algarotti, Count Francesco (1712–64), 92
America: 14, 81, 89, 110, 137, 144; prayer-book reform, 145–50; *Abridgement*, 15, 137, 148, 150, 151–3; fire-prevention, 113–14, 115–16; Stamp Act, 25, 26, 67, 68, 69, 70, 111, 114, 138, 140, 147
Amey, E., 27, 159
Amyand, Claudius (1718–74), 81
Ancaster Society, 108, 109
Anne, Empress of Russia, 9
Anson, George, 1st Bn., 160, 197, 198
Antiquaries, Society of, 14, 26, 94, 95, 100, 104–5, 106, 108, 109, 110
Archer, Henry (1700–68), 22, 50
— Thomas, 1st Bn., of Umberslade (brother of above), 109
— Thomas (uncle of above), 109
Arnold, Dr. Samuel (1740–1802), 120
Arts, public Academy of, 101, 121, 128–30
Arts, Manufactures, and Commerce, Society for the Encouragement of, 12, 14, 105, 110, 130
Asia Minor:
    D.'s tour, 9, 100–1
    Dilettanti expedition, 14, 100, 103–4, 116
    Skipwith's tour, 99–100
Atterbury, Luffham (d. 1796), 119–20
Austen, Sir Robert, 4th Bt. of Bexley, 9

Bacchus, temple of, at Teos, 116
Bache, R. M., on 'Franklin's Prayer-Book', 151, 152, 153
— T. H., 151, 152
Baker, E. A., editor of *Chrysal*, 135
Baltimore, Frederick Calvert, 6th Bn. (1731–71), 29, 30, 31
Bamfylde, Sir Richard Warwick, 4th Bt. (1722–76), 66

Banks, Sir Joseph, 132
Barrington, William Wildman, 2nd Visc., 51, 67, 197, 198, 199, 200
Barthélemy, Abbé Jean Jacques (d. 1795), 93
Bastard, John (d. 1778), 119
Bateman, James, 109
Bathurst, Henry, Bn. Apsley, 2nd Earl, 200
Bedford, John Russell, 4th Duke of, 62, 63, 64, 197, 198, 199
Belsham, William (1752–1827), 61, 140
Berkeley, Norborne, Bn. Botetourt, 56, 65
Berlin, 91–92, 99, 100
Besborough, William Ponsonby, 2nd Earl of, 198, 199
Bindley, John, 76, 84–85, 89, 184, App. IV(*b*)
Bisham Abbey, 131
Bishop's Castle, 64
Blackburne, Francis, 138–9, 140, 144, 157
Blackfriars Bridge, 27, 127, 128
Blackstone, Sir William, 39, 40
Bledlow, 130
Boerhaave, Herman, 106
Bogdani, William, 106
Bolingbroke, Henry Saint-John, 1st Visc., 7, 15, 16, 17, 98
— Lady (Marie-Claire de Marésilly, d. 1750), 27, 98
Book of Common Prayer, *see* Liturgy
Bordeaux, 98
Borgnis, Joseph, 117
Boston, Society at, 108
Boswell, James, 127
Bridge Hill House, Canterbury, 98
Bridgeman, Sir Orlando, 4th Bt. (d. 1738), 8
Bristol, George William Hervey, 2nd Earl of, 200
Brooksbank, Stamp, 77
Browne, Joseph (1700–67), 97

# Index

Fane of Wormsley (d. 1777) and niece of Thomas, who in 1762 succ. as 8th Earl of Westmorland and was great-grandson of Sir Francis Fane of Fulbeck, 3rd son of 1st Earl of Westmorland), 133

Stapleton, Sir Thomas, 5th Bt. (1727–81) (son of Sir William, 4th Bt. and his wife, Catherine Paul, dau. of William Paul and Catherine Fane, sister of Lady Mary Dashwood; his son Thomas, 6th Bt., became Bn. Le Despencer in 1788 on death of D.'s sister, Rachel), 132, 133

Stayner, Robert, 184
Stevens, Bishop, 151
Stifler, J. M., 152, 153
Stone, Francis, 140
Stormont, David Murray, 7th Visc., 2nd Earl of Mansfield, 200
Strange, James Smith Stanley, Bn., 5, 24, 47, 50, 58, 66, 78
— Sir John, 196
— Sir Robert (1721–92), 130
Stuart, James (1713–88), 14, 102, 103, 105, 106, 117
Stukeley, William, 106, 108
Suffolk, Henry Howard, 12th Earl of, and 5th of Berkshire, 51, 200
Switzerland, 26, 41
Symons, John, 184
— William, 194

Talbot, Charles, 1st Bn. (d. 1737), 17
— William, 2nd Bn., 1st Earl, 6, 10, 16, 17, 18, 19, 29, 32, 35, 43, 45, 50, 51, 64, 65, 78, 138
Tatham, Edward (1749–1834), 126
Temple, Richard Grenville-, Earl, 56, 57, 58, 63, 198
Thelème, Abbey of, 133, 134
Thomas, Sir Edmund, 65
Thompson [or Thomson], Dr. Thomas (d. 1763), 6
Thornton, William (d. 1769), 41
Thurlow, Edward, 1st Bn., 200
Thynne, Henry Frederick, 200
Tinney, John (d. 1761), 117

Todd, Anthony, 88, 89
Townshend, Charles, 49, 50, 51, 66, 84, 198, 199
— George, 2nd Marquis of, 12, 41, 42, 51, 62, 64
— Thomas (d. 1780), 125
— Thomas (d. 1800), 200
Treasury, 73, 74, 75, 76, 77, 88
Trevor, Robert Hampden-, 4th Bn. Trevor, 1st Visc. Hampden (1706–1783), 107, 198
Tucker, John (c. 1713–79), 67, 113, 133
Turnbull, Dr., 100
Turner, Sir Edward, 2nd Bt., 37

Vails, 73
Van Doren, C., 152–3
Venuti, Nicolo-Marcello, 93
Voltaire, 92

Wager, Sir Charles, 196
Wakefield, Gilbert, 138
Walcot, John, 9
Wale, Samuel (d. 1786), 130
Wallace, James, 200
Waller, Edward, 20, 32
Walpole, Edward, of Dunston (d. 1740), 107
— Horace, 4th Earl of Orford, 9, 19, 31, 36–37, 41, 46, 58, 70, 79, 91, 97, 98, 104, 105, 107, 132, 133, 135–6, 140
— Horatio, 1st Bn. W. of Wolverton, 107
— Sir Robert, 1st Earl of Orford, 4, 5, 7, 10, 13, 15, 16, 17, 19, 20, 21, 22, 25, 49, 60, 61, 86, 196
Ward, John, 6th Bn., 1st Visc. Dudley and Ward, 51
Warren, John Borlase, 132
— Sir Peter, 160
— Dr. Richard (1731–97), 125
Watson, Bishop Richard, 139, 141, 142, 143, 151, 154, 155, 156, 157, 193
Watts, Banister, 119
Wedderburn, Alexander, 1st Bn. Loughborough, 200
Wenman, Philip, 3rd Visc., 37

209

PRINTED BY R. & R. CLARK, LTD., EDINBURGH